COME AT ONCE—
ANNIE IS DYING

To Marianne

Come At Once-
Annie Is Dying

JACK DOUGHTY

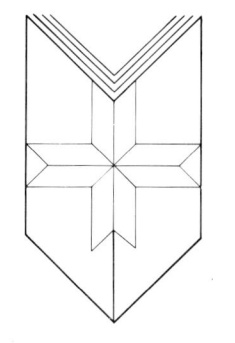

Pentaman Press Ltd

Published in Great Britain by
PENTAMAN PRESS LTD
Unit 18,
Kingston Mill,
Chestergate,
Stockport.

COPYRIGHT JACK DOUGHTY 1987

ISBN 0 9512449 0 6

PHOTOSET: Ashton Gaskell & Associates Ltd

PHOTOGRAPHS: Jack Ireland

Printed in Great Britain by
ANCHOR BRENDON LIMITED
Tiptree,
Colchester,
Essex.

CONTENTS.

CHAPTER		PAGE
1	WORKHOUSE	9
2	A MYSTERIOUS ILLNESS	26
3	A FAVOURED PRISONER	43
4	THE MASTERLY MR. COTTINGHAM	52
5	LETTERS TO THE EDITOR	79
6	FRIENDS AND NEIGHBOURS	86
7	EXHUMATION	96
8	PURCHASE OF POISON	108
9	A QUESTION OF MOTIVE	115
10	THE DOCTOR'S DILEMMA	137
11	VERDICT	170
12	'NO OFFICIAL KNOWLEDGE'	189
13	MRS. BERRY'S PAST	198
14	UNDER SENTENCE OF DEATH	211
15	UNEXPECTED VISITORS	221
16	THE EXECUTIONER	230
17	ENTER THE 'COLONEL'	237
18	A LETTER FROM THE DOCTOR	247
19	THE LAST WALK	252
20	MORE ABOUT THE 'COLONEL'	260
21	THE AUCTION	269
22	INCONCLUSIVE EVIDENCE	277
23	THE PRINCIPALS	284

ACKNOWLEDGEMENTS

In the early stages of my research for this book I was greatly encouraged by the Oldham author and historian Tom Webb, who sadly, has since died. Tom was extremely helpful in suggesting possible sources of information. Subsequently I received a great deal of assistance from the staff of Oldham Public Library, where I had access to the archives of the Oldham Standard and Oldham Evening Chronicle newspapers, and to a lesser extent, the staff of the Manchester and Rochdale Public Libraries.

In addition, the late Dr. William McManus, with whom I discussed the various medical aspects of the case, Colin Ashworth, solicitor, who advised on several legal points, Mr. Malcolm Bardsley, Registrar of Chadderton Cemetery, Oldham, Mr. John Lavin, Registrar of St. Josephs Roman Catholic Cemetery, Moston, Manchester, and Mr. Fred Hilton, formerly Assistant Director, Residential Day Care and Ancillary Services, Oldham, are just a few of the people who have helped to make this book possible.

Special mention must be made of photographer Jack Ireland, who was keenly interested in the project from the start and whom I dragged around various locations, including graveyards, in all weathers, even trespassing at one stage to get the most effective angles for his shots.

PREFACE

On Friday January 7th, 1887, the following item of news appeared in the Oldham Evening Chronicle.

> A girl named Ada Berry, aged 10, died on Tuesday at Oldham Union Workhouse under somewhat singular circumstances. She was on a visit to her mother who is a nurse at the Workhouse, and on Saturday morning was taken ill. She died on Tuesday. On Wednesday, Dr. Patterson, the Workhouse Medical Officer, made a post mortem examination of the body, the result of which will be made known at an inquest to be held at the Workhouse this afternoon.
>
> The mother, who is a widow, has not now her full liberty. These facts, coupled with the reticence on the part of the police and the Workhouse authorities on the matter, would seem to point to grave suspicion being entertained as to the way in which the girl met her death.

This brief report aroused little public interest initially, but upon further facts being brought to light and reported by the newspapers in greater detail, much excitement and speculation was generated in the town and indeed throughout the country as this remarkable case gathered momentum, finally to culminate in a highly controversial murder trial at Liverpool Assizes.

The first report was not entirely accurate. The deceased girl's name was not Ada, but Edith Annie, and the mother was not merely a nurse, but in fact head nurse of the female infirmary at the Workhouse.

Elizabeth Berry was thirty-one years old and had lost her husband several years previously after a long, agonising illness. Sometime after this she had broken up her home and boarded out her two children with relatives at Miles Platting Manchester, while at the same time she herself had commenced training as a nurse at the Manchester Royal Infirmary. About three years later one of the children, a boy named Harold, unfortunately died. The other child, Edith Annie, had settled in well at her new home. Her aunt and uncle, a Mr. and Mrs, Sanderson, were a kindly couple with no children of their own and were more than pleased to have her. Mrs. Berry, on completion of her training, was therefore in a good position to seek work further afield if necessary, and she did in fact find employment at various Workhouses up and down the country before applying for the position of head nurse at Oldham.

In her letter she described herself as a certified nurse and gave her address as being in the neighbourhood of Stretford Road, Manchester. She was able to produce excellent references and although there were several other candidates under consideration Elizabeth Berry was appointed in July 1886 at a salary of £25 per annum plus free accomodation, rations, fire and gas. For the times these were reasonable if not over-generous terms and meant that she would be well able to provide for herself and Edith Annie, whose board and lodging cost her three shillings per week.

The accomodation allotted to the new head nurse comprised a bedroom and sitting room situated on different levels and seperated by a courtyard, the sitting room being next door to the surgery, where all medicines, including poisons, were kept.

CHAPTER 1

WORKHOUSE

A brief look at the origins of the Oldham Workhouse and indeed the development of the notorious Workhouse system itself in towns such as Oldham might help to give a clearer picture of the backcloth against which the dramatic events described in this book were played out.

Before the Poor Law Amendment Act of 1834 the hungry and destitute were administered to by means of outdoor relief, and, where necessary, shelter in the local poorhouse. There was a poorhouse to be found in each parish, and though the comforts in these places were frugal and the buildings themselves often decaying and verminous, at least families remained together, had somewhere to sleep, and regular if somewhat meagre rations,

As well as housing the homeless the poorhouses also took care of families, who, though having somewhere to live, were nevertheless in distressed circumstances. To such people outdoor relief was given, and included among these were large numbers of able-bodied men, a fact which did not go down well in some quarters, for to maintain the poor a rate was levied on the better-off in the community, the majority of whom did not pay up willingly. They considered the poor to be a severe burden, not only upon themselves, but also on the economy of the country. To them the recipients of poor relief were nothing more than a rabble of indolent loafers who had come to regard pauperism as a way of life. The alarming thing, they said, was that the numbers of poor were increasing so rapidly that the point would soon be reached where food supplies would be exhausted altogether and the country bankrupted. These fears were not altogether unfounded, for unemployment was widespread, and as the population increased the number of persons claiming relief had reached an all-time peak.

It became clear that the problem would have to be tackled at national level if a solution was to be found to deal with the ever-growing scourge of pauperism, and in 1832 a Royal Commission was set up to look into the whole question of the Poor Laws. After a lengthy period of investigation and discussion it was agreed that the existing methods of administering to the poor were plainly out of date and would have to be replaced by a centrally controlled system whereby all the parishes in each district would be grouped together into Unions, which, it was believed, could be run much more efficiently and at far less cost to the ratepayers. A Board of Guardians, elected from and by the more prosperous citizens, and working within the framework of a set of rules and regulations laid down by the Poor Law Commisioners in London, would supervise the running of these Unions and make every effort to ensure that no relief should be granted except where absolutely necessary.

The hub of each Union would be a Workhouse, so named because it had already been decided that if the poor were to be sheltered and fed they must also expect to work. At this point it was not clear exactly what sort of employment would be found for them, but it was agreed that no longer should they be allowed to wile away their days in idleness. Besides, it was felt that a person living on charity year in and year out became lazy in body and dull in mind. Therefore, if life in the new institutions was made too cosy for the pauper he would have no incentive to rehabilitate and eventually support himself.

Bearing these facts in mind the Commissioners were determined that the Workhouse would be a fair but harsh taskmaster, and any person entering it with the idea of settling down to a life of ease and comfort would be in for a rude awakening. For one thing it was felt that no man being kept at the expense of the community could reasonably expect to be afforded a standard of living on a par with that of even the humblest labourer. As a working man of the labouring class existed on less than nine shillings a week at that time and the meanest of diets, it was quite obvious that the poor would have very little to look forward to when the new Workhouses opened their gates.

On August 13th, 1834 the new act became law and within months the grim forbidding fortresses began to appear in all parts of the country. When a Workhouse was ready for occupation all outdoor relief in that area was abolished and the poor either forced to somehow fend for themselves or enter the institution. If they chose the latter they were naturally required to show that such a course was the only one open to them, and on being admitted could at least be assured of food, shelter and clothing. On the debit side was the immediate feeling of incarceration, for the Workhouses were built like prisons, with high walls and huge iron gates, a feature which caused them to become known in most towns as the 'Bastille'

Once inside the poor were referred to as pauper inmates. Their clothes were taken away from them and fumigated. They were examined by the Workhouse doctor, then given a 'pow', or close haircut, after which they were issued with 'Union' garb, rough ill-fitting clothes which they were obliged to wear from that moment on. In later years, when conditions improved and rules became somewhat less stringent, Workhouse inmates were occasionally allowed to go out on liberty and were easily identifiable on account of their dress.

In the early days, the healthy, along with the sick, crippled and even the insane, were herded indiscriminately together into the same living quarters, often sharing beds. Only age and sex were taken into account when assigning newcomers to the various dormitories, and this in itself was to prove one of the worst features of the new system, for it inevitably led to the splitting-up of families. Once a person became separated from the other members of his or her family it was not always possible to remain in close contact with them. At mealtimes for instance, talking was forbidden, a rule strictly observed in most if not all Workhouses. It was often claimed that mothers could sometimes hear their babies crying and yet not be allowed to go to them. The mental torture these wretched women must have suffered can well be imagined.

There is little doubt that this breaking up of families was quite deliberate and just one more example of the authorities determination to make life for the Workhouse inmate as hard and uncompromising as possible. After all, it was argued, if a man had chosen to avail himself of the charity of the state he could hardly expect to enjoy a normal family life within the walls of the institution. Rules like this, it was believed, would make the pauper determined to get out of the Workhouse and stand on his own feet. No doubt there were many idlers among the ranks of those receiving charity, but what was apparently overlooked was the fact that the country was in an acute state of depression, with little or no work available even for those who were desperately anxious to obtain it.

For the mothers of illegitimate children the 'Bastille' held even further terrors, these unfortunates being forced to parade their guilt and shame by wearing a yellow frock at all times. This practice continued for many years, and even as late a 1887 the shabby treatment of unmarried mothers was the direct cause of a serious revolt at a Workhouse in the South of England, after the other inmates had been expressly forbidden to associate with them. This so angered the women that when several of the Guardians were being conducted around the premises by the Master they were suddenly attacked by a mob of irrate females, showered with stones and mud, beaten with sticks and forced to retreat to the safety of the boardroom. The police were called in and eventually quelled the rioters, but not before one of the visitors had received quite serious injuries.

Such a defiant spirit, however, was not in evidence in the early days of the Workhouses, when the inmates were far too cowed to resist even the most degrading treatment.

The person directly responsible for the running of a Union Workhouse was the Governor, or Master. No special qualifications were required for such a post, except that the man chosen had first and foremost to be capable of enforcing the strictest discipline. For this reason ex-military men were usually favoured by the appointing Guardians. In most cases assisted by his wife, who was known as the Matron, the Master undertook to follow the rules as laid down by the Commission, and ensure that such things as punctuality and cleanliness were rigidly observed. It was also his duty to read prayers morning and night, to inspect the wards after roll call each morning and to make sure that all able-bodied paupers were put to work.

After the rising bell at 6 a.m. (in the summer) the days work began at seven, following roll call and breakfast. The women were given jobs such as sewing shrouds and oakum-picking, an occupation that entailed the shredding of old ropes and led to many raw finger ends. Men were used to grind corn on a hand-mill which had to be turned manually by several inmates at a time and involved trudging around in a circle for hours on end. Bone crushing was another favourite of the authorities, the bones of animals being brought to the Workhouses to be ground down to dust for use as fertilizer. This was one of the most dreaded occupations of all and as punishing both physically and mentally on the operatives as the notorious prison treadmill.

There was a mid-day break for dinner, following which the tedious tasks were repeated until early evening, when the weary inmates trooped into the dining hall for supper. At the end of the meal prayers were read by either the Master or the Matron. There was very little time allowed for recreation, for all paupers had to be inside their dormitories not later than 8 p.m. and it was the duty of the Master to see that everyone was in bed and lights and fires extinguished by nine o'clock.

The wretched inmates, often too hungry to sleep, would lie

awake thinking of their families locked up in some other part of the building and praying for the miracle that would release them from this life of soul-destroying monotony and hopelessness. Of course they were not deemed to be serving a sentence, and any man was therefore free to leave at any time, provided he took his entire family with him. Having once made the break however, that family would not be entitled to any kind of relief, nor would an application for re-entry be looked upon favourably either by the Guardians or the Master, as the business of re-processing would obviously entail further unnecessary expense to the community.

So, having nothing better to go to on the outside, the pauper, once inside the gates, was virtually a prisoner and only a more tolerant attitude on the part of the Master and his staff was likely to ease his lot. In almost every instance such tolerance was not forthcoming, for if the rules were to be carried out to the letter the Workhouse Master had to be a very hard man indeed. Unfortunately some were positively inhuman and often meted out severe punishments for trifling misdemeanors. From time to time these cruelties came to light, but were seldom acted upon by the authorities, even when little children were the victims. The pauper was never allowed to forget that he only existed at all by courtesy of the state. If he failed to adher to the rules of the institution he must suffer the consequences. The root cause of this attitude was undoubtedly the fact that the men who represented the benefactors, namely the Guardians, did not in the main look upon the poor with sympathy and understanding, but more often than not with undisguised contempt.

At Andover in Hampshire in 1845 however, a scandal too shocking to be ignored was uncovered through the terrible stories circulated by former inmates, who told of the pitiful conditions prevailing in the institution there, allegedly aggravated by a ruthless Master, who had carried out his duties in such a tyrannical manner as to make the lives of his charges utterly unbearable. A former army Sergeant-Major and a man given to excessive drinking, he had systematically stolen from the paupers already meagre rations. According to the reports this had created such hunger amongst the inmates that men had been seen to fight over the scraps of rotting meat still clinging to some of the bones delivered for crushing.

It had been the practice of those employed at this work to attempt to break the bones in half before throwing them into the crusher, for the purpose of extracting the marrow which they found to be very nutricious, no doubt reasoning that this had been well protected and was therefore fit to eat. However, they had become so ravenous that even the few miserable bits of meat on the bones were in great demand, despite the fact that they were invariably putrid and gave off the most nauseating stench.

Unlikely as the stories appeared at the time they were proved to be factual in practically every sordid detail, and though the culprit managed to escape punishment, due mainly to the support of the Guardians, he had no option but to resign, much to the relief of the emaciated inmates.

. . . .

The new act did not come into effect in Oldham until 1847, when the Oldham Union was formed. The new body was endowed with the grand-sounding title of 'Guardians of the Poor of the Oldham Union'. Its first Chairman was a Mr. George Barlow, with the Reverend Richard Durnford and Mr. John George Blackburne being elected Vice-Chairmen. Mr. Kay Clegg was appointed Clerk to the Board and meetings were fixed for each Wednesday at 2 p.m. It was further arranged that a Mrs. Fawcett of the Angel Inn should provide the Guardians with a plain dinner for the sum of one shilling per head.

In existence at this time were six parish poorhouses, covering the districts of Chadderton Crompton Royton Thornham Middleton Alkrington Tonge and Oldham itself. They dated back at least as far as the early eighteenth century and the people who found shelter in them must have been desperate indeed, for these places were described at the time as 'small dirty and altogether comfortless, and of little credit to the townships in which they exist'.

The Crompton poorhouse, situated close to the junction of the Manchester and Oldham roads, was one of the worst, being inadequate in size, badly ventilated and insanitary. Oldham's poorhouse, at Mount Pleasant or Workhouse Croft, as it came to be known, was little better. Built around 1730, it occupied the site of the present Black Horse* public house and adjoining property in the Lees and Glodwick roads, and was sadly overcrowded, for poverty in the town had reached chronic proportions, a situation not helped by the mass influx of Irish labourers and their families into the area,

In 1847 the Master and Matron at the Oldham Poorhouse received a salary of £50 per annum between them, while those in charge of the smaller houses in outlying districts were paid at a lower rate, the custodians at Chadderton Royton and Tonge earning as little as £15 per year. When it is taken into account that these people had to deal with the chronic sick and the aged it was indeed small reward even for those times.

It was hardly surprising that one of the most pressing subjects for discussion on the new board's agenda should be the deplorable state of existing accommodation for the poor, and it was unanimously agreed that a new Workhouse, incorporating the six parish poorhouses, was an urgent necessity. A sub-committee was formed without delay to find a suitable site, while in the meantime tenders were obtained for the bulk purchase of supplies, including such items as fustian cloth, check neckerchiefs and calico

*The Black Horse was demolished in the early part of 1986

shirts for men, red flannel for men and women, linsey petticoats, calico chemises, red twill neckerchiefs and linen caps with cambric borders for women. The women were to be provided with gingham for outer garb, adult females to wear such dresses fashioned as a bed gown. It all sounded very fine, but when made up the women's dresses were said to resemble sacks. Clogs were supplied by John Swires of Oldham, who charged at the following rates;–

> Mens 2s 11d, Large boys 2s 3d, Small boys 1s 8d.
> Womens 2s 3d, Large girls 1s 11d, Small girls 1s 8d.
> Extra Small girls 1s 1d

In 1848 plans were submitted to the Board for the erection of a Union Workhouse at Northmoor. A tender of £10,000 was accepted and work completed in 1851, the final cost being £13.305 - 2s - 2½d.

While the new Workhouses were in many ways a distinct improvement on the old poorhouses they soon came to be regarded with dread by those unfortunate enough to find themselves in distressed circumstances, and the new institution at Oldham was no exception. It was well-equipped, with a large kitchen, dining hall, surgery and female hospital. But the homeliness of the old parish poorhouses was missing. In its place the first inmates found only strict discipline, regimentation and a cold impersonal approach on the part of the staff. On the other hand the records do not reveal any evidence of cruelty or such horrors as were uncovered at Andover, but the Oldham Workhouse certainly experienced its share of controversial, not to mention unsavoury, episodes. For example, the discovery of the decomposed body of a lunatic inmate in a cistern of drinking water, or the scandal of the toothless old man who choked to death for the want of a knife to cut his food with. These incidents naturally led to questions being asked, but were speedily dealt with and soon forgotten. In the early 1870's, however, a series of quite unrelated events took place which severely shocked the public and caused quite a furore at the time.

In January 1872, the death occurred at Oldham Workhouse of Betty Hilton. A pauper inmate for quite a number of years, she had been a native of the nearby township of Shaw, and it was to the Trinity churchyard there that the old woman's remains were conveyed for interment. A small band of relatives and friends stood around the grave as the vicar solemnly read the burial service. Then, as the roughly made coffin was about to be lowered into the ground, something happened which completely stunned the spectators and left them gasping with horror. As the coffin was suspended above the hole it suddenly started to fall apart and the ghastly corpse in its humble shroud became exposed to view. What had happened in fact was that the rings attached to the wood for the purpose of lowering had come adrift, causing the coffin to drop suddenly, twisting almost onto its side and striking the top edge of the excavation before crashing down into the grave, the lid coming off as it fell. The service was abruptly terminated and the burial hurriedly completed, the coffin being repaired under the supervision of a rather agitated sexton. The Oldham Standard reported:-

> Poor old Betty. For 81 years she had sojourned on earth
> battling with the vississitudes of an oppressed life, and
> all for a paupers funeral - and what a funeral!

Who was to be blamed for this very unsavoury and upsetting spectacle? No one perhaps except the contractor responsible for the knocking together of poor peoples coffins. But of course old Betty had been a pauper, and as such was fortunate to warrant a coffin at all.

Within a matter of weeks came another scandal involving the Workhouse, when Thomas Simpson, a pauper aged 71, was found dead in the imbecile sick ward. Dr. Samuel Jackson, the institutions medical officer at that time, was rather perturbed at the circumstances surrounding the death and called for a post mortem examination, a request which was promptly rejected by Mr. Milne, the Workhouse Master. The doctor, who had never been on very good terms with Milne, suspected that Simpson had been ill-treated by some of the nurses and refused point-blank to issue a death certificate. The whole affair was eventually thrashed out at the inquest, at which several of the staff and paupers were in attendance.

The deceased, a coal dealer in his younger days selling from a horse and cart, had been an inmate for over a year.

"He was not subject to fits or aggressiveness", stated the doctor, "but was rather weak in his mind."

Simpson, who was also blind and very frail, had been found dead on the floor of the ward. Just above one eye was a bruise, which the doctor believed could have been caused by a fist. One of the attendants claimed that Simpson had fallen over while sitting in a chair. After several other witnesses had been heard it was decided that a post mortem could be dispensed with and that the old man had died from concussion of the brain caused by injury to the left eye. But when how and by what means there was no conclusive evidence.

Only two months later a new scandal erupted which was not so easily explained away. Simultaneous with the arrival of a letter from the Poor Law Inspector in London, severely censuring Milne for preventing the post mortem on Thomas Simpson, an act of gross carelessness was brought to light which was to place the Master in a very awkward position indeed.

The principals in the affair were Caleb Walsh, aged 85, and an old woman named Betty Jones, both of whom died at the Workhouse on the same day, Friday June 7th, 1872. Incredible as it may seem, the old man, with face unshaven, was inadvertently placed in Betty Jones's coffin, conveyed to the cemetery and buried as a woman.

Early on the morning of their deaths the bodies of the two old paupers were placed in the 'dead house', as the mortuary was then known. At 10-30 a.m. that day the relatives of Caleb Walsh were informed of his demise by John Taylor, an inmate of the Workhouse, who, when he delivered the message, enquired if it was their intention to fetch the body away and arrange burial themselves. He was informed that this would in fact be done. Richard Wild, a relative of Caleb Walsh, immediately contacted Thomas Lowe, a local undertaker, and made the necessary arrangements, later informing the Workhouse authorities that the body would be collected on the Monday, the funeral having been set for Wednesday June 12th at St. Pauls churchyard Royton.

Meanwhile, the Workhouse undertaker had been instructed to make the usual arrangements for the burial of Betty Jones and sent a coffin, which, though intended for a man, would do for a woman just as well. Old Betty's funeral was to take place on Monday the 10th, and as she had been a Weslayan the appropriate minister was duly notified that her remains would be brought for interment to Chadderton Cemetery on that day.

However, by some unaccountable mischance the body of Caleb Walsh was placed in the old woman's coffin and taken to Chadderton. The ceremony was proceeded with – ashes to ashes dust to dust and so on, the supposed mourners of Betty Jones looking on reverently as the minister droned on. The coffin was then lowered and as the gravediggers began to cover it with earth the relatives dispersed, having unknowingly paid their last respects to a total stranger.

Back at the Workhouse the mistake had already been discovered, the Master being immediately informed. Mr. Milne had barely had time to acquaint himself with the facts when he was told that a grandson of Caleb Walsh had called to say that the body would not be removed from the Workhouse that day after all, but would instead be collected on the Tuesday. Milne's relief turned to alarm when he learned that the grandson was at that moment waiting at the gatehouse, having asked to see the corpse. The Master, without giving an explanation, sent word to the gatehouse that the body could not be viewed, and the young man left the Workhouse rather puzzled and annoyed.

Mr. Milne, after giving his staff a severe dressing-down, attempted to rectify the blunder by getting in touch with the registrar at the cemetery with a view to having the bodies exchanged. But that gentleman proved to be the officious type, and it very soon became clear that nothing short of a written order from the Secretary of State would induce him to part with that of which he had been made custodian.

While all this was going on preparations were being made to do honour to the last mortal remains of Caleb Walsh, for though he had died in the Workhouse, his surviving relatives had helped support him there, and were now determined that he should be accorded something more creditable than a paupers funeral.

The old man had been something of a local celebrity in his day, being best known in Royton, where he had lived for many years.

Born in Bacup in 1786, the son of a customs officer, he had arrived in Oldham as a young man, working as a hand-loom weaver in Holden Fold, Royton. Being an excellent penman he passed a good deal of his time as a kind of village adviser and letter writer, becoming well known among the uneducated people in the area. Up to the age of seventy-five he had earned his own living, but after that time had been assisted at intervals by various members of his family. His constitution gradually weakened until he became too feeble to attend to himself and eventually had to go on outdoor relief, receiving 1s 6d per week.

Since the death of his wife Caleb had lived with his daughter, Betty Mellor, in Flake Lane, Royton, but having eight children and a husband to occupy her, Mrs. Mellor was finding things more and more difficult. Eventually, Dr. Drummond, the local G.P., ordered the old man into the Workhouse. He was admitted seven weeks before his death and did not take kindly to the idea. Betty Mellor was in no position to help support her father, but Mr. Byrom, the Relieving Officer for the district, applied to his son and eldest daughter, who had previously contributed one shilling per week towards his upkeep. This was subsequently increased to four shillings and sixpence upon his entering the Workhouse.

Inside the 'Bastille' old Caleb was none too happy and lost no time in requesting liberty. He was told to settle in first and re-apply at a later date, which he did, being allowed out on Monday June 3rd. Once outside the gates he drank freely at several public houses while discussing the forthcoming elections, politics having been one of his main interests in his younger days. Although leaving the Workhouse in the morning he did not arrive at his daughter's house until late that night, and was in such an unsteady condition that his relatives thought it wiser to return him to the Workhouse as quickly as possible. The authorities were contacted and on the following day a van was sent. Old Caleb was helped aboard and taken back to the institution, where he died three days later, having more than likely accelerated his own end by his over-indulgence earlier in the week.

With the registrar of Chadderton Cemetery quite immovable, Mr. Milne now found himself in a most awkward dilemma, for the muddle was undoubtedly his responsibility, if not his fault. The Master therefore sought the advise of the Guardians and even went up to Oldham to see the Town Clerk. But the law was unrelenting and it certainly seemed at this point as if Caleb would have to remain in the grave as Betty Jones unless proper authority could be obtained for the exhumation of his body.

The dead man's family now got wind of what was going on and demanded that the error be corrected. They were told that as the old man had been a pauper the Governor had every right to bury him as one and that they ought to have kept him at home if they were so sensitive about his being buried in a paupers coffin. However, the matter was not allowed to end there and the unfortunate mistake was eventually rectified, Betty Jones being finally laid to rest in Chadderton Cemetery and old Caleb in more familiar ground at Royton.

Despite such outrages as those already referred to, and one or two others that were never made public, the Oldham Workhouse was by no means among the worst in the country, far from it. For by the middle 1850's various improvements had been made and the institution at Oldham was often held up to other Unions as a model to be copied. We have seen just a few examples of what could occur in a 'well run' Workhouse. One shudders to think what some of the others must have been like.

In 1872 there were 535 inmates at the Oldham Workhouse, including 74 males and 54 females in the imbecile wards. Poverty was still so acute that the authorities were often hard pressed to accomodate all who were in need of food and shelter. In addition to those in the Workhouse over 1,000 persons were receiving outdoor relief at this time. But the Guardians were extremely cautious when it came to parting with the ratepayers money, and Relieving Officers would even go to such lengths as touring the areas under their jurisdiction at night on the off-chance of seeing some recipient of outdoor relief entering or leaving a public house. When this occurred the matter was immediately reported to the Guardians and relief to that person would be terminated forthwith. If he then failed to find employment he would have no alternative but to bring his family into the Workhouse, and though it would now cost even more to keep that family, at least the Guardians could be sure that the money was not being squandered on drink.

As time went on and conditions improved somewhat children in the Workhouses received some sort of basic education, usually within the institution itself, where they were often taught by teachers who were themselves in a way paupers, in that they lived on the rates but also received a small salary. Unfortunately these people were not always of the highest calibre, for though some had simply fallen on bad times there were others who had gravitated to the Workhouse from good positions, often through the evils of alcohol.

In 1884 plans were made for a new school at the Oldham Workhouse, to be built at a cost of £15,000, and in 1888 Casual Wards were erected along with a Washouse and a Hospital for male paupers. All this was a far cry from the old parish poorhouses and the humble beginnings of the Union system. Yet the stigma still remained. To enter the Workhouse was to have reached the very bottom of the heap. The ultimate in human degradation. And though great strides had been made since those early desperate days it cannot be claimed that the life of the pauper was ever at any time lived in pleasant and comfortable surroundings. The proof of this can be found in a statement made by a man named William Wheeler, who worked as an attendant at the Oldham Workhouse for many years, commencing in 1923. In 1957 Wheeler told the Oldham Chronicle —

"It had to be seen to be believed. Bare floors, black ceilings, unpapered walls. Men dressed in white cord trousers, blue rufile jackets and striped Union shirts. Women in thick print dresses and shawls. Porridge for breakfast, bread and jam for tea, with a substantial dinner ...... They were hard days."

In 1929 the Oldham Board of Guardians was abolished and their duties transferred to the Public Assistance Committee. Though by this time the number of actual inmates at the Workhouse had shrunk to less than a hundred, most of them getting on in years, the casual wards remained quite busy, catering mainly for tramps passing through town. By the mid-fifties however, the number of tramps on the road had so diminished that the casual wards were hardly being used. They were eventually demolished and the site cleared to make way for a row of garages.

In January 1957 forty old people were moved out of the Boundary Park Annexe at Rochdale Road Oldham. They were the Oldham Workhouse's last remaining charges and were taken under the care of the Welfare Services Committee, being transferred to the Westlands home at Grange Avenue, whose former residents had been removed to a newly-built old peoples home at Limeside.

Since then the buildings at Boundary Park, much improved and extended, have served only as a general hospital, which includes a psychiatric block.

Though the casual wards have gone and the interior of each building has been vastly altered, the outside of the old Workhouse remains virtually the same now as on that fateful day in 1886 when Elizabeth Berry first entered its gates to take up her duties.* It was to be a brief and highly eventful stay.

---

*At the time of going to press, in the Spring of 1986, the former Workhouse part of the hospital, including the old clock tower and gatehouse, was in the process of being demolished, having stood for 135 years.

CHAPTER 2

A MYSTERIOUS ILLNESS

Elizabeth Berry did not take long to establish herself in her new position. Within a matter of weeks she had shown herself to be thoroughly efficient industrious and resourceful. She had about her a quiet firmness, which was often very necessary when dealing with some of the older inmates, while at the same time exhibiting a love for children that was said to have been nothing less than remarkable.

An early riser, she would begin the day by making a round of the wards under her charge, following which she would issue such items as bandages ointments and cod liver oil. She would then make out the dinner note and when Dr. Patterson arrived at noon would assist him in taking surgery. During these sessions treatment would be given to inmates and new arrivals examined. The doctor would then go into the wards to attend to bedfast patients. He would usually stay for about an hour before departing to attend to his practice in Middleton Road Oldham, leaving Mrs. Berry to deal with any problems that might arise before his next visit, which would be on the following day unless he received an urgent summons in the meantime.

Shortly before Christmas 1886 Dr. Patterson noticed that Mrs. Berry was looking rather worn out and suggested that she take a break from her work. This she agreed to do, and after receiving permission from Mr. Lawson, the Governor, Mrs. Berry worked over the Christmas period and left for Miles Platting on December 27th to spend a quiet two days with her daughter at the Sandersons.

On Wednesday the 29th, as she prepared to return to the Workhouse, Edith Annie, who did not see her mother all that often, pleaded to be allowed to accompany her to Oldham for a short holiday. Mrs. Berry agreed to this and also suggested that

Annie should bring along her friend, Beatrice Hall. Mrs. Sanderson hurried round to nearby Vicar Street to talk to Beatrice's parents, returning within a few minutes to say that Beatrice could go. Annie was delighted, and with Mrs. Sanderson's help was soon packed and ready to leave. After kissing her aunt and uncle goodbye she left with her mother to collect Beatrice Hall and set off for Oldham. At this time, according to the Sanderson's, she was in perfect health.

Mrs. Berry and the two excited little girls travelled to Oldham by horse-drawn tram and arrived at the Workhouse around 6 p.m. While Mrs. Berry unpacked, Annie and Beatrice went off to explore the corridors before supper. The following two days were spent in further exploration of the Workhouse buildings and grounds and the two friends had a fine time while Mrs. Berry got back to her duties. They were bright youngsters, full of high spirits, very talkative and great favourites with the staff and inmates. On the Thursday they left the Workhouse to visit the local shops, returning with their pockets full of coconut chips and chocolates. Later they attended a party given for the paupers and their children.

That evening a dance was held in the Workhouse at which Mrs. Berry proved to be something of a star attraction, so immaculately was she turned out. It was a night she had obviously been looking forward to, having travelled to Manchester the previous week to buy a rather stunning gown of red silk, with accessories.

Before going to bed the two girls took great delight in helping her to dress, trying on the dainty pink dance shoes and taking turns to pose in front of the looking glass with the elegant black fan. The following day they went to Oldham Market, where they spent most of the afternoon. Before returning they bought some fish from a stall which they ate for tea, sharing it with Mrs. Berry. Afterwards they played for an hour or two, and before going to bed both ate a rather large helping of cheese and apple pie. On the following morning Annie was not her usual self. She said she did not feel well and refused breakfast. She was ill all that morning, a Saturday, and spent most of it either being sick or lying down.

When Dr. Patterson arrived for daily surgery he was asked by Mrs. Berry if he would see her daughter. He found the little girl in her mother's sitting room, lying on a sofa in front of the fire.

"She was taken ill about breakfast time.", Mrs. Berry informed him. "She has vomited frequently since then."

Mrs. Berry showed the doctor a vomit-stained towel streaked with blood. "She has also vomited a considerable quantity of blood, which I've emptied away."

The little girl complained of pains over the stomach and after giving advice on the case Dr. Patterson made up a mixture of iron and quinine and left it with Mrs. Berry.

At about 9.30 that evening he received an urgent request to visit the child again and arrived to find that she had been removed from the sitting room to the mother's bedroom. She was no better, the pain was still there and the vomiting, which had continued, was again tinged with blood. The doctor asked Mrs. Berry if she had given Annie the medicine, and was told; "I gave it to her twice, but she brought it back again."

He then told her not to continue with the medicine and went away, returning the following morning, Sunday, to find that although the vomiting continued, it was less frequent, and that the general condition of the patient had improved. He made up another mixture and told Mrs. Berry that there was now 'a fair chance of recovery'. However, on visiting the sickroom that evening he found the little girl much worse. Her pulse was very weak and her eyes sunken. Several new features now presented themselves which struck the doctor very much. Previously the pain had been above the stomach. Now she complained of pain all over the abdomen. Dr. Patterson had previously understood Mrs. Berry to say that the child had not been purged. Now she told him that Annie had been violently purged, that the straining occurred every fifteen minutes, and that the evacuations from the bowels contained blood. The doctor asked to see the evacuations and was told that they had been washed away. While he was in the sickroom on this occasion he saw the patient vomit matter stained with blood. He also noticed that the edges of her mouth were red and swollen, and asked the mother what had caused this.

She replied; "I gave her a piece of lemon with some sugar. It must have been that."

At this point the doctor, apparently at a loss, decided to seek a second opinion. Leaving the Workhouse he travelled the short distance to Oldham town centre and returned later that night accompanied by a colleague, Dr. Robertson of King Street.

The child was very exhausted, but conscious. Dr. Robertson examined her and after a brief consultation the two medical men decided on a fresh course of treatment, Dr. Patterson making up a new mixture which he left with dosage instructions. The two men then returned to Dr. Robertson's home, where they spent some time that night in discussing the case.

....

Ann Sanderson was rather startled by the sharp unfamiliar rap on her door on Monday morning January 3rd. She was even more surprised to find a telegraph boy standing on the step. The contents of the telegram which he handed over left her so badly shaken that it was some minutes before she could fully grasp the significance of the brief message.

COME AT ONCE, ANNIE IS DYING ... E. BERRY, OLDHAM UNION.

A less resourceful woman would probably have flown into a panic. Mrs. Sanderson remained as calm as was possible in the circumstances. After locking up the house she hurried to the nearby works where her husband was employed as a letterpress printer and showed him the telegram. John Sanderson went pale as he read it. He then explained the situation to his employer before leaving with his wife for Oldham.

The Sandersons were not only stunned by the message, they were also very puzzled. For only two days previously a letter had arrived from Annie which indicated that she had been in excellent health and spirits at the time of writing, Friday December 31st. In it she had informed them of her safe arrival at the Workhouse and related that she and Beatrice had attended a Christmas party and watched the children 'get their prizes.' She also described the Christmas decorations at the Workhouse, and went on to say; "Mamma was splendidly dressed for the ball last night. Beatrice and I are enjoying ourselves very much."

Around mid-day the Sandersons arrived at the Oldham Workhouse and were directed to Mrs. Berry's bedroom, where they found the little girl with her mother. Although very low by this time Annie immediately recognised her aunt and uncle and seemed pleased to see them. Mrs. Sanderson kissed her on the cheek and asked; "Are you poorly love?"

Annie replied, "Yes ... my belly hurts."

Mrs. Sanderson then turned to the mother and asked; "What's wrong with her?"

"She's suffering from acute stoppage of the bowels, "Mrs. Berry replied.

"How did it come about?"

"I don't know. She had a heavy supper the night before she became ill. That might have caused it."

The little girl motioned Mrs. Sanderson to come closer to her, and whispered; "I've bought you a brooch. You'll find it in Mamma's sitting room. On the mantlepiece."

Little Beatrice Hall left for home that day, presumably with Mr. Sanderson, who also returned to Miles Platting, leaving his wife behind at the Workhouse. Ann Sanderson remained at the bedside of her niece throughout Monday. There was very little she could do beyond comforting the child, who was showing very little sign of improvement.

During the afternoon various nurses from other parts of the Workhouse called in to see how Annie was, and several of the inmates who were employed as servants were on hand to bring in tea, mop up when the vomiting occurred and deal with any other chores. They all appeared very anxious and concerned about Annie, having got to know her well during her brief stay at the Workhouse.

Mrs. Berry continued to perform her duties, but spent long periods in the sickroom. She seemed very worried and had hardly slept for two days. When the doctor arrived sometime between nine and ten that night he suggested she should take some rest, but she refused.

Dr. Patterson, who had made an earlier visit that day, now examined the child's mouth and noted that the redness around the lips had developed elevated blisters. He again asked to see the bloodstained towel which Mrs. Berry had shown him the previous day. He examined it closely, then told the mother that he would call again the following morning, and left, taking the towel with him.

Mrs. Sanderson, who had remained in the room during the doctor's visit, now accompanied Mrs. Berry to her sitting room, where they had supper. They were away for about fifteen minutes, during which time, Ellen Thompson, a Workhouse servant, stayed with the patient. On their return Ellen Thompson offered to sit up all night along with Sarah Jane Knight, another inmate. Mrs. Berry thanked them, but said that it would not be necessary as she and her sister-in-law would not be going to bed. According to Mrs. Sanderson the child had not taken any food all that day, but was given a drink of tea cooled with milk. She was also given injections of cold milk.

After midnight the little girl grew steadily worse and was obviously in some pain. Several times she told her aunt; "My belly hurts me", and, putting her hand on her chest. "It hurts me here."

She continued to be sick, although the vomit was not copious, but small in quantity. The sickness was difficult and accompanied by such pains as to make the child exclaim, "Oh Mamma Mamma!" However, after about one o'clock in the morning all pain seemed to leave her. There was no more vomiting and she became very calm, eventually drifting off into unconsciousness. Her pulse was by now very faint and it became clear that she was slowly sinking. At about 4 a.m. Mrs. Berry rose and left the room, saying; "I cannot bear to see the last." An hour later Annie was dead.

. . . .

A message was sent round to Dr. Patterson's home informing him of the child's death. He did not, however, arrive at the Workhouse until quite late in the morning, being no doubt impeded by the dense freezing fog which enveloped the town. This was so bad that those in charge of traffic were in constant peril, and later in the day the steam trams were forced to cease operations.

On reaching the Workhouse Dr. Patterson went straight to Mrs. Berry's bedroom and examined the body. At this stage he did not communicate any suspicions he may have entertained, but probably commiserated with the bereaved mother. He then covered up the little girl's head and left the room.

Sometime after this Mrs. Berry approached the doctor in his surgery and said; "I shall need a certificate from you."

The doctor, however, was not prepared to write out a death certificate on the spot. Nor did he feel inclined to discuss the question just then, as several patients were present. He therefore replied, "Yes, and I shall talk to you presently."

When surgery was over he told Mrs. Berry, "Neither Dr. Robertson nor myself are clear as to the cause of death. We would like your permission to make a post mortem examination."

According to Dr. Patterson's later statement Mrs. Berry hesitated before replying, but this could of course have been merely due to a natural reluctance on the part of the mother to have her child's body mutilated in any way. In any event Dr. Patterson added; "We shall confine the examination to the abdomen."

After further hesitation Mrs. Berry consented to this. The doctor then asked if the child was insured, and stated later that the mother's reply was; "Not a penny. I shall have to pay for everything out of my own pocket."

That night the freezing fog gave way to a terrific snowstorm, and morning found the grimy cobbled streets covered by a six inch blanket of white. Comparatively few vehicles were to be seen and the road surfaces became so treacherous that the horse-drawn trams had to be withdrawn altogether. Nevertheless Dr. George James Robertson, Bachelor of Medicine and Master of Surgery, somehow managed to make his way down from King Street, meeting his friend Dr. Patterson at the Workhouse, where they embarked on the post mortem. At the end of it they held a lengthy discussion on their findings and decided that it would now be necessary to apply to the Coroner for an order to make a complete post mortem examination. In the meantime, and this was to cause much controversy later on, a death certificate was issued to the mother, stating that death was due to gastro-enteritis. The Coroner's order being duly granted, a second post mortem was arranged for the following day, and the news quickly leaked out that Dr. Thomas Harris, of the Royal Infirmary Manchester, would travel to Oldham to assist the two local doctors.

Dr. Harris, a very distinguished man in his field, had only a few months earlier been a witness at the famous Britland Poisoning trial, when Mary Ann Britland of Ashton-Under-Lyne Lancashire was indicted for three murders at Leeds Assizes. The victims were her husband Thomas, her daughter Elizabeth and Mary Dixon, wife of Thomas Dixon, Mrs. Britland's lover. She was tried only for the murder of Mrs. Dixon and was found guilty of having poisoned her with Harrisons Vermin Powder, or 'mouse powder' as she called it, a substance containing strychnine and arsenic. She was hanged in Manchester on August 9th 1886.

Following his last visit to the stricken child on the Monday evening, Dr. Patterson had taken the blood-stained towel to Oldham Police Station, where he had discussed the case with the Chief Constable, who then forwarded the towel, at the doctor's request, to Mr. Charles Estcourt, the well known Manchester analyst.

On the afternoon following the initial post mortem, Mrs. Berry, alone in her sitting room, was visited by the Workhouse Master. Behind him stood two policemen. They were introduced by Mr. Lawson as Chief Constable Charles Hodgkinson and Inspector Purser of the Oldham Police.

Mrs. Berry appeared rather taken aback by the sudden intrusion and asked what they wanted with her.

"As Chief Constable," Hodgkinson told her, "it is my business to inquire into the circumstances attending the death of your child, whom I believe died rather suddenly."

"Very well." replied Mrs. Berry. "What can I tell you?"

After taking down details of the child's name etc., Hodgkinson asked to see the body. Mrs. Berry led the way across the courtyard and upstairs to her bedroom in the block opposite. On the way there she told the Chief Constable that Annie had been living with her aunt in Miles Platting, and added; "She was unwell when I brought her here last Wednesday. She was constipated. I've spoken to my sister-in-law about this and she tells me that Annie was often like this. She usually gave her a pill or a powder to relieve it, and whenever she did the child passed blood."

On reaching the bedroom Mrs. Berry let them in, then remained by the door with Mr. Lawson as the Chief Constable stepped forward and uncovered the little girl's face. He seemed rather shocked at what he saw. In the dimness of the gaslight he could just make out what appeared to be an ugly red eruption around the edges of the mouth. It seemed to extend for about half-an-inch above and below the lips and stood out vividly against the chalky white cheeks.

"Have you seen the state of her mouth?" Hodgkinson asked the mother.

"Yes I know." she replied. "Before she died her mouth was badly ulcerated."

Hodgkinson now informed her. "The doctors suspect foul play. They think she's been poisoned."

At this Mrs. Berry turned to Mr. Lawson. "Oh Govenor! Why should I kill my darling?"

The Workhouse Master tried to calm her down, but she went on; "Haven't I only recently doubled my insurance in favour of her? Didn't I ask if she could come here and live with me when the Workhouse is enlarged in a year or two. Didn't I?"

The three men just stared back coldly at her. Mr Lawson took her by the arm and led her out, the room being then locked up again.

That same afternoon Dr. Harris arrived from Manchester, and with the two Oldham doctors carried out an extensive post mortem examination, when parts of the organs were removed from the body and placed in bottles. These were then labelled and passed on to Mr. P.A. Estcourt, son of the analyst. It was arranged that Dr. Harris would make known his findings within a few days. In the meantime an inquest had been set for the following day, at which Dr. Patterson would be the medical witness.

....

The inquest was opened at 2 o'clock on the afternoon of Friday January 7th by Mr. F.N. Molesworth, District Coroner, in the boardroom at the Workhouse. In addition to the jury, of which Mr. James Henderson was the foreman, Alderman Kelsall and Mr. W. Horrobin, two members of the Board of Guardians, were also present, together with Mr. J.W. Mellor, Clerk to the Guardians, the Chief Constable and the Workhouse Master.

Because of the seriousness of the situation, Mr Joseph Whittaker, an Oldham solicitor, had been engaged by Mrs. Berry to look after her interests, and he in turn had retained Manchester barrister James Cottingham, who had previously appeared on the Oldham scene in 1883 as defender of Harry Swindells, the Shaw Road murderer.

James Cottingham was born into a distinguished old Anglo-Irish family. His father was James Courtney Cottingham of Somerville, County Cavan, while his grandfather, James Henry Cottingham, became a Freeman of the city of Dublin for services rendered during the rebellion of 1798. As this honour was handed down from father to son, the Manchester barrister's name was, at a later date, duly inscribed on the Dublin Freemasons roll.

His mother also had something of a pedigree, being descended from Sir Hercules Langrish, a leader in the Irish House of Commons before the Act of Union.

James Cottingham was educated at Trinity College, Dublin,

and subsequently entered for the Bar at Lincolns Inn, being called in 1854. An extremely well-read man and a gifted orator, he had acquired an outstanding reputation in the criminal courts of the North, and, though getting on in years, remained as formidable as ever.

Shortly after 2 p.m. Mrs. Berry entered the room. She looked quite pale and seemed somewhat distressed as she took her seat beside Mr. Whittaker. Close by sat Mr. and Mrs. Sanderson. There appeared, however, to be a marked coolness between them and the bereaved mother.

Twice during the hearing Mrs. Berry left the room, first with Mr. Whittaker and then with Mr. Cottingham, for the purpose of consultation. On each occasion she was accompanied by Inspector Purser. All the time she appeared abashed and ill-at-ease, her eyes wandering from one object to another but resting on none.

After Ann Sanderson had told the inquest her story, from the child leaving her until her death at the Workhouse, Dr. Patterson was called. Mrs. Berry now began to take a keener interest in the proceedings and listened intently as he gave his evidence.

"On the morning of Saturday January 1st", he told the court. "I was asked by Mrs. Berry to go and see her daughter. When I first examined the child I thought her illness might possibly be attributed to an ulcer of the stomach, which is not uncommon in young girls, and which would cause vomiting accompanied by blood. I treated the patient accordingly and at the time of my third visit on the Sunday morning she seemed to be well on the way to recovery. However, on returning that evening I found the child much worse. I then formed the opinion that the patient was not suffering from any ordinary disease."

At this a murmur ran through the courtroom and Mrs. Berry held a whispered consultation with her solicitor.

"Under these circumstances", continued the doctor "I went

to Oldham and took counsel with Dr. Robertson, who then came down to the Workhouse with me and examined the girl. He found nothing beyond what I had described to him. We made up a new mixture for the patient, then left. I saw the child twice on the following day - that was Monday. On Tuesday morning she died, and on the Wednesday Dr. Robertson and I made a post mortem examination. As well as redness and blistering around the lips we found that the inside of the mouth was coated white. We found the stomach and intestines heavily congested. The stomach was very much contracted, and both it and the lower bowels contained quantities of a dark brown fluid.

"On the following day we assisted Dr. Harris in performing a complete post mortem. Passing over minor matters, one remarkable feature attracted our attention. On opening the gullet we found on it a spot, which presented a black and corroded appearance. This spot was about an inch in diameter. There were similar but smaller marks over the lining of the gullet. Dr. Harris, who is an expert in this field, has taken away with him the whole of the stomach and intestines for further examination and analysis."

Dr. Patterson was then asked by the Coroner. "What is your opinion as to the cause of death?"

He replied; "The corrosion of the gullet, independent of anything else, would be sufficient to cause death."

"And what is the cause of that?"

"There is no room for doubt." said the doctor. "An irritant or corrosive poison has been administered to the child."

This statement caused quite a sensation in the Courtroom, and Mrs. Berry, who had remained calm up to this moment, now set up a loud screaming and had to be restrained by her counsel. After order had been restored the Coroner asked; "This is your considered opinion doctor?"

"Yes." replied Dr. Patterson. "It leaves no doubt in my

mind."

Mr. Cottingham now took it upon himself to cut in with a sharp "What?"

"That a corrosive or irritant poison has been given to the girl."

"That is not an answer to your question." said Mr. Cottingham, addressing the Coroner.

"It is quite satisfactory to me sir." was Mr. Molesworth's curt reply. He then turned to the jury. "Gentlemen, I think you will agree with me that we ought to have the experts evidence on this matter. As you have heard, his examination is not yet completed. I intend therefore to adjourn until sometime next week."

The date set was the following Thursday, Mr. Cottingham stating that he would postpone his cross-examination of Dr. Patterson until then.

Mrs. Berry now appeared to have regained her composure somewhat, but when the Chief Constable suggested that she be moved to the Oldham Police Station she broke down completely and wept like a child, pleading to be allowed to remain at the Workhouse. The Governor was then asked if he would be prepared to incur the responsibility of having the woman on the premises. He replied that he would, provided that a police officer remained there also to keep her under surveillance. This was agreed upon and a constable duly sent for.

Mrs. Berry was therefore placed under what might be termed 'house arrest', with a female attendant her constant companion and a policeman posted day and night outside her door. Under these conditions the head nurse spent a most depressing weekend, and who knows just what thoughts must have run through her confused mind as Monday dawned, for this was to be the day of the funeral; a funeral she was not permitted to attend.

Monday January 10th 1887 turned out to be a bleak and bitterly cold day, and few Oldhamers paid much heed to the tiny cortege as it made its way from the Oldham Workhouse to Chadderton Cemetery. Anyone out on the streets on such a day was more eager to get home and in front of a roaring fire than to stand in the icey wind and watch a funeral procession trundle by. Possibly they were unware that the interment was that of Edith Annie Berry. In any event the funeral excited little if any interest among the public, and no more than a handful of people looked on as the burial rites were read and the coffin lowered into the ground. The mourners in fact numbered only five; the child's uncle and aunt, another aunt and two cousins. Mrs. Sanderson was very deeply affected and sobbed bitterly as she was led away by her husband.

It was to be several weeks before 'The Oldham Poisoning Case', as it came to be known, was to really capture the imagination of the public. The death of a child in those days was a commonplace occurrence. That very week an inquest was held at the Star Inn public house in Oldham on a seven month old baby, believed to have been suffocated in bed. This was hardly surprising considering that the infant had shared the bed with three other children plus the father and mother.

At least the people concerned in that sad little case had a bed and a roof over their heads. These were not things to be taken for granted in the eightcen-eighties, when life was unbelievably hard for poor people, who were very much in the majority. A glance at the Police Court proceedings in any newspaper of the period bears testimony to this.

When one Joseph Higginbottom was brought up at Oldham Police Court in February 1887 on a charge of deserting his wife, Mrs. Higginbottom told the court that she was in distressed circumstances. As she was unable to pay the rent her flockbed had been seized and she had nothing to lie on.

Another plantiff, Betty Read, charged her husband, John Samuel Read with deserting her and their children. They lived in a court off West End Street Oldham and she admitted that she was in the habit of sending her children out on the streets at night to beg from passers-by.

Of course, it was often said that the poor did little to help themselves, and it is a true fact that many did contribute to their own misery. In those days public houses remained open all day long and most of the night and were never short of customers. Drink was cheap and extremely potent. For a few pence men and women could drink themselves into a state of insensibility and find escape for a few hours from the bitter realities of life. Another case, taken from the files of the Oldham Standard, is a typical example of this.

A middle-aged woman, Annie Megee, was charged with being drunk and incapable, a police constable stating in court that he had found her lying in a passage off Jacksons Pitt near the town centre at 12.30 a.m. In the snow beside her was a child without shoes or stockings. With the assistance of another officer he removed them to the Police Station, where the infant was found to be in a state of exhaustion and suffering from exposure, it's hands and feet being like blocks of ice. The prisoner, who held the child in her arms in the dock, still without anything on it's feet, had nothing to say for herself. She was fined five shillings and costs or seven days.

But drink was by no means the only form of excape in towns like Oldham, where there was always an abundance of colourful and varied entertainment. The visit of a travelling circus was one highlight, when the entire troupe, including animals, would parade through the streets led by a band, prior to opening. There were also such places as the People's Concert Hall, where it was 2d in the pit, 4d in the circle and the cost of a box one shilling. The inevitable music hall was held at the Gaiety, while at the famous Theatre Royal, Horsedge Street, Mr. Lindo Courtenay presented popular melodramas of the day such as 'Alone in London' and

'The Famine'.

On the evening of January 10th 1887, the day of Annie's funeral, the 'Original Drury Lane Company' headed by Mr. Henry Neville, opened there in 'Human Nature', a favourite play of the period. That night the theatre was packed to suffocation, and in fact a touch of 'human nature' was shown by a member of the audience during a scene involving the proprietors of a baby farm, who were in the process of ill-treating a waif named Dick, when the proceedings were suddenly interrupted by a factory lass up in the gods, who shouted out "Let the child be!" A request which was received with laughter and cheering by the audience.

CHAPTER 3

A FAVOURED PRISONER

During that fateful January the Board of Guardians attempted to play down as much as possible any sensationalism the case was likely to evoke. It did not take long, however, before the rumours began to fly thick and fast. These mainly took the form of wild stories and speculation concerning the Workhouse staff, who were now viewed with suspicion by some members of the public. When a woman inmate died within a few days of admittance it was whispered that foul play was suspected. This rumour no doubt owed its origin to the fact that Dr. Patterson had found it necessary to carry out a partial post-mortem on the body, it being at first supposed that the woman had received a kick in the stomach. The doctor, however, decided that there were no grounds for such a supposition and wrote out the death certificate.

The Guardians were naturally most anxious to avoid having the Workhouse staff shown up in a bad light and were therefore more than a little perturbed when it was brought to their attention that a complaint had been received from a number of Roman Catholic inmates, who claimed that for several weeks past they had been prevented from attending their own church on Sunday mornings, having been stopped at the gatehouse and told that no one was allowed out unless they were over sixty years of age. The Guardians promised to look into the matter.

The complaint may well have been a legitimate one, yet there is little doubt that many of the rumours and stories circulating were due partly to the readiness of some people to magnify even the most trifling incident concerning the Workhouse following the death of Edith Annie and the subsequent police investigation.

. . . .

The adjourned inquest was resumed on January 13th, and this time Dr. Harris was present, as also was Mr. Charles Estcourt, the analyst, who, like Dr. Harris, had been a witness at the Britland trial. Their appearance in the room was followed by that of Mrs. Berry, who looked remarkably well considering the ordeal she was undergoing. She was again in the charge of Inspector Purser, who remained by her side throughout the hearing.

Dr. Patterson told the court: "I have a dispensary at the Workhouse in the female infirmary. There is no resident doctor and in my absence Mrs. Berry has charge of the dispensary. There is a cupboard which contains such poisons as opium, strychnine and prussic acid, as well as other poisonous substances. That cupboard I keep locked up, and hold the key myself. As far as I know I am the only person having access to these drugs. All the poisons are not kept in the cupboard however. I have here a list of those that were not locked up on the 1st of January and I will swear that the poisons named were outside the cupboard on that date. I made up this list on January 9th.

"Mrs. Berry had a key to the dispensary and she would admit a servant daily to light the fire. On a cold morning the patients who came up from the house were let into the dispensary to sit by the fire until I attended to them. I do not think any persons would be admitted to the dispensary unless either myself or Mrs. Berry were there."

" But how can you be certain of that?" the Coroner asked him. " You said that when you arrived you sometimes found people waiting for you."

"I have found people waiting in the lobby." replied Dr. Patterson. "I may have sent them into the dispensary until I could attend to them."

At this point the Chief Constable made an observation, which prompted Mr. Cottingham to make the first of many indignant attacks on Mr. Hodgkinson. He told him; "Be good enough not to interpose any observations without the leave of the Coroner." To which a red-faced Mr. Hodgkinson replied; "I am not doing."

Dr. Patterson's evidence being concluded, Mr. Cottingham said that it would save the time of the court if he waited until all the medical evidence had been heard before putting any questions to the witness.

Dr. Thomas Harris, of the Royal Infirmary, Manchester, and physician of Owens College, stated; "I made a post-mortem examination on the body at the Workhouse, which was that of a fairly well nourished child, not a robust one. The abdomen had been opened and the stomach and part of the bowels, together with other organs, removed. There were dry patches all round the mouth. These were brown in colour and quite different from the rest of the skin, which was quite healthy. The tongue, mouth and throat presented no abnormal appearance, but the upper part of the gullet was fairly, though not heavily, congested. At the junction of the lower middle thorax was a black and corroded patch. The right lung was somewhat congested and in the upper part of the left lobe was a small cheesy nebule the size of a pea. On the morning of the same day I examined the contents of three bottles handed to me by Dr. Patterson in the presence of Dr. Robertson. The first was marked 'Edith Berry, Stomach and contents, January 5th 1887'. The other two bottles were labelled 'Large and Small intestines, unwashed'.

Dr. Harris now went into great detail regarding his examination of these parts of the body and ended by telling the court that he had then placed them, along with various other organs, into several jars, and after labelling these, had passed them on to Mr. Estcourt junior for analysis by his father. He was then asked by the Coroner; "What, in your opinion, was the cause of death?"

"Corrosive poison." replied Dr. Harris.

"Can you say what the corrosive poison was?"

"Possibly sulphuric acid, but I cannot say for certain."

"Would sulphuric acid affect the teeth?"

"Not necessarily."

"If sulphuric acid had been administered, would it necessarily be found in the stomach?"

"No, not at all. It would depend on the symptoms during life, and the treatment."

"Then your opinion is that the cause of death was corrosive poison?"

"Yes."

"Do you say it was a corrosive poison as distinct from an irritant poison?" asked Mr. Cottingham. "Because I believe an irritant poison may not be a corrosive one. Is this not so doctor?"

"I say it was a corrosive poison." replied the doctor emphatically.

"And you suggest it was sulphuric acid. Can you tell us the probable quantity?"

"No."

"Was any of this sulphuric acid you speak of found in the organs?"

"Not as they were handed to me, no. But it might have been present in the vomited matter."

"Do you give it as a decided opinion or merely as a suggestion, that corrosive poison was the cause of death?"

"As a decided opinion."

After further evidence had been given by Beatrice Hall and Dr. Robertson, who stated that he agreed with Dr. Harris as to the cause of death, the court was informed that although Mr. Charles Estcourt was present he was not yet ready to report on his findings. Mr. Cottingham therefore suggested that a further adjournment would be necessary. The jurymen were considering what would be the most convenient time to meet again when one of them remarked that he thought all were agreed that death was due to poisoning. The Coroner reminded him that it was the duty of the jury to hear all the evidence before giving an opinion. It was then decided to adjourn until the following Thursday.

Mrs. Berry was now informed that the Guardians could not take upon themselves the responsibility of having her remain at the Workhouse, and that she would therefore have to go to the Town Hall. At first she was much put out, but was told that she had better bear it as well as possible for it could not be helped, and this advice she seemed to accept. She was then led out by Inspector Purser and taken by cab to Oldham Town Hall, where she was placed in a cell. It is recorded that a flock mattress was allowed her along with a pillow, so presumably this was not the usual practice.

On the following Thursday, the day set for the resumed inquest, Mrs. Berry was concerned in a further drama, again involving a child. In order that her removal from the Town Hall to the Workhouse might attract as little attention as possible, she was conveyed in a horse drawn cab, again accompanied by Inspector Purser. As the vehicle was nearing the bottom of Barker Street, which is quite steep, a little girl, who had been standing at the kerb, suddenly decided to cross the road and ran straight into the path of the cab. The driver, who fortunately was proceeding down the hill at a slow rate, managed to veer to one side and avoid running over her. He could not, however, prevent the splinter bar catching the child a glancing blow on the head. The little girl was carried to her home nearby, where she was found to have a small but not too serious head wound from which she subsequently recovered.

At the inquest that afternoon various inmates and members of the staff who had had contact with the deceased during her stay at the Workhouse gave evidence. During the questioning of one, Alice Alcroft, an old Workhouse servant, a further clash occurred between the Chief Constable and Mr. Cottingham. As the old woman related her recollection of events on the morning Annie first became ill, she mentioned that;

"The children came downstairs and talked for a few minutes to some of the inmates in the corridor."

Whereupon the Chief Constable chipped in; "Yes that's correct. It was the public corridor."

"If you have anything to say", Mr. Cottingham told him, "please put it through the Coroner. I must object to you interfering with the witness in this way. It is not for you to do so."

Turning to Alice Alcroft again, Mr. Cottingham asked her; "Does the corridor lead from Mrs. Berry's room?"Yes it does". she replied..

"Then it is the public corridor as I said", cut in the persistant Mr. Hodgkinson, ignoring Cottingham's angry look. He then remained silent for some time as the inquiry continued. However, a little later on he felt constrained to again take a hand in the proceedings, when the witness was asked by a juror. "Did you see the children in the surgery?"

"Yes I saw them in once, washing their hands."

"Was the mother in the surgery at the time?"

"No, I never saw Mrs. Berry in the surgery."

At this the Chief Constable asked, "Did you hear the question?"

This was just too much for Mr. Cottingham, who protested angrily to the Coroner.

"I really must object to a constable of the police acting as advocate. Any assistance he may be called upon to give you I do not object to, but I do not feel that he should be allowed to interfere with a witness."

"I hardly think he is interfering with the witness", replied the unsympathetic Mr. Molesworth. "The witness was asked if Mrs.

Berry was in the surgery with the children and she answered 'not at the time'."

"She says she did not see her in the surgery at all that morning." Mr Cottingham corrected him.

The Manchester Barrister then asked the old woman; "You're very familiar with the surgery, aren't you?"

"Oh yes sir. I go in every day to light the fire and clean up."

"Is there a counter in the surgery?"

"Yes there is."

"How high is it?"

"Well .... not too high."

"Could a child reach anything off it, do you think?"

"Oh yes, easy."

"Have you ever seen bottles on the counter?"

"No I don't think so."

"I mean medicine bottles."

"Oh yes, I've seen medicine bottles."

"I did not mean beer bottles or anything of that kind", quipped Mr. Cottingham, a remark which caused some laughter in the court.

"Nor did I", repled the old woman, just as dryly.

Another witness, Sarah Jane Knight, was asked by a juror; "When the child was lying ill and you were with her, did she complain of anything having been given to her?"

"No", was the reply.

"I should like to have that recorded", said Mr. Cottingham, resuming his seat.

Later the evidence of Mr. Charles Estcourt was heard, and was no more that a substantiation of Dr. Harris's findings. After

Mr. Cottingham had cross-examined the medical witnesses the jury arrived at their verdict, which was recorded by the Coroner as 'death by poisoning'.

Mrs. Berry was now formally charged with murder and escorted from the boardroom by the Chief Constable and Inspector Purser. As she left the building, grim-faced but impassive, she appeared reasonably calm and collected, but the strain on her was beginning to tell. Twice she complained of feeling faint, first on leaving the Workhouse and again at the Town Hall. She was helped down to the cells by the Inspector and a young constable, who was detailed to keep an eye on her.

The next step in this chain of legal events would be an inquiry at Oldham Police Court. In the meantime Mrs. Berry settled down as best she could in surroundings rather more austere than her comfortable quarters at the Workhouse. She had little cause to complain about her treatment however, every effort being made to ensure that she had all she needed. She was in fact a favoured prisoner and was allowed to spend a good deal of time outside her cell in the space provided for exercise. She was also served with excellent food, brought in from a nearby restaurant. But despite all these concessions she remained very low in spirits and did not enjoy the best of health during this period of her confinement.

In the week preceeding the Magistral Inquiry she was visited by friends from Manchester, with whom she talked freely about the charge brought against her. According to them her sorrow over the loss of her child was very profound, and they were quite moved as they left the Town Hall. Another frequent visitor during the week was George Robinson, a young man serving his articles with Joseph Whittaker, Mrs. Berry's solicitor. Robinson became a close friend of the prisoner, who seemed to have a great deal of confidence in him. Throughout her imprisonment he was to be a constant visitor and the main link between her and the outside world

After carefully considering the grave position in which she now found herself, Mrs. Berry requested pen and paper for the purpose of writing to her employers. The letter was read out at a meeting of the Board of Guardians on Wednesday January 25th, two days before her appearance at the Magistrates Court. It ran;

Gentlemen,

Considering my present unfortunate position I hereby tender you resignation of my appointment at the Oldham Union Workhouse. I beg also to inform you that immediately on release from my difficulties I shall apply to be reinstated.

It was moved that the resignation be accepted and that her salary due, amounting to £2. 1s. 6d, be sent to her. The motion was seconded, carried and the question of appointing a successor discussed. Finally it was decided that Dr. Patterson should be requested to make temporary arrangements to see that the work was carried out satisfactorily and the matter allowed to rest for the time being.

CHAPTER 4
THE MASTERLY MR. COTTINGHAM

Thursday January 27th 1887 turned out to be a bitterly cold and blustery day, but the biting icey wind did not prevent an extremely large crowd assembling in Mill Street outside the Oldham Town Hall and it quickly became evident that the accomodation was likely to fall short of that required. This in fact proved to be the case and many people were subsequently refused admittance.

The number of women present was quite remarkable. Apart from occupying a large part of the courtroom they were also packed into the two side balconies, or ladies galleries. These were only used on rare occasions and admission to them went by favour. Whether the female section of the audience had come to gloat or lend their support to Mrs. Berry was not yet clear. More likely they were like the rest of the public, just curious. Not having heard the evidence they had not had an opportunity to make up their minds as to the prisoners guilt or innocence, but this would soon be rectified.

The magistrates made their appearance on the bench a few minutes after ten o'clock. Already seated in their places were Mr. J.W. Mellor, prosecuting on behalf of the treasury, and Mr. Joseph Whittaker. Mr. Cottingham, however, was not with him, and had still not arrived when Mr. J. Wild, Chairman of the bench, opened the days proceedings. The case of embezzlement against James Crouch, former Magistrates Clerk, was first of all dealt with and was nearing its conclusion when Mr. Charles Estcourt arrived, accompanied by his son Philip, who also acted as his assistant.

At ten minutes past eleven the name of the prisoner was called and an expectant hush fell upon the court as the spectators awaited the appearance of the now well known Mrs. Berry. Every eye in the room was fixed on the door leading into the courtroom from the cells as the prisoner made her entrance, accompanied by two constables. Female necks craned forward eagerly to get a better look at the former head nurse as she made her way to the dock, to stand there looking pale and drawn before the intense glare of what must have seemed to her a sea of curious faces. Faces that took in every minute detail of the fashionable morning attire she wore; from the handsome black silk fur trimmed dolman to the high buttoned kid gloves. Elizabeth Berry was a most attractive woman. Small in stature and very dark, she possessed a neat trim figure and wore her hair in a smart fringed style. But the thing which struck the gathering most about the prisoner was her bearing. Somehow, despite the gravity of her position, she still had about her an air of quiet dignity. And yet she looked so very vulnerable up there alone in the dock, so helpless. As far as the spectators were concerned, especially the women, it was an unbeatable combination. Could this be the monster about whom they had all be reading? Could this meek-looking little woman with the pale face and dark wistful eyes possibly have poisoned her own child? No, they just could not believe it, and during the ensuing two days the prosecution would produce nothing to convince them otherwise.

The short silence was broken by the Magistrates Clerk, Mr. Hesketh Booth, who announced that the Chief Constable would not be present due to illness. Mr. Whittaker then informed the magistates; "Mr. Cottingham, instructed by myself, will appear on behalf of the prisoner, and although he has not yet arrived he is expected during the course of the day. In the meantime I shall conduct the case for Mrs. Berry. I feel confident that in Mr. Cottingham's absence every consideration will be given to myself and my unfortunate client. However, I would ask the bench to allow cross-examination of the witnesses to be reserved until Mr. Cottingham's arrival. As the bench are no doubt aware the Manchester Assizes are now in session, and it is of course quite a privilege to have the services of a man such as Mr. Cottingham, who is a much sought after advocate. Therefore I beg the courts indulgence and hope that my request will be granted."

The Chairman asked Mr. Mellor if he had any objection, to which the prosecutor replied; "I have nothing to do with it. It is in the hands of the bench entirely." The Chairman intimated that this arrangement would be acceptable.

"As it is likely to be rather a long case", said Mr. Whittaker, "might I also request that my client be allowed to leave the dock and sit with me on the solicitor's bench so that I may take instruction for the purpose of cross-examination. It is necessary that I be in constant communication with her".

"I thought you said you were not going to cross-examine", piped up the Magistrate's Clerk.

"I mean instructions to pass on to Mr. Cottingham."

"The bench can see no objection to that course." said the Chairman. "However, if Mr. Cottingham does not turn up it will be at your own risk Mr. Whittaker."

"In that eventuality", replied the local solicitor, "I shall be quite prepared to act without him. Although I am confident that this will not be necessary."

With a sprightly step Mrs. Berry now left the dock and took a seat beside her counsel, obviously relieved to reach the comparative anonymity of the solicitors bench.

Mr. Mellor, on opening the case for the prosecution, stated; "The prisoner Elizabeth Berry is charged with causing the death of her daughter Edith Annie by adminstering poison to her. I shall abstain from attempting to attribute motive or do anything which would seem to press heavily upon the prisoner. It is common knowledge that at the Coroner's inquiry on the 20th instant a verdict was found that the deceased died from poison, and the jury then found as against the mother a verdict of wilful murder. Upon that she was taken into custody and now stands before you on this charge.

"It is my duty as representative of the Crown to lay the facts before the bench, and having done so to ask them to say that there is a prima facie case upon which they will commit the prisoner to take her trial."

He then went on to outline in detail Mrs. Berry's visit to her sister-in-law's house at Miles Platting and her return two days later with the children, emphasising that Mrs. Sanderson would swear that Edith Annie had left her in perfect health. He then explained to the court the complete layout of the Workhouse buildings, mentioning that the two girls had been seen by several witnesses, apparently in good health, playing in one of the corridors on the morning of Saturday January 1st.

"On that day Mrs. Berry came downstairs first, having had her breakfast before the children awoke. Afterwards Edith Annie and her friend came down together, and a witness will tell you that somewhere between nine and ten o'clock that morning Mrs. Berry and the deceased were observed together in the surgery without the presence of any other person. Now on that morning the witness Beatrice Hall will tell you that her friend became ill and was unable to eat her breakfast. That she suffered from sickness and vomiting. This will be abundantly proved by several other witnesses. As might reasonably be expected the mother was alone with the deceased for much of the time during her illness, and it will be my duty to show you these times.

"The circumstances of this illness were such as to arouse the suspicion of Dr. Patterson, the attending physician, that the child was suffering from poisoning. He watched the case carefully and his suspicions were increased. He therefore requested the assistance of a colleague, Dr. Robertson, who came to see the patient and agreed with him that there was something quite unnatural about the child's illness. Following her death a post-mortem examination was carried out by Dr. Thomas Harris, and although no actual trace of any specific poison was found in any portion of the remains of the deceased, there were certain internal appearances which produced a profound conviction in the minds of the medical men that this girl did in fact die from poisoning. They will tell you that it is not at all unusual in death from poisoning that no absolute trace of poison as such should be found in the body, because it is common knowledge among pathologists that where, as in this case, there is great vomiting and purging, the poison is often eliminated from the body."

Ann Sanderson of 68 Albion Street, Miles Platting, was the first witness and related her story to the court, during the course of which she mentioned that the child had been insured in a 'penny club' at the Prudential office.

"By that I mean a penny a week was paid for the insurance. The payments were entered on a card by the agent and the card kept at my house. Mrs. Berry repaid me once a quarter at the same time as she paid me the three shillings a week for Annie's keep. She also paid for the clothing and schooling of the child. The school money was also a penny a week.

"Two days after Annie's death the prisoner called at my house and asked me for the insurance card. That would be on the 6th of January between one and two o'clock. The child was not buried at the time."

Ann Dillan, a pauper inmate of the Oldham Workhouse, stated; "I have been an inmate of the Workhouse for the last three years, employed as an assistant working under Mrs. Berry. My duty in the Infirmary is to take the patients their meals. I knew Edith Annie very well, as she'd come to see her mother a few times before. I saw her with her little friend on the Thursday going about the place as merry as possible. They seemed quite hearty. On the Saturday - that was New Years day, I saw them coming down the stairs about nine o'clock in the morning. At about a-quarter-to-ten

I went to look for Mrs. Berry to ask her for the dinner note and found her in the surgery along with her child. I was in the surgery about five minutes waiting for the note."

"Was Beatrice Hall in the surgery also?"

"No", was the reply. "The mother and the child were there alone. I saw the little girl again later that morning in her mother's sitting room. She was leaning against Mrs. Berry, who had a drinking glass in her hand which contained some sort of liquid. White, I think it was. Mrs. Berry was saying 'Drink this love, it'll make you better'. The child said 'Oh no Mamma, I can't drink it, I can't.'"

At this point the court was adjourned until 2 o'clock for lunch, but but a large number of spectators preferred to sit through the break rather than run the risk of losing their seats, so keen was the interest in the case. The only ones in fact who could be sure of their places were those directly involved in the proceedings, and when the magistrates re-appeared at ten minutes past two the courtroom was as densely packed as it had been in the morning.

After Ann Dillan had concluded her evidence, Ellen Thompson took the stand and explained to the court that she was employed as an assistant to the prisoner, being an inmate of the Workhouse owing to the fact that her husband had gone off to Australia, leaving her with six children.

She had seen Edith Annie early on the morning of Saturday January 1st, when she appeared to be in good health, but at sometime after eleven she had gone into Mrs. Berry's sitting room to find that;–

"Annie was very sick indeed. She was standing up, leaning against her mother's bosom. The poor little thing vomited at least three times while I was there. About five minutes would elapse between each attack."

"Did you see the vomited matter?" Mr. Mellor asked her.

"Yes, it was streaked with blood, and some of it was on the carpet?"

"Did you see Mrs. Berry give anything to the child?"

"No. She gave her nothing while I was there."

After Dr. Harris had given his evidence, which was simply a reiteration of his findings as stated at the Coroners court, Mr. Philip Anderson Estcourt told of receiving seven bottles from Dr. Harris which he passed on to his father.

Mr. Charles Estcourt now took the stand and told the court that he had taken a chemical analysis of the contents of the bottles. This had occupied a period of eight days, at the end of which he had found no trace of poison of any sort. However, in his opinion a corrosive had been present in the body before death. The details of his analysis took quite some time to relate, after which Mr. Whittaker, still lacking the services of Mr. Cottingham, asked him; "You say you found no trace of poison whatsoever?"

"No," replied Mr. Estcourt, "but death may be occasioned by corrosive poison, yet no trace found in the body after death."

"But how can you say that that is the case here?"

"I can tell from the state of the gullet."

At the conclusion of Mr. Estcourt's evidence Mr. Cottingham still had not put in an appearance, but as it was now well on into the afternoon the Chairman decided to adjourn until the following day.

....

Mrs. Berry entered the courtroom at ten-fifteen next morning to face another big turnout.

Again the majority of spectators were ladies, who appeared to take the greatest interest in the proceedings, no doubt because the accused was one of their own sex, and although the body of the court was not quite so crowded, the galleries were again packed to overflowing.

Mrs. Berry stepped lightly into the prisoners dock, through which she passed, to again take her seat next to Mr. Whittaker. She shook hands with Mr. Cottingham, who had arrived early, having failed to get away in time from the Manchester Assizes the previous day.

Mr. Mellor called for the witness Beatrice Hall. but she did not appear to be present. In her absence, Alice Alcroft, the old inmate who usually lit the fire in Dr. Patterson's surgery, was called by the defence.

She stated; "Between nine and half-past on Saturday morning January 1st I saw Edith Annie coming down the stairs. She was in the company of Beatrice Hall."

"Did you speak to them?", asked Mr. Cottingham.

"Yes, I told them I would warm 'em for coming down so late for breakfast."

"And what did they reply?"

"They laughed and said they would warm me."

"And when did you next see the deceased?"

"It was later on that morning. I was in the kitchen when Mrs. Berry called out to me. I went into her sitting room and saw some vomit on the carpet and hearth rug. She told me to get a cloth and wipe it up,which I did. She then told me to go into the surgery next door and fetch a mineral powder."

"Was the surgery door unlocked then?" Mr. Cottingham asked.

"It was ajar. I went in and took a box containing the powders from the counter. She then sent me into the kitchen for a glass of water. I didn't see Edith Annie again till after dinner when she was in bed, and Mrs. Berry told me she was a little bit better."

"Did you see what was done with the glass of water or the

powder?"

"No sir."

"I understand Mrs. Alcroft that most of your time is spent in the kitchen. Is that correct?"

"Yes it is."

"Could you tell us exactly where that kitchen is situated?"

"It's very nearly opposite the sitting room and surgery. If the door's open I can see the surgery from the kitchen."

"Was the door open that morning?"

"It's open practically all the time."

"But was it open that morning?"

"Yes sir."

"How can you be sure of that?"

"Well, I'm a bit hard of hearing, and if the door hadn't been open I wouldn't have heard Mrs. Berry call me, would I?"

"So the whole of that morning you were in the kitchen. That is except for the time Mrs. Berry called you into the sitting room and then sent you into the surgery for the powder?"

"That's right."

"Do you know a woman called Ann Dillan?"

"Yes."

"Did you see her that morning?"

"Yes, she came down to the stores to get some clean linen. The stores are a bit further along the corridor."

"To get to the stores she would have to pass the kitchen. Is that not so?"

"Yes she did. That's when I saw her."

"Did you see her enter the surgery?"

"No."

"Did you see her go into the surgery at all that morning?"

"No I didn't."

"Thank you." said Mr. Cottingham, and sat down."

Mr. Mellor now asked the witness; "Who keeps the key to the surgery?"

"That question", cut in Mr. Cottingham, getting to his feet again, "does not arise out of the cross-examination."

"Very well" said Mr. Mellor "I will not press it."

Thirteen year old Beatrice Hall, who had arrived during the cross-examination of Alice Alcroft, was now questioned, and stated;

"Yes, I came downstairs with Edith Annie that morning and was with her all the time till she was sick."

Mr. Cottingham was well satisfied with the evidence of these two witnesses, for what Alice Alcroft had told the court certainly cast doubt on Ann Dillan's story of having seen the prisoner and the deceased alone in the surgery, while Beatrice Hall's assertion that she had not left Edith Annie up to the time she first became ill was a further indication that Mrs. Berry had had little opportunity to administer anything that morning which might have caused the sickness.

It was now clear that if Dillan's story was true, then Beatrice Hall was mistaken. For the Workhouse servant had been quite adamant that she had seen the mother and daughter alone in the surgery in the early part of that morning. In other words *before* the child became ill.

Sarah Jane Knight, aged thirty-four and an inmate of the Workhouse for over three years, was the next to give evidence. She explained to the court that part of her duties had been to act as Mrs. Berry's servant, while at the same time looking after the lying-in wards in that corridor.

"I went into Mrs. Berry's bedroom on the Sunday about five o'clock and stayed with the child for an hour or so."

"Did she say that anything had been given to her which made her feel worse?" Mr. Cottingham asked her.

"No, she never complained to me."

"Did you notice anything unusual about her lips. Any redness or anything of that nature?"

"No I didn't. They may have been red, but I can't say I noticed it."

Cross-examined by Mr. Mellor, the witness was asked to give her opinion on the condition of the child during the hour she had spent with her.

"How do you think she was?". asked Mr. Mellor.

Mr. Cottingham was on his feet in a flash. "I object to that. She is not an expert."

"Very well", sighed Mr. Mellor, "I withdraw the question."

Dr. Patterson was now called. but had barely stepped into the witness box when Mr. Mellor informed the Chairman that the Chief Constable had arrived and that as he was unwell it might be a good idea to take his evidence first. This was agreed to and Dr.Patterson stepped down. Mr Hodgkinson said that he was too ill to stand and was allowed to give his evidence seated.

Mr. Mellor said that to make things easier for the police chief he did not intend questioning him, but would leave him to state his evidence in his own time and in his own way. Mr. Cottingham, however, was not nearly so sympathetic and soon made it perfectly clear that he had no intention of allowing the ailing Chief Constable any quarter whatsoever. Mr. Hodgkinson had hardly begun to speak when the hard hitting Manchester barrister interrupted him.

"I notice that the Chief Constable is looking at some papers. I object to that."

"I was not looking at them for the purpose of giving my evidence", snapped back Hodgkinson. "I was just looking for an envelope marked in pencil, and it does not seem to be here."

"I saw him looking at some papers.", insisted Mr. Cottingham. "As he was doing so before giving his evidence the obvious conclusion is that he is reading from them."

"I have not read a word", replied the Chief Constable, rather embarrassed.

"You were looking at them."

"He is entitled to look at them", cut in Mr. Mellor.

"No, he is not.", said the persistant Mr. Cottingham. "He is not entitled to look at anything except for the purpose of refreshing his memory. He must not read direct from the notes."

"Well, if you see anything improper while he is giving his evidence", said the Chairman, "then you can object."

This seemed to pacify Mr. Cottingham for the moment and a rather flustered Mr. Hodgkinson proceeded to give his evidence as best he could, without the assistance of his notes. After describing his visit to Mrs. Berry's sitting room and the viewing of the body, he told the court that when he had placed the prisoner under arrest following the adjourned inquest, she had told him "I did not do it."

"I may state", said the Chief Constable, "that on the 3rd of January Dr. Patterson brought me a towel smeared with blood and made a statement to me. The towel I sent to Mr. Estcourt in Manchester, for analysis. Dr. Patterson had further communication with me regarding the death certificate. On the day following the child's death I had photographs taken of her face. These pictures clearly showed the condition of the lips."

"Those photographs are not evidence", cut in Mr. Cottingham.

"I did not intend to put them in here", replied Mr. Mellor, "but I reserve the question as to whether they are evidence in the case of a committal."

"It will be the evidence of the photographer", said Mr. Hodgkinson.

"Yes it would be in that case", said the Magistrates Clerk.

After the Chief Constable had thankfully removed himself from the witness box, Dr. Patterson was recalled and described himself as 'Doctor of Medicine of the Queens University Ireland, and Surgeon'.

"I have been Medical Officer at the Oldham Union Workhouse for the past twelve years. I do not reside there, but visit the institution almost every day."

He now proceeded to go over his evidence as given at the Coroners inquest, though in far greater detail. In doing so he mentioned something which was to result in considerable controversy later on.

"I visited the patient on the Sunday morning and found her much improved. I was handed a towel stained with vomit and noted that it gave off a strong acid smell. Because of this acidity I decided to make up a mixture of bicarbonate of soda and water, to which I intended to add a small amount of creosote. However, I found the creosote bottle empty and made out an order to have it filled, which I sent to Mr. Goodall, the chemist in Manchester Street, telling the mother that when the creosote arrived she was to disolve eight drops in a 12 oz. bottle of water and give the patient one tablespoonful every two hours. Before the empty bottle left me I filled it with water and rinsed it out. This solution I added to the bicarbonate of soda. The mixture therefore contained just a trace of creosote."

The question of the creosote bottle, which was very soon to place Dr. Patterson under fire from a prominent local medical man, was not gone into any further at this stage. The doctor simply went on to relate the sequence of events which had followed, stating that on the Sunday night he had first noticed the redness around the child's lips. He went on; "Previously I had suspected ———"

"Will you be good enough not to tell us your suspicions". snapped the ever alert Mr. Cottingham. "Just give us your diagnosis of the case as a medical man."

Having been firmly put in his place, the doctor continued with his evidence, explaining that during his visit later on the Sunday night, when he was accompanied by Dr. Robertson, he had again found it necessary to change the medicine, this time prescribing a mixture of morphia and bismuth, which he made up himself and gave to the patient.

"On visiting the patient the following morning, Monday, I found her much worse. I saw her again that evening, but there was no change. She continued to sink until her death, which took place on the Tuesday morning."

"What is your opinion as to the cause of death?" Mr. Mellor asked him.

"The administration of an irritant or corrosive poision", replied the doctor.

"Is there any known disease which could cause the symptoms observed after death?"

"No", was the reply, "there is no known disease which could possibly produce the appearances we were met with."

Cross-examined by Mr. Cottingham the doctor stated that he had taken notes of all that had occurred during his visits to the deceased.

"Have you got those notes with you?" he was asked.

"Yes".

"Allow me to look at them please."

The notes were handed over and as Mr. Cottingham glanced through them Mr. Mellor remarked that when the defence had finished with the notes he wished to have them marked as exhibits.

"You will do nothing of the kind", said Mr. Cottingham, without looking up, "I have not put them in as evidence."

"But your cross-examination will partly arise out of them", said Mr. Mellor.

"I cannot say yet whether it will or not."

"Well I contend that the notes ought to be exhibited", argued Mr. Mellor.

"And I submit", replied the Manchester barrister, "that you cannot make the private notes of a doctor exhibits in a murder case. Of course if Mr. Mellor wishes to enter into a discussion on the laws of evidence ...."

"Very well", said Mr. Mellor, declining to accept the challenge. "I will wait until any questions regarding the notes are asked."

Referring to the notes Mr. Cottingham now asked the doctor; "This towel you mention ... did you actually examine it for acid?"

"No, but there were indications of acid. This is the reason I prescribed bicarbonate of soda."

"But why did you later, if you thought poison had been administered, prescribe bismuth to stop the vomiting?"

"The patient was in great distress. I prescribed morphia and bismuth to relieve the pain, without reference to the poison."

"At the expense of her life?"

"It does not follow. It was the most likely thing to help her through."

"You prescribed to allay the vomiting, and left the poison to do its work?"

"No, I will not have that put down."

"That is what it amounts to", insisted Mr. Cottingham.

"I do not agree with you." said the doctor.

"Well I ask you. What would be the effect of bismuth on the stomach?"

"It would allay the vomiting."

"But surely vomiting would have the effect of getting rid of any poison which had not been absorbed ...wouldn't it doctor?"

"Yes ... if it was there."

"Now your diagnosis on Sunday night, when Dr. Robertson was present, was that the patient was suffering from poisoning."

"Yes, which I thought had been administered in the afternoon. I considered that the child had been given poison which led to the illness, but after finding her much better on the Sunday morning, and then seeing her condition that night, I concluded that something had been administered between my visits."

"In that case why did you not apply yourself in attempting to eliminate the poison. Why did you not try to get it out of the stomach?"

"Dr. Robertson and I agreed that we should relieve her suffering at once, and on that account prescribed morphia and bismuth."

Mr. Cottingham sighed deeply and referred again to the doctor's notes, thumbing through them slowly and deliberately. At last he looked up and turned his attention to the witness again.

"Is it usual for medical men to consult suspected persons as to what to say on the certificate of death?"

"I did not consult Mrs. Berry as to what I should write on the certificate."

"You discussed the matter with her before making out the death certificate. How is it that you did not suggest to her at the time that the child had been poisoned?"

"I give no reason for that."

"You did not suggest at that time that the child had been poisoned. Neither did you allude to it on the death certificate."

"No I did not", replied the doctor, now quite incensed, "but I wish to explain —"

"I don't want an explanation", snapped Mr. Cottingham.

Mr. Wild, the Chairman, now took a hand; "I think he ought to be allowed to give his reasons."

"No", said Mr. Cottingham defiantly. "He is not at all entitled to do so."

Mr. Cottingham was not to have his way this time though, and the doctor explained to the court; "On the certificate the cause of death is assigned as gastro enteritis, that is, acute inflamation of the mucus membrane of the stomach and bowels. Without any explanation that suggests disease, and there was no evidence of any disease, but when I spoke to Mrs. Berry about the certificate on the day the child died I had not then got a Coroners order for a post-mortem examination. I had to ask Mrs. Berry for the privilege."

"Is it not true", Mr. Cottingham asked. "that you told Mrs. Berry it was merely for scientific purposes that you wished to carry out a post-mortem?"

"Yes I did say that. I was anxious not to mention anything about poison until the last possible moment."

"One more question doctor. As you suspected on the Sunday night that the child had been given poison between your visits, did you take steps to have her watched after that?"

"No, it was too late then."

Shortly after this the court was adjourned for lunch. On resuming, the evidence of Ann Partland, a widow and pauper inmate of the Workhouse, was taken. She told the court that she had emptied and cleaned out a vessel containing a dark brown fluid, presumably vomit. She had also observed blisters around the patient's mouth.

She was followed into the witness box by Dr. George James Robertson, Bachelor of Medicine of the University of Aberdeen and one of the surgeons of the Oldham Royal Infirmary, who stated;

"In consequence of a communication made to me by Dr. Patterson on Sunday January 2nd, I went with him to the Infirmary at the Workhouse and there saw the deceased. She was lying on her back, conscious, but extremely exhausted. I asked the prisoner if I might see the evacuations from the bowels, but was told that they had been emptied away. I saw the redness around the child's mouth and formed the opinion that the poison was probably administered by the mouth in liquid form. I thought at the time that it might have been oxalic acid."

"Along with Dr. Patterson you prescribed bismuth and morphia", said Mr. Cottingham.

"That is correct."

"Was it prescribed as an antidote, or to allay the pain and vomiting?"

"It was prescribed to meet the requirements of the case."

"Will you answer the question?", snapped Mr. Cottingham, glaring across at him.

"I am not aware that we had settled what the poison was, but we agreed upon the medicine."

"Did you give anything to antagonise the poison?"

"I said I did not know what the poison was."

"You said you thought it was oxalic acid."

"Yes, but that opinion was more in the nature of a guess. However, I now agree with Dr. Harris that it was probably sulphuric acid."

"But at the time you thought it might be oxalic acid."

"Yes."

"So what did you do to antagonise the poison?"

"We gave morphia and bismuth."

"Do you mean to say that if you were called in to treat a case of oxalic acid poisoning you would give bismuth as an antidote?"

"Yes I would give bismuth."

"Would that be the best treatment?"

"Yes,"

"What would be the most appropriate treatment?"

"I cannot say."

"Was morphia and bismuth given to deal with the pain, or to allay the poison in this case?"

"It was given to allay the irritation."

"That is not an answer to my question. Was it given to stop the vomiting?"

"Yes, partly."

"Did you give anything specifically to antagonise the action of the poison?"

"As I have already stated we did not know what the poison was."

"Did you give anything to combat the poison?"

"No we did not."

"Now doctor, why did you not return to see the patient after your visit on Sunday?"

"I was not asked. When I saw the child I gave it up from the first. But had I been in charge of the case I would have treated the patient in exactly the same way Dr. Patterson did."

On Dr. Robertson's evidence being completed, Mr. Mellor announced that the case for the prosecution was now closed.

Mr Cottingham, apparently confident that the Crown had failed to prove its case, asked the bench whether or not they had formed any decided opinion. If they had come to any conclusions it was not his intention to address them he said. However, if they were still undecided it was his duty to put to them his clients side of the case. After a brief consultation with his colleagues the Chairman said that the bench would be glad to hear what Mr. Cottingham had to say. He began;

"Gentlemen, I can scarcely imagine a more onerous duty which could befall a bench of magistrates. You have before you a gentlewoman of unimpeached character. A woman who has not only held a responsible position in this borough, but who came here with the very best of credentials. Upon her character not a shadow of suspicion has ever rested. She is a widow. She had one surviving child. This little girl was beloved by her mother. There has been no suggestion even here in this court which would contradict that. There has not been a suggestion throughout this case that the mother was ever negligent of her child, or that she was ever forgetful of her duties as a mother.

'At Christmas time she decided to have her child near her, which is not unnatural. So she brought her to Oldham along with her friend Beatrice Hall. During the time they were at the Workhouse the children seem to have amused themselves, going about and playing as children do.

'Now the deceased was not a strong child. We have heard Dr. Harris tell us that although she was fairly well nourished she was by no means robust. But she seemed to have been in good spirits, and delighted in everything that was going on. With her mother going to the ball and with other things as we have heard.

'On the Saturday morning, two days after the ball, the child was suddenly seized with violent vomiting ... I ask you to pause here and carefully consider the facts. We have it in evidence that until the child was taken ill that morning she was in the society of her companion, who slept with her, and who, from the time Mrs. Berry left them in the bedroom to go downstairs to breakfast and then begin her duties, to the time the deceased was taken ill, was never away from her side for a second. One of the witnesses here has attempted to show that Mrs. Berry was alone with the deceased in the surgery on that morning, but her evidence is contradicted by that of Beatrice Hall and also by the woman occupying the kitchen. The door of the kitchen is almost opposite to that of the surgery, so she had ample opportunity of seeing anyone who went in there. As we have heard, Beatrice Hall never left her friend from getting up till the commencement of the sickness. Therefore it was not possible for Mrs. Berry to have administered poison to the deceased.

'The first time she gave the child anything was after she had already started to vomit, and she sent a woman into the surgery to get it. As soon as she realised that her child was ill she at once sent a servant to the gatehouse, so that the doctor might be told as soon as he arrived that Mrs. Berry's daughter was ill. Did you ever hear of a mother who poisoned her child and then sent for a doctor at the earliest opportunity?

'The doctor at that time had no suspicions of foul play. He has admitted that his diagnosis was hardly correct. He came to the conclusion that the patient was suffering from ulceration of the stomach. The child vomited before him, and he prescribed a medicine for her. On Sunday morning the patient was much better and Dr. Patterson altered the treatment. He gave her bicarbonate of soda and the rinsings of a creosote bottle. It seems to me peculiar treatment on the part of a doctor to give a patient the rinsings from a bottle. Now up to that time the doctor had not suspected foul play, but reposed confidence in the mother. When he visited that evening though, the symptoms had changed he tells us, and he came to the conclusion that an active irritant poison had been administered between his visits. The child was at this time so convulsed with the irritant that her condition was now absolutely hopeless.

'Under these circumstances what does he do? The line I took in my cross-examination of the doctor was not for the purpose of attempting to suggest that he treated the child ignorantly, but to show that he did not himself believe that there was any irritant poison at work then, because had he so believed it would surely have been his duty to have given the child an antidote, promptly. When a doctor has come to the conclusion that a patient has been poisoned I put it to the medical fraternity of Lancashire whether bismuth and morphia is the proper thing to administer. Obviously the first thing to be done in such a case is to get rid of the poison, or to neutralise it. Instead of that the two medical men prescribed bismuth and morphia to relieve the pain, which would have the effect of keeping whatever was in the stomach still there to do its deadly work.

'That was the treatment the doctor adopted and persevered with right up to the child's death. Yet he tells us he believed the girl had been given poison, and whats more he suspected that the poor lady sitting here beside me was the person responsible for this monstrous act. I'd like to know, if these were his conclusions, why he did not take active steps to save the life of the child? Why first of all did he make no attempt whatsoever to antagonise the poison, and why in the second place did he not withdraw the child from the custody of the mother? I defy the doctor to escape from this dilemma.

'I will not do him the injustice of believing that he was capable of treating the child in the way he did with the conclusion in his mind that she was suffering from poisoning. I would also point out that the child was visited by quite a number of other persons, several of whom were left alone with her. Yet she never complained of anything she had been given. I would like to know how the poison could have been administered without the deceased being aware of it. Sulphuric acid? This is the suggestion remember. Sulphuric acid would surely have burnt her mouth very badly and caused her to complain, wouldn't it?

'I am not suggesting that Dr. Harris was mistaken in his findings, although there is a great deal to be said against some of the conclusions he has arrived at. But supposing the post-mortem appearances did suggest that death was due to poisoning. How does the prosecution connect Mrs. Berry with it? She has never attempted to conceal anything. On the contrary. She sent for the doctor promptly. She kept the towels stained with vomit and showed them to him each time he visited. Is this the way a poisoner behaves? This woman has acted the way you would expect a mother to act. As any loving and solicitous mother would. Are we expected to believe that she became the murderer of her own child? And for what motive? For surely no motive has been shown. The imputed motive, so contemptible that I will pass over it with just a bare mention, is the miserable insurance money of £10. That amount was drawn for the purpose of paying the funeral expenses, which in fact came to more than the sum received. Is that a motive? To suggest that a woman in her position should not only have murdered her own child, but to have done it for such a paltry sum of money only goes to show the mares nest into which the prosecution has fallen. I ask the bench; Does the accused look like a murderess? Are her anticedents such as would lead you to suppose she is capable of this terrible crime? Let us assume for the purpose of argument that a crime was committed. Can you connect Mrs. Berry with it? If not, the question to ask yourselves is this; If we send this lady for trial, would a jury of Englishmen convict her? If you have no reasonable belief that they would, and yet you still send her for trial, then I say, with the greatest deference to the bench, that you would be guilty of a violation of public duty. If, however, you feel that there are sufficient grounds to justify committing her, I for one will have no complaints. But before submitting her to such a trying ordeal you should once again ask yourselves these questions; Is there a single portion of the evidence which points to complicity on the part of the prisoner? Remember, it will not do to say that she was there and had access to the poison. No, no, the question must be this; Is there any proof that she administered it?

'Now one final word regarding Dr. Patterson, who seems to have been rather more officious in this case than doctors usually are. And I must say that I have never known of a medical man fraternising with a woman he believed to be a murderess in the way he did. Giving her advice as to the funeral, asking her to allow a post-mortem for the benefit of medical science, and then handing her over to the police – I feel that his conduct was a little inconsistent to say the least. I do not see that he had any reason to consult the mother regarding the death certificate. He had his notes and the post-mortem examination to assist him. If he was so certain that poison was the cause of death why did he not state it on the certificate? I can only suggest to you that the doctor's conduct was very peculiar, and the bench certainly ought not to join him in the suspicions he has thrown out when these suspicions are destitute of any facts.

'I am quite certain", concluded the very eloquent Mr. Cottingham, "that I have the honour of addressing four humane and intelligent English magistrates, who will not pause to speculate on what further evidence might be obtained if the prisoner were committed for trial, but who will do no more than consider the evidence before them now. Gentlemen I confidently await your decision."

With that Mr. Cottingham resumed his seat and Messrs. Wild, Waddington, Collinge and Lees left the court to consider their verdict.

Mr. Cottingham's presentation of his client's case had been extremely skilful. He had come into the hearing a day late, yet he had been the dominant figure from the moment he entered the courtroom. He was the acknowledged expert criminal lawyer and the rest had seemed overawed by his presence. Even the Crown's representative, Mr. Mellor, had shown a decided reluctance to tangle with him, preferring to take the easy route wherever he could, rather than face a head-on clash. He could not be blamed for this of course, being a local official with a somewhat limited knowledge of the law. Mr. Cottingham on the other hand was a thoroughly experienced advocate and veteran of many courtroom skirmishes. Yet allied to this was the sheer magnetism of the man. His built-in confidence, natural aggression and bold handling of the witnesses had obviously impressed the onlookers. If the ladies in court had shown a decided leaning towards the prisoner previously, and this much had become quite evident during the course of the hearing, it was a safe bet that they were now completely won over following Mr. Cottingham's very compelling closing speech. It might truthfully be said that he had poured it on rather thickly in using such terms as 'a jury of English gentlemen' and 'four humane and intelligent English magistrates', but this was standard courtroom procedure, and Mr. Cottingham certainly knew his magistrates and how best to handle them. Apart from the obvious expertise though, the fact remained that he had defended his client in an extremely able manner, and in doing so had presented his case in such a clear cut way that even the humblest layman could follow it step by step and draw his own conclusions. Whether he had impressed the magistrates as much as he obviously had the spectators was yet to be seen, but there was no denying the fact that his arguments had contained as much logic as skill in presentation.

Although the witness Dillan claimed she had seen Mrs. Berry

alone in the surgery with her child, there had been no one to corroborate her evidence. In fact, the testimony of Alice Alcroft had appeared to cast some doubt on her story of having gone into the surgery at the time mentioned, or in fact at any other time that morning.

In addition to this the conduct of Dr. Patterson had certainly left much to be desired when looked at in retrospect. But perhaps the defence's most telling argument was the one regarding motive. It seemed inconceivable that any woman would even consider murdering a child for so trifling a sum as the £10 mentioned. Mr. Cottingham had in the end made it appear that Mrs. Berry was the injured party, and had clearly aroused much sympathy for her among those present.

It was now 4.20 p.m. and a hush descended upon the gathering as the four magistrates filed back into the room, having been out no more than fifteen minutes. Amid the greatest silence Chairman John Wild addressed the court;

"We have given this case our very careful consideration. And we have arrived at the conclusion that the evidence, as laid before us, is not sufficient to warrant us sending the prisoner for trial."

There was a momentary pause, then suddenly a loud burst of cheering from the body of the court and shouts of "Hurrah". On hearing the verdict, Mrs. Berry, who had remained calm throughout, now appeared greatly moved, and hung her head, trying vainly to stifle the tears. The relief she must have felt at that moment was not the only thing which had its effect upon her, for it was clear that the feelings of the audience were to a considerable degree in her favour, and this she must have found quite touching. The tremendous din continued for some minutes and eventually had to be suppressed by the constables.

On being congratulated by Joseph Whittaker and young Robinson, Mr. Cottingham just nodded his acknowledgement and gathered up his papers. He was under no illusions. After getting the worst of it at the inquest they had merely won round two, and he was well aware of it. For what many of the spectators did not realise was that Mrs. Berry would not be released, but would remain in custody, charged on a Coroner's warrant with wilful murder. However, bearing in mind the result of the magistrial inquiry, the prisoner's final acquittal would, in normal circumstances, have been no more than a formality; but it would not now be that simple, as Mr. Cottingham realised only too well. For during the latter part of January the police had been very active indeed, and several new and hitherto unknown facts regarding Mrs. Berry's past were beginning to come to light.

CHAPTER 5
LETTERS TO THE EDITOR

It was during an interview with Ann Sanderson that the name Mary Ann Finley was first mentioned. According to Mrs. Sanderson the woman had died at Castleton, near Rochdale, some twelve months previously, and as she had been the mother of Elizabeth Berry, Inspector Purser paused for a moment to wonder if her death, which had apparently been rather sudden, could possibly have any significance in the light of the current investigation at Oldham. Probably not, but he made a note of it anyway and passed it on to the Chief Constable, who seemed to think the matter might be worth persuing. One of his men, a Detective Rawlins, was sent over to Castleton with instructions to make a few discreet inquiries. His visit was followed several days later by that of a colleague, Detective Lamb, and information gleaned by the two of them subsequently passed over to the Coroner. Mr. Molesworth, after studying the report carefully, decided to forward it to the Rochdale Police.

Of course the press very quickly got wind of what was going on, but despite persistent requests for information, both the Coroner and the police remained silent on the matter, apart from admitting that a lengthy interview had taken place between Mr. Molesworth, Dr. Harris and Superintendent Tindall of the Rochdale Police.

On the Wednesday following the Magistral Inquiry a letter was printed in the Oldham Evening Chronicle severely criticising Dr. Patterson's treatment of his patient and applauding the Magistrates action in dismissing the case. It was written by a former local doctor named John Kershaw, who had obviously followed the court proceedings very closely and who now felt it his duty to bring to the notice of the public what he felt had been a gross mis-handling of the medical side of the case. The letter ran;

Having watched with considerable forensic interest the

progress of the so called Oldham Poisoning Case, I feel it is my duty, in the interests of justice, first to congratulate the presiding magistrates on the sound sense and judgement they have shown in exonerating Mrs. Berry from the serious charge brought against her by the Medical Officer of the Oldham Workhouse. I will also, with your kind permission, draw your attention, as well as that of my medical bretheren, to the extraordinary evidence of the Medical Officer, particularly that relating to the creosote and the unscientific manner in which it was prescribed. Also to the results possibly arising from its mode of administration.

In his evidence Dr. Patterson says that after the first medicine he prescribed (tincture of iron and cinchona bark) had been vomited back by the patient, he gave her a mixture of bicarbonate of soda with the rinsings of a creosote bottle. He also mentions that he sent this bottle to the chemists to be filled, and instructed the mother to disolve 8 drops in a 12 oz. bottle of water and give the patient a tablespoonful every two hours. That same evening he found the child worse and noticed the reddening around her lips. He now tells us 'I came to the conclusion that between my morning and evening visits an irritant and probably corrosive poison had been administered.' Up to that point he does not appear to have entertained or expressed any suspicion of foul play.

The medical interest in this case appears to me to depend chiefly on the inflamed condition of the mouth and lips. Has it never occurred to the various medical witnesses that the irritant poison creosote, administered in the way described by Dr. Patterson, would fully account for the state of the child's mouth?

Let us for a moment examine into the character of creosote. It is described as a mixture of volatile oils obtained by the destructive distillation of wood, having a strong empyreumatic odour and burning taste, sparingly soluable in water. It is frequently adulterated with carbolic acid, and its action and uses are those of carbolic acid.

Now, from the evidence of Dr. Patterson, it does not appear that he took advantage of the pharmaceutical mode of administering the drug as recommended and authorised by the College of Physicians, but gave the oil in its crude state, as received from the chemist, water only being the medicine used. This being so, the creosote or 'oil of tar', would, from its specific gravity (1071) be unmixable with water, and would therefore settle to the bottom of the bottle. If the mixture was shaken well before taking, the creosote would, in its concentrated state, come into contact with the lips and skin around the mouth, and would then give rise to all the symptoms described.

The dose of creosote is from one to two drops for an adult and for a child of eleven should be about half a drop. Is it not possible from the foregoing evidence that the child was inadvertently given more than the authorised dose, and that too in its concentrated form, owing to its administration in the crude state?

With regard to the case in its legal aspect I have nothing to do, but from motives of humanity, as well as saving the poor woman from the approbation of the uncharitable, I have presumed to place before you a matter which I believe has not received that attention which the vital importance of the case deserved.
The letter was signed;

Yours truly,
JOHN KERSHAW, F.R.C.S. L.R.C.P. & etc.,
late medical officer of health for Royton.
Sedgley Park, Prestwich, Manchester –
January 30th, 1887.

The public criticism of such a well known and respected man as Dr. Patterson was certainly a very serious matter and there is no doubt that he was extremely disturbed by it. He was also very hurt and angry, and made up his mind immediately to draft out a reply. Before he could put pen to paper, however, a further letter was received by the Chronicle, this time speaking out in the doctor's defence. It was signed C. Granville Wood, Associate of the Pharmaceutical Society, 30 High Street, Oldham. In it Mr. Wood claimed that;

> Dr. Kershaw has evidently not tried to disolve eight drops of creosote in twelve ounces of water, or he would not have made the statement as to its insolubility. I have made the mixture in the proportions Dr. Patterson ordered and got a presentable mixture, quite clear, and in fact a permanent solution. (No separation has yet taken place and the mixture has been at rest about fifteen hours). The solution is perfectly in accordance with the laws and rules of accurate dispensing.

The letter certainly appeared to be quite a strong vindication of Dr. Patterson's actions, and to have let the matter rest there would have been the wisest and certainly the most dignified thing to do. But Dr. Kershaw's scathing indictment had obviously stung the Workhouse Medical officer very badly, and he was determined to follow up the chemists letter with another, more cutting one, of his own. Sure enough, on the Friday, there it was. It began as a brief analysis of Dr. Kershaw's criticisms, went on to answer them in detail, then proceeded to deliver the coup de grace in rather vicious and defamatory terms. It is worth reproducing in its entirety;

Sir, I cannot think that motives of humanity alone prompted Dr. Kershaw to write that letter in Wednesdays Chronicle. Had his objective been to benefit the 'poor woman' I think he would have accomplished it better by observing the usual prudence of silence while the matter is still under judgement. Besides, I understood that Mrs. Berry had in Mr. Cottingham an experienced and able advocate to whom Dr. Kershaw could have communicated his valuable suggestions, which I will briefly examine.

1   Dr. Kershaw says my prescription of creosote was unscientific - only his ignorance. Let him try to make it and he will find that the solution is perfect. Not only so, but that it can be made of greater strength than that prescribed by me. His statement is therefore untrue.

2. He suggested that undiluted creosote would blister the lips. There was no undiluted creosote, for the mixture prescribed was never made. But it would not blister the lips in any case. I painted the edges of my own lips with raw creosote, and could not blister them. I also painted the lips of four children of the same age as the deceased, keeping the creosote on for six minutes. I did not put a blister on any one of them. Statement number two is therefore also untrue.

3. Dr. Kershaw suggests that I had no suspicion of poisoning until the Sunday night. On the contrary, I told Mr. Cottingham at the Workhouse enquiry that I suspected poison on the Saturday evening, but he took good care not to ask me any questions

regarding this at the Magistrates Court. So statement number three is untrue also.

The blistering of the lips, the vomiting and purging of blood and intense pain in the abdomen in life, in conjunction with the corroded spot on the gullet found at the post-mortem, told the story pretty well. And now in conclusion, how has Dr. Kershaw 'from motives of humanity to the poor woman', benefited her by writing such an umprudent letter made up of absurdities and untruths?

Alas dear Dr. John! it has been so with you for many years now. The rattle of your relatives money in your pocket, has, I fear, turned your poor weak empty head.
T. PATTERSON.

The letter was rather strong to say the least, with the last paragraph something of a blow below the belt. Perhaps Dr Patterson's anger was not to be wondered at, bearing in mind that his professional knowledge and integrity had been questioned. Yet it seems a pity that he should find it necessary to be so petty and personal in his closing remarks, especially as he had already dealt with Dr. Kershaw's criticism so convincingly earlier in his letter. In any event the tirade apparently had the desired effect, for it does not appear to have elicited a reply from the former Royton Medical Officer.

While the two local doctors scribbled away feverishly, the case against Mrs. Berry was slowly strengthening. Along with several other items, a piece of carpet, on which the deceased had vomited, had been removed from the sitting room and sent for analysis. So that the Jury would have a clearer picture of things, a plan of the prisoner's sitting room and the surgery had been drawn up, as well as other drawings of the block of buildings in which her bedroom was situated.

Had the magistrates hearing been concluded a day or two

earlier, Mrs. Berry's case would have been referred to the Manchester Assizes, then in session, and she would have been required to travel only a matter of seven miles or so to stand trial. As it was the case would now be heard at Liverpool Assizes later that month. The prisoner was therefore transported to Walton Jail on the outskirts of Liverpool, there to sweat it out for the next three weeks in the knowledge that further investigations were taking place, which, though not directly connected with the death of her child, might well have a great bearing on the case against her.

CHAPTER 6
FRIENDS AND NEIGHBOURS

Since the circumstances surrounding Mary Ann Finley's death had been brought to his attention Superintendent Tindall had been informed by the Coroner that nothing further could be done until a certain document arrived from the Home Office. The Superintendent, however, was not the sort of man who took kindly to the idea of waiting around. He therefore set about gathering as much information as possible regarding the deceased woman.

She had lived in the neighbourhood of Bury Road, Rochdale in 1883, but in 1884 had moved to Back Albion Street in the nearby village of Castleton. Twice married, she was then living apart from her second husband, a man named Finley, and though this was her legal surname she was still known to some people as Mrs. Welsh, this having been the name of her first husband.

Mrs. Finley supported herself by working as a weaver at Phythians Mill, Castleton, and among her fellow workers and neighbours was highly respected, her friendly disposition and general steadiness gaining her many friends. Despite her affable manner, however, it was obvious that she was not an altogether happy woman, and not long after moving to Castleton she confided to some of her closest friends that the cause of her sadness was the fact that she was at variance with her daughter Lizzie, who had not 'owned' her for some time past, although she was not clear as to the reason.

Around Christmas time 1884 however, Mrs. Finley received a letter from her daughter's sister-in-law Mrs. Sanderson, inviting her to go to Miles Platting and visit her grand-daughter Edith Annie. She showed the letter to a neighbour who urged her to accept the invitation as it might possibly lead to a reconciliation with Lizzie. She decided to take the neighbours advice, and on returning from Miles Platting announced that she had made it up with her daughter and all was now well between them.

It was more than a year after this episode that the neighbours first set eyes on Lizzie. When they did they were very impressed, one remarking, 'She was quite a lady, who knew Latin and foreign languages and such like."

According to the villagers in Castleton she had arrived to stay with her mother in February 1886 and had remained until Mrs. Finley's sudden death just ten days later. She had talked to several of them over tea one day and told them that she had recently returned from Birmingham Union Workhouse, where she had gone to take up an appointment, but on turning up had found that the person she was to replace was not due to vacate her position for another week. Mrs. Berry had therefore taken the opportunity to travel up to Castleton so that she might spend a few days with her mother, who had not been well.

At the time of her daughter's arrival, Mrs. Finley, who had been troubled by nose bleeds, was feeling much better, but within a matter of two or three days she became ill again, this time developing rather alarming symptoms. Several times over the next few days she seemed to recover somewhat, only to become suddenly worse again. On the thirteenth of February she died, and was buried two days later at Moston Cemetery, Manchester.

It was said that after the funeral Mrs. Berry and another relative had returned to Castleton and started to "sell up the house", the first things to go being Mrs. Finley's clothes. The sale was proceeded with so speedily that within a couple of days the place was stripped completely and Mrs. Berry gone from the village, after which nothing was seen or heard of her again until reports of the Oldham Poisoning Case began to appear in the newspapers almost a year later.

Mary Ann Finley's death had come as something of a shock to her neighbours. Yet if any of them had harboured suspicions regarding the circumstances of it there does not appear to be any record of their having voiced them at the time. Since the news of

Mrs. Berry's arrest had been made public, however, the wagging tongues were working overtime, more especially in view of the fact that Back Albion Street, Castleton, had recently been visited by detectives from Oldham.

Superintendent Tindall now decided to take the investigation a step further, and made the short journey to Castleton for the purpose of talking to the neighbours himself and going into their stories in greater depth.

At some time after the last century the block which formed Albion Street and Back Albion Street was completely altered and renovated, so that the front doors of Back Albion Street became the rear exists of Albion Street,

In 1886, when Mary Ann Finley lived there, these were two sets of seperate back-to-back cottages, at the end of which was a fire station, where horse-drawn wagonettes were kept. This later became a cobblers shop. The whole block, which stood at the lower end of what is now the busy thoroughfare known as Queensway, was demolished around 1980.

The Blue Pitts Inn, of which more will be heard later, stands on the main Rochdale-Manchester Road, and is no more than a hundred yards or so from where Back Albion Street stood, while Phythians Mill, where the unfortunate Mrs. Finley earned her living, is now a part of the premises of Whipp and Bourne Ltd. It is below the Blue Pitts Inn, going in the direction of Manchester, and the old Phythians section of it, which must be just about as ancient as anything in the district, is now in quite a bad state, the brickwork crumbling and bellying out, causing huge cracks to appear in the walls..

In the latter part of the nineteenth century Phythians was a small but busy little mill, employing a good number of people, living mostly within yards of its big gates. They were honest hard-working folk, earning just about enough to get by on, with very little to spare for luxuries or entertainment. Some were born and died in the village without ever travelling much further than Rochdale in an entire lifetime. Certainly, these people experienced almost nothing in the way of excitement, and the arrival of the law in Back Albion Street, the third such visit within the space of a week, was more than enough to keep them talking, and to increase speculation as to how Mary Ann Finley had met her death.

At Number 6 the Superintendent spoke to 29 year old Mary Ann Lyons, wife of Thomas Lyons, a carder, who told him that she had known Mrs. Finley well, and saw her practically every day when she was alive. She was sure that the first sign of illness had been a bleeding from the nose, which had started in the early part of February 1886. She seemed to recover from this, but soon after had become ill again and "taken to her bed". Mrs Lyons had not seen her after that until she had gone to the house to visit on Tuesday February 9th. At that time Mrs. Finley's daughter was staying there, and the mother seemed to be in a poor state of health. However, when Mrs. Lyons went in again on the Friday she found the older woman much brighter, and said to her;

"I think you're getting better love."

Mrs. Finley smiled and agreed that she was.

"I left her at 10 o'clock that night in quite good spirits," said Mrs. Lyons, "and got a real shock the next day when I was told she had died at seven that morning. I helped to lay her away, and noticed that the lips were very much swollen and bluish in colour."

After leaving Mary Ann Lyons, Tindall knocked at Number 11. Sarah Ann Wolfenden opened the door. Mrs. Wolfenden, whose husband worked as an overlooker at a local cotton mill, had been one of the dead woman's closest friends. She told him;

"I remember Mrs. Berry calling at my house on the 3rd of February last year. It was a Wednesday, and she had come to visit her mother, not knowing that Mrs. Finley had gone to Manchester that morning.

'I went into Mary Ann's house often and saw her every day while she was ill. Early in February she had a nose bleed, but Dr. Sharples attended her and she got well of that. But this other illness was very strange. I saw her on the Tuesday morning as she died on the Saturday, and she seemed well enough then. In the afternoon she came in here and brought me some tea and toast. That same night she was taken poorly after she got home from my house, and I went in to see her. She told me she had felt bad after having her tea. I saw her on the Friday, the night before she died. She was still in bed but looked a lot better, and said she felt it.

'I left her at eleven o'clock that night and went back at seven, or it might have been a few minutes before, the next morning. Well …. I had a shock. She was dying. She lay there twitching all over her body. Every nerve seemed to be at work. Her breast was rising and falling and her tongue hanging out of her mouth. I remarked on the difference from the night before and asked Mrs. Berry when her mother had taken the change. She said it took place with the turn of the night. I offered to go and fetch Mrs. Lever who lives at the endmost house, but Mrs. Berry stopped me at the door and said I must not bring anybody, as she had no wish to let people see her mother like that. Soon after this the poor woman stopped twitching. She was dead."

"Did you help to lay her away?" Tindall asked her.

"Yes I did."

"Did you notice anything about the lips?

"No … apart from the fact that they were a bit swollen I think."

Superintendent Tindall thanked her, and at Mrs. Wolfenden's suggestion called at Number 14, where he interviewed Alice Eaves, who clearly remembered the events leading up to Mrs. Finley's death. She recalled Mrs. Berry coming to stay with her mother.

"She arrived on the 3rd of February, and on the 9th, that

would be the following Tuesday, Mrs. Finley became ill. That afternoon I saw her at Sarah Wolfenden's house and she did look poorly. I told her to go home and get to bed, which she did. I went in to see her later that night and she was very bad. In a dreadful state she was."

"Was she conscious?", asked Tindall.

"Well I think so, but she seemed like she was in a fit or something. I was so upset when I saw her I ran out and fetched my husband. I thought she was dying. I sent word to Sarah's as well."

"Was Mrs. Berry there?"

"Yes", replied Mrs. Eaves. "She took a small bottle off the mantlepiece while we were in and gave her mother a spoonful out of it. After she'd taken it Mary Ann went a bit quieter. We were all gathered round the bed, but she didn't seem to know us. There was a lamp in the room and I held it up near the bed to show a light, but Mrs. Berry said she didn't need a light and told me to take it away. Before we left Mary Ann's eyes were shut and she looked all flushed."

"How long did you stay?"

"Oh about half-an-an-hour I think. I offered to stop all night, but Mrs. Berry wouldn't let me. She said she wasn't frightened and would manage on her own.

'On the Friday morning I was at the house again when I took the Prudential agent in, because Mrs. Finley had told me she wanted one of her policies endorsed. When we got in Mrs. Berry was washing her mother, who was still in bed. I was having a conversation with her when Mrs. Berry said "Don't talk to her. Her pulse is beating faster than it should." Mary Ann told her daughter where to find the policies and she went and fetched them.

'I went in again that night and found Mary Ann alone with her sister, a Mrs. Pemberton. Mrs. Berry had gone out."

"This was on the Friday night?"

"Yes, early on."

"How was she at that time?"

"Oh much better. She was sitting up in bed eating some cake, and asked me to get her a drink of beer."

"Beer?"

"Aye that's right. She liked a drink did Mary Ann. She told me there was a bottle in the cupboard but Lizzie had forbidden her to have it. Mrs. Berry had gone to Rochdale to fetch her some nourishment and was expected back any minute, and she wanted a drink before she came."

"Did you get it for her?"

"Course I did. Well she had such a longing for it, poor thing. Wasn't a drunkard or owt like that, but she liked a sup."

"Did you go back in next morning?"

"Aye .... but she was dead then. I got the shock of me life when I heard. Mrs. Berry said there'd been a great change in the night."

"Did you see the body?"

"Yes."

"Is there anything you can remember about the mouth or lips?"

"No, I didn't see her face. It was covered up."

Mrs. Finley's next door neighbour, Harriet Dorrick, confirmed most of the details of the other women's stories and told of having met Mrs. Finley in the street on Friday February 5th, a week before her death.

"She said she hadn't been well and that her daughter Lizzie was staying with her for company. She said Lizzie had given her some medicine and she had felt sick and queer after drinking it. I said perhaps it would make her feel better. She showed me a jug of bitter which she had under her shawl and said she'd been to fetch the supper beer. She said she thought the walk would do her good."

The medicine was again referred to when Tindall questioned Alice Chorlton, who had been in the habit of calling at Mrs. Finley's house on her way home from work.

"I saw Mary Ann on the night before she died. It was six o'clock in the evening and she was in bed, but seemed much better. She called me to her bedside, putting her finger to her lips, as much as to say she was dry. I turned to Mrs. Berry and said - "Lizzie, your mother wants a drink." Mrs. Berry told me she would not have the medicine from her and asked me to try and get her to take it. She poured some stuff from a bottle into a cup. I added water to it and lifted Mary Ann's head up off the pillow. She drank it straight off and said – 'Oh dear that's bad. It's worse than poison."

"Did you see Mrs. Finley after she was dead?", asked the Superintendent.

"Yes", was the reply, "but I didn't look closely at her."

So far each account of Mrs. Finley's death had been consistent with the others, and apart from the fact that the dead woman had apparently been partial to a gill of bitter, several other points had now been established. First, the onset of Mrs. Finley's fatal illness had coincided with the arrival of Mrs. Berry to Castleton, give or take a day or two. All the women questioned agreed that it had come on rather suddenly, and had been quite startling in its severity. On several occasions the patient had appeared to be on the verge of recovery, but each time had experienced an unaccountable relapse During this period she was looked after by her daughter, who, if the neighbours were to be believed, had discouraged visitors as far as she possibly could. She had also been seen to administer a liquid of some kind which the mother had found most disagreeable. The word 'poison' had even been mentioned.

From experience Tindall knew that in retrospect it is often a simple matter to make a set of circumstances fit a crime, or in this case a suspected crime. And although the former neighbours of Mrs. Finley had seemed very sure of their facts, there were certain little embellishments that did nothing to lend credulity to their stories. This account, given by Henrietta Morton, of nearby Cross Street, is a good example.

"Mrs. Finley and her daughter came to visit me on the 5th of February last year. While we were having tea Mrs. Berry told me she had had a dream, and that when she had a dream of this sort there was always a death in the family. She said she dreamt she had gone to a new situation and was walking down one of the wards. She noticed that the beds were placed feet to feet. When she reached the end of the ward she saw that one bed had been reversed and there was a person lying in it. She asked who it was, and then saw it was her mother. Her mother didn't speak, but lifted herself up on one elbow. Mrs. Berry then saw that there were marks of blood on the bed."

Mrs. Morton seemed to consider that her story of the dream had some significance, and found it difficult to understand why the Superintendent did not persue the matter. To Tindall of course it was simply a question of encouraging the neighbours to talk in the hope that something of importance might be uncovered.

From Henrietta Morton he also learned that Mrs. Berry had had in her possession a prescription, which she claimed had been torn out of a doctor's book, presumably at one of her places of employment. She had not produced it, but had asked Mrs. Morton if there was a pharmaceutical chemist in Castleton. and had been told that there wasn't, but that she could get the prescription filled at Mr. Highley's shop in Rochdale.

If the prescription note had in fact been removed from a doctor's pad, it had no doubt been a blank one, the Superintendent reasoned, which would then have to be filled in before presentation.

If this was so it could mean only one of two things. Either Mrs. Berry had had very little faith in Dr. Sharples, who had treated her mother, or she had been intent on obtaining some mixture which was not calculated to aid the patient's recovery. If the note was still in existence, or if a record of it had been kept by the chemist, Tindall would in all probability learn precisely what had been administered to Mrs. Finley during the last fatal week of her illness.

With this in mind he returned to Rochdale, but was disappointed to learn that Mr. Highley had no such record, nor could he recall having served a woman answering Mrs. Berry's description. There was nothing for it but to make the rounds of all chemists in the area, and Tindall had barely begun this tedious exercise when he received an urgent summons to contact the Coroner. As usual the newspapers were well aware of the Superintendent's movements, and after his second meeting with Mr. Molesworth he was inundated with requests for information, which he still insisted he was not at liberty to divulge.

It was then that the newspapers began to draw their own conclusions, some even going so far as to state that the body of Mrs. Berry's mother would very likely be exhumed. The Oldham Chronicle, which claimed to have received information from 'a reliable source' substantiating this, decided to dig a little deeper, and sent one of their best reporters to Moston Cemetery with instructions to find out all he could regarding the rumoured exhumation.

CHAPTER 7

EXHUMATION

St. Josephs Roman Catholic Cemetery, Moston, was opened in 1875 and stands roughly midway between Oldham and the centre of Manchester. It has been for many years the chief burial ground of the Catholics of Manchester and is quite extensive, covering the best part of thirty acres. It is also one of the finest and best laid out cemeteries in the area, although many parts are now falling into decay due to lack of funds.

From its inception the cemetery was administered by a brotherhood of monks known as the Alexians, who undertook to 'bury the dead and help the infirm', and who still maintain a nursing home at St. Marys Road, Moston.

Some of the tombstones that mark the graves of the more prominent or prosperous Catholics are quite grandiose in size and character, whilst the burial ground of the priests, which stands next to the church and dominates the approach from the main gate, is marked by a massive stone cross and encircled by a series of stones inscribed with the names of those buried there.

Not far from this spot stands a towering monument to three reckless young men who have gone down in history as Irish patriots. Their names were Allen, Larkin and O'Brien, and they were members of an organization known as the Fenian Brotherhood, a group of revolutionaries formed in the middle of the last century.

The trio in question were among the ringleaders in a raid on a police van in 1867. In the fracas that ensued a police-sergeant was shot and killed; an act for which the three young Irishmen paid with their lives. One of the three, along with several other Fenians, had been defended by Mr. James Cottingham.

A short distance away, just beyond the church, is a lengthy path, at the end of which stands what can best be described as a huge temple. This is known as a Campo Santo. It is a copy of a similar one in Genoa, Italy, and houses the vaults in which lie the bodies of bishops and other dignitaries of the church. In 1886, when Mary Ann Finley was brought to Moston for burial, there was also a 'Calvary', which stood close to the church. Intended as a re-enactment of the crucifixion, it comprised a cross with the nails in position , a ladder and a hammer and pincers. There was another just like it which stood some distance away in a different section of the cemetery. Being carved in wood, these have long since disintegrated and no sign of them now remains.

Section D, where Mrs. Finley was interred, is only a short walk from the priests burial ground, but to go from one spot to the other is like passing into another cemetery. For this is one of the neglected areas and contains row after row of public or 'inscription' graves, all exactly the same design, like war graves, except that they are marked by a stone slab rather than a wooden cross. Though blackened by time the tiny white crosses cut into them still stand out vividly, and when visited at dusk have a weird and sinister appearance. Some of the headstones have now toppled over and lie forlornly in the coarse grass, the names of the long since forgotten people buried there being slowly but surely covered over by the gathering moss.

The Oldham Chronicle's reporter arrived at Moston on a cold and windy February afternoon in 1887 and sought out the Brother Superior, who immediately denied all knowledge of any exhumation. He had not heard a word about it he said, apart from what he had read in the newspapers. "In fact", he told the reporter, "its extremely unlikely that the body of Mrs. Finley will be exhumed, for there are eleven others in the same grave."

The reporter, though now somewhat doubtful, asked to see the grave, and followed Brother Kleppell as he rather reluctantly led the way to Section D. The first thing the reporter noticed was the fact that only nine names appeared on the headstone, and on pointing this out was told that in these graves lay the remains of those whose relatives could afford no more that the bare cost of such a burial, which in 1887 amounted to six shillings and sixpence, plus an extra few shillings if an inscription was to be cut upon the stone. Although only nine names appeared on this particular one, three others, whose names were not inscribed, had also been buried there.

"Only four of the other bodies were put down before Mrs. Finley's," Brother Kleppell informed the reporter. "The three children and four others were interred after her. So you see, if an exhumation did take place, seven bodies would have to be raised before the one in question was reached. In any case the relatives of these poor people would most certainly object very strongly to any interference with the dead, and on their behalf I shall oppose any such steps being taken."

With that the reporter left the cemetery and returned to Oldham, fairly certain now that an exhumation was most unlikely. However, on the following day, a Tuesday, two policemen visited the cemetery and talked to the Brother Superior, and though every effort was made to keep the meeting secret, the news inevitably reached the newspapers. The Chronicle, which did not receive this information until Wednesday, promptly despatched their man to Moston again, where he was received with very little enthusiasm by Brother Kleppell, who was beginning to find the whole business extremely annoying.

"No, I cannot tell you anything more than I already have", he told the reporter.

When asked if there was any truth in the story that he had received a visit from the police, Brother Kleppell replied that his 'mouth was closed', by order of the board. When it was suggested that the body had already been exhumed, he denied this, but eventually admitted that it would be disinterred on the following day. This was all he was prepared to say, and as it was now quite dark and a further prowl around the cemetery did not particularly appeal to him, the reporter decided to let things rest for that night and return the next day, although he had been unable to elicit from Brother Kleppell the time arranged for the exhumation.

On leaving the cemetery the reporter paused for a moment outside the gates. He was not entirely satisfied that the Brother Superior had told all he knew, and before returning to Oldham the reporter decided to seek information elsewhere. After making inquiries in the neighbourhood, he was directed to the house of Matthew Tyson, foreman gravedigger, who was just home from work, but who insisted that he could be of no help. The abruptness of his manner, however, made the reporter more than ever certain that something was going on, and after leaving Tyson he returned to the cemetery, which he now found locked up. Leaving the road, he crossed a neighbouring field, to where a thorn hedge ran between it and the north-east corner of the cemetery. At this point he found himself no more than fifteen yards from the grave of Mary Ann Finley, and a small light immediately attracted his attention. From his position behind the hedge he could make out three dim figures apparently working at the graveside. Unfortunately, as he leaned closer to peer through the thicket, he stumbled, and the slight noise caused the workmen to stop and listen. They must have seen him, for they immediately concealed themselves behind a nearby gravestone, where they waited for quite some time. Eventually one of them appeared carrying a lantern and crossed to the hedge, asking; "Who are you and what's your business here?" When told, he did not appear too pleased, and when asked what he himself was doing there in the dark, the man replied that he was a watchman. Judging from his dress, however, the reporter took him to be a gravedigger, and asked; "How long have you been digging?" This he would not answer, nor would he reply when he was asked., "What time do you think the body will be taken out?"

Having failed to discourage the unwelcome spectator the lantern carrier returned to the graveside, where the work was silently resumed, while the reporter remained by the hedge for a while longer watching them. It was now well past nine in the evening and he was very cold. So as the work did not appear to be nearing a conclusion, and also because he felt dubious about his position there, the reporter decided to end his vigil and return to Oldham with his story. If he had stayed much longer he would no doubt have been cleared off by the Brother Superior in any case, for Kleppell appeared shortly afterwards and stayed for some considerable time watching the diggers at work. Later that night other reporters arrived on the scene and hung about for a while before being dispersed by the Brother Superior.

Meanwhile the gravediggers toiled on, their work being made all the more laborious on account of the fact that much rain had fallen over the previous two days, leaving the ground very soggy and the clay wet and glue-like. Eventually the first coffin was reached and the job of raising each one begun. It was well after midnight before this was done. By that time, seven coffins, including several very small ones, lay on the path, and the night's eerie work was completed.

. . . .

At seven o'clock next morning a group of people met outside the Blue Pitts Inn, Castleton. They included Dr. Sharples, fifteen jurymen and Superintendent Tindall, who had assembled them together for the purpose of holding an inquest. At five minutes past eight the Coroner arrived and the jurymen were sworn in, after which they boarded a horsedrawn wagonette and set off for Moston. Also in the party were Mary Ann Lyons and Sarah Ann Wolfenden, whose odious task it would be to identify the body.

The party reached Moston Cemetery shortly before nine o'clock, to find Dr. Harris waiting for them with Brother Superior. When all were gathered around the graveside the ropes were placed in position and the coffin slowly raised out of the ground.

As they watched, the expressions on the faces of those present showed that they were very uneasy, especially the two women, who seemed rather unnerved by it all.

The coffin was laid on the path, and after lumps of clay and soil had been scraped away the nameplate could be clearly seen;

MARY ANN FINLEY
Died 13th February 1886
Aged 55 years
"Rest in Peace"

Two trestles were brought and the coffin lifted onto these, so that it was now at waist height. The lid was removed, and to assist identification, a bucket of water was carried to the spot and poured over the face of the dead woman. The fifteen jurymen then filed past the coffin to view the remains. When this had been done the two women were asked to step forward, which they did somewhat reluctantly. They were obviously very much affected as they looked down once more upon the face of their former friend, and each took no more than a hurried glance before nodding and turning away again.

Their revulsion was hardly surprising, for the face of the deceased was by now swollen and grotesque, the body being in an advanced state of decomposition.

The identification having been satisfactorily concluded, the party re-boarded the wagonette amd was driven back to Castleton to open the inquest, Dr. Harris remaining behind to begin the post-mortem examination, which was to be carried out on the spot, the cemetery being closed to the public for that day. The work took several hours and was not completed until the early part of the afternoon, by which time parts of the stomach had been placed in bottles. Dr. Harris then announced that the body was ready for its second interment, and left the cemetery, taking with him the bottles and also samples of soil from around the coffin.

At ten minutes past eleven that morning the crowded wagonette arrived back at the Blue Pitts Inn, where its occupants disembarked and filed solemnly into the bar parlour, which was just about large enough to accommodate them.

On taking his seat, Mr. Molesworth, District Coroner, explained that the body of Mary Ann Finley had been exhumed at the request of the County Police Authorities and with the sanction of the Home Secretary.

Mary Ann Lyons was called first, and told the assembly;

"Mrs. Finley died on the 13th of February last year. She was fifty-five I believe. I never knew her husband and to the best of my knowledge never saw him in my life. I have no doubt that the dead body I've seen this morning is Mary Ann Finley."

She was followed by Sarah Ann Wolfenden, who said;

"The body lying there at Moston Cemetery is that of Mary Ann Finley. I'm quite certain about it. I laid her away."

At this point some uncertainty arose as to the number of the deceased's house. Mrs. Wolfenden said it had been mentioned that it was number 6, but she did not think this was correct. However, as there was no number on the door she could not be positive. She said she thought it was really the back door of a house in another street, which only served to add to the confusion. The Coroner, impatient to get on with the case and not wishing to be bogged down by insignificant, if necessary, details, sent a constable off to check the house number. He returned within a short space of time with the information that it was in fact number 4.

The Coroner then told the gathering;

"I do not intend to take any further evidence today. The identification has been satisfactorily dealt with and we must now wait until the doctors have made their report."

He was asked by a juror how long this would take and replied that it could be as much as ten days. It was therefore decided to adjourn until February 14th.

As far as Superintendent Tindall was concerned the first part of the operation had been successfully completed and the scales of justice now seemed to be balanced rather ominously against Elizabeth Berry. For some reason Mrs. Berry's solicitor was apparently ignorant of all that was going on at this time, and by all accounts did not hear about the exhumation until sometime later that morning. After ascertaining that his source of information was a reliable one, he decided that expert assistance was called for, and immediately sent off a telegram to none other than Dr. John Kershaw of Prestwich, requesting him to be present at the Cemetery on Mrs. Berry's behalf.

Dr. John was only too pleased to oblige. He was already somewhat deflated following those two rather telling replies to his letter and was not eager to see his theory demolished completely. Within minutes he was enroute to Moston, where he intended to introduce himself to Dr. Harris as an official representative for the defence. He was therefore very disappointed indeed to find on his arrival, the post-mortem completed and the reburial already well under way.

....

Joseph Whittaker was a very worried man as he sat in his St. Peters Street Chambers later that day and considered the events of the morning.

Whatever the post-mortem on Mary Ann Finley revealed he knew only too well that the very fact of its taking place could be prejudicial to Mrs. Berry's case. By that evening it would be common knowledge, for the newspapers would obviously give it wide coverage, and he felt it was totally wrong that the Castleton investigation should be opened at all while his client was still held in custody pending what he hoped would be her formal dismissal.

After all, the same woman might be involved, but it was a completely different case and should not be allowed to have any bearing on the trial of Mrs. Berry at Liverpool Assizes.

As he ruefully considered the grave implications of the affair at Castleton, he thought of his client languishing there in Walton Gaol. A previously bright and vivacious woman, she had appeared lifeless and depressed on his last visit, and even the arrival of friends from Burton-on-Trent had done little to lift her spirits.

This was not really surprising, for many things were troubling her, not the least of which was the fact that an appeal to the public for money with which to pay for her defence had met with very little response. Considering the magistral hearing had shown the majority of the people in court to be in sympathy with her, there had been every reason to expect support for the appeal, which was made through two local newspapers. Unfortunately for the prisoner it had barely been launched when rumours of the Castleton investigation began circulating, and there is little doubt that this had the effect of altering public sentiment towards her and seriously hampering all efforts to raise money on her behalf.

The day prior to the exhumation had seen the opening of the Liverpool Assizes, with Mr. Justice Hawkins delivering his charge to the Grand Jury. In these days when we are constantly informed that the crime figures are increasing at an alarming rate, it is interesting to note that the calender at Liverpool in the spring of 1887 contained the names of no fewer than 90 persons, three of whom were charged with murder, three with manslaughter and eight with offences against women with children.

Referring to the Oldham Poisoning Case, Mr. Justice Hawkins pointed out that although the Coroners Jury had given a verdict of wilful murder against the defendant, the magistrates had not seen fit to commit her for trial.

"Nevertheless", he told the jury, "the bill will be presented to you in order that your judgement may be given on the matter."

In passing briefly over the known facts of the case he made a point of mentioning that the child's life had been insured "at the Prudential Office", and that she had been in perfect health on her arrival at the Workhouse. These are points to be noted, as his Lordship was later to be accused by some newspapers of having a decided leaning towards the prosecution.

He also mentioned in his opening speech, however, that although in the deposition it was stated that a powder had been brought from the surgery on the morning the deceased had first complained of feeling unwell, there was no evidence that the prisoner herself had gone into the surgery to get it. "But", he said, with great emphasis, "the mother and child were seen in the surgery together just prior to the time the girl was seized with a fit of vomiting, which continued more or less until a short time before her death. The prisoner has said that her child was always weak, and there are other statements attributed to her, such as - "I cannot bear to see her draw her last breath" - when the child was approaching her end and the mother left her. Not that these statements are any proof of the allegations against the prisoner, but they must be taken into account. They may be innocent expressions, but are still part of the story which will be told to you. After the child died an analysis was made of the contents of the stomach, and although no trace of any poison was discovered, there are three or four medical gentlemen who will give evidence that the child died of some corrosive poison. The question therefore is by whom and how was that poison administered. Was it by the prisoner? If it is not proved that it was, then there is no case to answer."

After giving the jury a full outline of the depositions, the judge passed on to other cases on the calender. It would be some days before the Oldham Poisoning Case came up, but as far as the defence was concerned the crucial question was when. Mr.

Whittaker had been given to understand that Monday of the following week was a likely date, and this was perfectly acceptable, as it would then take place several days prior to the resumed inquest at Castleton, and so would be less likely to be affected by it. However, the defenders of Mrs. Berry were to meet with a disappointment here, for several of the cases preceeding hers turned out to be somewhat lengthy affairs.

Ironically enough, one which occupied a good deal of time also had its roots in Oldham and concerned a youth named Alfred William Turner, who was charged with shooting at a policeman with intent to kill, the constable in question having been hit in the back whilst standing with another officer late at night outside the Bulls Head public house, Bottom o'th Moor, Oldham.

Apparently it had been a case of mistaken identity, Turner being under the impression that he was firing at a certain P.C. Bottomley, against whom he harboured a grudge.

P.C. Howton, the victim, sustained five pellet wounds in his back, but the force of the blast had been somewhat deadened due to the amount of clothing he was wearing at the time. Considering that his apparel included a cape, overcoat, tunic, cardigan, woollen shirt and flannel vest, it seems rather surprising that the swanshot reached his body at all. In any event his injuries were no more than superficial, although his companion was marked around the eyes.

The would-be assassin, a wild lad of sixteen, was immediately seized by a third constable who happened to be in the vicinity and conveyed to the nearest police station. It was stated in evidence that he had purchased the gun earlier the same day, foolishly informing the vendor that he intended using it on a policeman. Counsel for the defence pointed out in mitigation that the prisoner was of previous good character, but had unfortunately taken to reading light literature which had had a bad effect on him. This was substantiated by his mother, who told the court that she attributed her son's rash act to the reading of penny dreadfuls and similar books which had tended to excite his imagination.

Turner stood in the dock dressed in his Sunday best, though minus collar and tie, and heard the judge sentence him to six months with hard labour. A harsh sentence perhaps for a lad of only sixteen, but certainly a well merited one.

When it became clear that there was no possibility of the Poisoning case being opened on the expected date, witnesses standing by to travel to Liverpool were advised that they would not be required that week at all. As the Castleton inquest was set for the following Monday, February 14th, it was now virtually certain to be held in advance of Mrs. Berry's trial at Liverpool, which was bad news for Mr. Whittaker.

The Oldham solicitor was now forced to leave all preparations for the approaching trial entirely in the hands of Mr. Cottingham, while he himself directed his attention to looking after Mrs. Berry's interests at Castleton, in an effort to ensure that nothing emerged which would adversely affect their chances at Liverpool.

CHAPTER 8

PURCHASE OF POISON

As the parlour of the Blue Pitts Inn had proved totally inadequate on the first occasion a much larger room would obviously be needed when the inquest was resumed. It was therefore arranged that the clubroom be made available and this proved spacious enough to accommodate the gathering.

At ten minutes past two the names of the jury were read over and the Coroner proceeded to take evidence.

Mary Ann Lyons was again called and related in detail her recollections of Mrs. Finley's fatal illness, concluding with the words; "Of course we all had our suspicions, because on the Friday she seemed to be getting better. Yet she was dead the next morning."

"If you had your suspicions, why did you not make them known at the time?" Mr. Whittaker wanted to know.

"I didn't say anything because I was afraid to.", answered the witness. "You know, none of them would like to say anything, but they all thought it strange."

"You say you saw a lot of the deceased during her illness?"

"Oh yes, I went in every day while she was in bed."

"Did she ever complain of anything?"

"Well, she never said nothing, no. But she was suffering, you could tell that."

"But did she complain of anything?"

"She said she wasn't well."

"Just that. She wasn't well?"

"The only complaint she made to me was about her nose, which still troubled her a bit."

"And when you laid the body away", asked Mr. Whittaker finally, "were there any marks on the deceased?"

"No, except for her lips. They were blue and swollen up."

She was asked by a juror if she had noticed whether the dead woman's hands had been straight or not, and replied that they were.

Sarah Ann Wolfenden then told her story, and on mentioning that she had offered to bring a neighbour in, but had been forbidden to do so by Mrs. Berry, she was asked by Mr. Whittaker; "Was any attempt made by Mrs. Berry to prevent you or any of the other neighbours from going into the house to see Mrs. Finley?"

"No", was the reply, "but she didn't encourage visitors".

"Did she raise any objection to you or any of the others going in there on the Saturday morning, after her mother had died?"

"No", admitted Mrs. Wolfenden, "I can't say as she did."

Questioned by a juror about the day Mrs. Berry arrived in Castleton and called at her house, Mrs. Wolfenden stated that she had invited the nurse in and given her a cup of tea. During the conversation Mrs. Berry mentioned her dream, and said she had the strange feeling that she had come to Castleton to bury her mother.

"At that time, was Mrs. Finley in good health?" asked the juror.

"Yes." replied the witness. "She was all right as far as I know."

Alice Eaves, who had been a close friend of the deceased, told of the startling change in Mrs. Finley over a period of little more than a week.

After telling the court of her visit to the house with the Prudential Agent, she mentioned that Mrs. Berry had requested about a week earlier that the policy should be endorsed. On going back to the house that night she had found the patient alone with her sister-in-law, Mrs. Pemberton, and had talked to the two of them while Mrs. Finley sat up in bed, eating cake and drinking beer. Alice Eaves said that the cake "looked like a plain teacake", and that it had been given to the deceased by Mrs. Pemberton.

"She looked champion that night". said the witness.

"You say you were a good friend of Mrs. Finleys?" asked Mr. Whittaker.

"Yes I was."

"Then you'll recall that she had been quite ill only a week or two before, when Dr. Sharples attended her."

"Yes, I was with her till two o'clock in the morning that time. It was when her nose bled. But she got better of that."

"Did you stay late with her on the night before she died?"

"No, there was no need was there? As I say, she was quite well then. I left her about seven o'clock. But I never saw her alive again."

Alice Chorlton, of Five Arches, Spotland Bridge, told the court that she had lodged with Mrs. Finley from June 1884 until January 1885, and had called to see her regularly after that. According to her the dead woman had been in quite good health, apart from minor ailments, and had worked in the cotton mill until shortly before her death.

After Harriet Dorrick had given evidence, Henrietta Morton was called and related to the court the story of the dream, as told to her by Mrs. Berry.

John Taylor, chemist, of Yorkshire Street, Rochdale, was the next witness. His evidence proved to be quite startling, and must have given Joseph Whittaker a severe jolt.

"On the afternoon of February 9th 1886", he told the court, "I remember my late apprentice, Fred Butterworth, handing me a slip of paper on which was written in Latin - Liquor Atropia Sulph. From the handwriting it looked as if it had been written by a medical man. The translation is Sulphate of Atropa. I was in the dispensing room at the time and asked my assistant what he wanted it for. He said there was a woman in the shop and I went out to speak to her, asking her the reason she wanted such a solution. She told me it was for dropping into the eyes. I thought I'd seen the woman before and in answer to my inquiries she told me she was an Infirmary or Workhouse nurse, I forget which.

'I asked her if she knew it was poison and she replied that she did. I told her she'd have to write her name in the book along with her address, and she wrote down the name Ellen Saunders, Freehold, Castleton. I made up the prescription. It amounted to 1oz, and I labelled the bottle 'Poison, not to be taken'. I then returned the prescription to her, which is usual, and she left the shop.

'Three days later she returned and handed me the same prescription note, asking for a further supply. I asked what had become of the other as I didn't think it could have been used in the time for dropping in the eyes. She answered, 'I knocked it over'.

'I went into the dispensing room to prepare it, leaving the door ajar, and she called out; "What will double the quantity be?" I told her the price and she said she'd take it, to save her coming back again so soon.

'The woman looked to be about 28 to 30 years of age and was of a dark complexion. I don't remember how she was dressed."

William Henry Lawson, Master of the Oldham Workhouse, was then called, and stated; "Elizabeth Berry has been employed at the Oldham Workhouse since July last year."

Asked if he knew her handwriting, he replied that he did. He was then shown the chemist's sales book, along with a letter, which he confirmed was a notice of births and deaths, written out by Mrs. Berry, and handed to him at the Workhouse.

"In my opinion", he told the court, "the two signatures, Ellen Saunders, in the chemist's book, are also in Mrs. Berry's handwriting,"

Frederick Wallwork, district agent for the Wesleyan and General Assurance Society, told the court;

"Mary Ann Finley was insured in my society for £100. The policy had been running for about four years when she died. I don't know who took out the insurance, but the premiums, which I collected from a Mrs. Heap, came, I believe, from Mrs. Berry.

'I received a certificate of the death of Mrs. Finley in February last year, and I believe the insurance money was paid through our Manchester Office, but to whom I don't know."

Following Wallwork came another insurance man, Prudential agent Harry Jackson, who stated that Mrs. Finley had been insured by his company for the sum of £27. 6s. "She paid the premiums herself to begin with, but they were later taken over by her daughter. On her death the money was paid out to Mrs. Berry."

The Coroner now informed the jury that as the medical men who had the case in hand had not yet completed their analysis, he thought it better not to take any medical evidence at all that day, and therefore proposed a second adjournment.

. . . .

Elizabeth Berry now found herself in a position almost unparalleled in the annals of British legal history. If found guilty of the murder of her daughter she would pay the extreme penalty and there would be little point in charging her with a second murder. If acquitted, however, there could be no question of her being released from custody, the probability being that she would be immediately re-arrested on suspicion of causing the death of her mother.

As the trial was now definitely set for the following Monday, it was almost certain to be over and done with before the inquest at Castleton was resumed, and in one sense this would be helpful to the defence. They could now concentrate their efforts on dealing with the charges already in hand and worry about the Castleton affair in due course. For this reason the adjournment must have come as something of a relief to Mr. Whittaker. Despite this, however, it was quite clear that the damage had already been done. It was common knowledge that Mrs. Berry was suspected of poisoning her mother, and although this should, in theory, have made no difference to the jury at Liverpool, it was inevitable that it would be in their minds both before and during the course of the trial.

In addition to this a new witness had emerged who was almost certain to be called by the prosecution. For although he had no direct connection with the Oldham case, the Rochdale chemist could swear that a woman answering Mrs. Berry's description had purchased poison from him on more than one occasion, and such a revelation was not calculated to help the defence's case any.

At this stage things were as black as they could possibly be as far as Elizabeth Berry was concerned. Both the Oldham Chronicle and the Oldham Standard continued to appeal for funds, which, it was stated, were urgently needed to ensure that the best defence possible was obtained for her. Not that these newspapers were taking Mrs. Berrys side. They simply felt that the interests of justice would best be served if no expense was spared in procuring any evidence that might be available to assist in defending her, and this would not be possible unless money was raised quickly.

Despite the appeals, however, very little in the way of hard cash was forthcoming from the public, whose sympathies Mrs. Berry now appeared to have lost.

So with very limited resourses with which to dig for further evidence, and possibly new witnesses, it was becoming clearer as each day passed that the defence would once again be pinning its hopes on the vast experience and skill of the redoubtable Mr. Cottingham.

CHAPTER 9
A QUESTION OF MOTIVE

The last case but one on the Assize Court Calender was completed on Saturday February 19th, leaving only the Oldham Poisoning case to be heard, and Monday morning found the courtroom packed to capacity.

That same evening the drama 'Blind Justice' opened at the Oldham Theatre Royal. Whether this was to have any significance as regards the outcome of the trial remained to be seen, for there was no doubt in peoples minds that the recent goings-on at Castleton had seriously affected Mrs. Berrys chances of acquittal.

Leading for the prosecution would be Mr. W.R. McConnell, a well known member of the Liverpool Bar, assisted by Mr. F.H. Mellor and instructed by Mr. J.W. Mellor, who, it will be recalled, had been involved at the magistrates court. They had marshalled no fewer than twenty-seven witnesses. Surprisingly, however, John Taylor, the Rochdale chemist, was not among them, it being reported in that days newspaper that he was now suffering from 'an aberration of the mind'. Whatever this might mean it could only have come as good news to Mr. Cottingham and his colleagues, who themselves had only nine witnesses to call upon.

At ten minutes to eleven the court rose as Mr. Justice Hawkins made his appearance. A rather severe looking man who always demanded and received the respect commensurate with his position, he was a very well known figure in legal circles, having acted as leading counsel for the Crown in the famous Tichbourne perjury case, in which his opponent, Dr. Keneally, was afterwards disbarred for his conduct in the same trial. He was to find Mr. Cottingham something of a handful, and there would be quite a number of clashes between the two of them before the trial was over.

Mr. Hawkins solemnly took his seat, and shortly afterwards

the prisoner's name was called. An expectant murmer ran through the packed courtroom as Mrs. Berry appeared and stepped lightly into the dock. As usual she was very smartly turned out, the dominating feature of her attire being the long black gloves with white cuffs which she showed off very prominently. Looking calm and confident she stood very erect in the dock as the charge was read out. Then in a firm clear voice answered; "Not guilty."

Whilst the jury was being sworn in a last minute consultation took place between the prisoner and Mr. Cottingham, after which Mrs. Berry sat down in the cane bottomed chair allowed her in the dock. Directly behind her stood a formidable looking wardress and close by a male warder.

Although the prisoner displayed her usual impassivity, a closer scrutiny of her features told another story. Somehow she did not have quite the same look as on her last public appearance, her complexion being not nearly so clear as it had been, and there was now a suggestion of weariness about the eyes.

Seated just in front of Mr. Cottingham, notebook at the ready, was Dr. John Kershaw, while no more than a couple of yards away sat Dr. Patterson. The two medical men did not communicate, apart from occasionally casting sharp sidelong glances at each other. The former Royton doctor was no doubt fervently hoping not only to see Mrs. Berry proved innocent, but also to be ultimately vindicated in his criticism of Dr. Patterson.

Opening the case, Mr. McConnell addressed the Jury; "Gentlemen, you have heard the charge on which the prisoner is arraigned. It is one of the most serious on which any person can stand before a jury."

In the course of his lengthy opening speech the prosecutor made a clear attempt to establish motive.

"In the April previous to the child's death", he told the jury, "a proposal was made by the prisoner that she should insure herself and her daughter for the sum of £100. The agent put forward this proposition to his directors, but it was not accepted, and the insurance was therefore never carried out. But the prisoner had not been informed of this fact at the time of her daughter's death.

'Now she had to pay for the insurance, clothing, maintenance and education of the girl, so it can be taken as a material fact that the child was costing the mother something in the region of twelve or thirteen pounds per annum out of the £25 she was receiving as salary at the Oldham Workhouse."

Later Mrs. Berry was to claim that the statement regarding her earnings was incorrect. In addition to the £25 per annum she said, she also received £10 for midwifery, plus £5 for dispensing medicine, and that with other odd perquisites her salary was in fact almost doubled. Dr. Patterson, however, who appears to have been a compulsive letter writer, stated in the Oldham Standard that this was positively untrue, and that any extra salary Mrs. Berry received would amount to no more than £7 per annum. Even this though was quite an advance on the sum mentioned by McConnell, and would appear to place a big question mark against his suggestion that Edith Annie had been something of a financial burden on her mother.

"In addition to the insurance proposal which was never accepted." went on the prosecutor, "the prisoner had also taken out a policy through her sister-in-law, Mrs. Sanderson, although she informed the Workhouse Medical Officer that the child was not insured at all. And I shall prove that the insurance money from this second policy was drawn by her only two days after the death of her daughter."

Alexander Banks, an Oldham architect, was the first witness. He stated that he had made a plan of the infirmary at the Workhouse showing details of the two counters in the surgery, each of which was 2ft. 10ins. from the floor. The cupboard containing the poisons was said to be 2½ feet high. It was also established that there was no direct access from the sitting room to the surgery.

Cross-examined by Mr. Cottingham, Banks stated that there was a small window in the surgery. On the instructions of the judge the plans were passed over for the jury to examine in order to save time later.

William Henry Lawson came next and told the court that he had been Master of the Oldham Union Workhouse for the past ten years. "The window in the surgery", he said, "is there for the purpose of serving medicines through. It looks out into the corridor and slides open. The glass in it cannot be seen through."

He was handed a sheet of paper and told to look at it very carefully. Mr. McConnell then asked him if he recognised the handwriting.

"Yes I do", he replied. "It was Mrs. Berrys duty to prepare a dinner bill every morning for the inmates of the Workhouse Infirmary. The note I see now is one of those bills, and it is definitely in her handwriting."

Ann Sanderson came next and explained that the prisoner was her sister-in-law, having been married to her brother, Thomas Berry, now deceased.

She was asked to produce the letter which she had received from her niece during the childrens stay at the Workhouse, and was very much affected when it was read out to the court.

Mr. F.H. Mellor took her through her evidence very gently and painstakingly, dwelling for some moments on the point regarding Mrs. Berrys having left the room just prior to the child's death. Much was again made of the fact that the bereaved mother had lost no time in calling on Mrs. Sanderson to claim the insurance money, and the witness was adamant in stating that Edith Annie had been in the very best of health on leaving her house. "In fact I never had reason to give her more than the occasional Gregorys Powder." she said.

Mrs. Sanderson gave her answers in a very low voice, the judge remarking that he was having great difficulty in hearing her. She seemed rather overwhelmed by the occasion. The prisoner on the other hand did not seem at all affected by her sister-in-law giving evidence against her, but appeared quite detached and unconcerned.

Mrs. Sanderson was the first to feel the lash of Mr. Cottingham's tongue, for when Mr. Mellor had finished with the witness, the Manchester barrister took the floor and set off in his usual aggressive style.

"Mrs. Sanderson," he began, "you tell us that Mrs. Berry left the room only a short while before her daughter died. But the child had been low for many hours before this. Is that not so?"

"Yes", was the reply.

"Is it not a fact that Mrs. Berry had hardly been to bed at all during the whole of the time the child was ill?"

"Yes, that's true."

"And is it not also true that the doctor had ordered her to take some rest on his last visit?"

"Yes."

"Now regarding the prisoner's husband, Thomas Berry, your late brother. Can you tell us how he died?"

"He was always very weak.", replied Mrs. Sanderson. "He had a weak inside."

"Prior to his death he was confined to bed for some considerable time I believe?"

"Yes, for about two years."

"And before he died he was very much emaciated, wasn't he? ... Very thin?"

"Yes he was."

"Edith Annie was not the only child of the marriage, was she?"

"No.", replied the witness. "There was a baby, which died at four months old."

"What was the cause of death, do you know?"

"The child died from teething."

"I see. When was this?"

"It would be about three years before my brother's death."

"But at the time Mrs. Berry was made a widow she had two children. Is that not correct?"

"Yes, there was a third child, a boy. who died in 1882."

"What did he die of?"

"I beg your pardon sir."

"The little boy. What was the cause of his death?"

"I think it was brain disease or something like that."

"Brain disease?"

"Yes ... I think that was it."

"Did you hear tubercular disease mentioned as the cause of death?

"No."

"Will you swear that you did not state to a person that death was due to disease of the brain and tuberculosis of the bowels?"

"I never said anything like that to anybody", replied Mrs. Sanderson, rather taken aback.

"Then how do you account for it getting into this paper?", said Mr. Cottingham, waving a sheet of notepaper under her nose.

"Really, Mr. Cottingham." interrupted the Judge. "This is most irregular, you know."

The defence counsel did not bother to apologise. Neither did he press the point any further. He did manage, however, to get an admission from Mrs. Sanderson that both the deceased boy referred to and Edith Annie had suffered from severe vomitting on one occasion following a trip to Blackpool. He then passed on to the question of the Gregory's Powders, asking how often they had been given to the child.

"Every few months", was the reply.

"Why, did she complain of pains in the stomach?"

"No, she never had any pains."

"Then why did you give her the powders?"

"I gave them to her when her stomach was out of order."

As it was now past one o'clock the court was adjourned for lunch and resumed an hour later, when Mrs. Berry re-entered the dock after a brief consultation with Mr. Whittaker. Throughout the morning she had listened to the evidence, particularly that of her sister-in-law, but had shown no sign of emotion, not even when Edith Annie's letter was read out.

The prosecution re-opened by calling Beatrice Hall to the stand. She told the court that she had been a school friend of the dead girl, and as her evidence was given a clearer picture of Edith Annie began to unfold, which showed her to have been a warm-hearted and very loving child. It was apparent that a strong bond had existed between the two friends, and the sudden severence of it and succeeding events had naturally left little Beatrice Hall in a somewhat confused state of mind. Nevertheless she answered each question put to her clearly and intelligently.

"On the first of January", she said, "we got up about nine o'clock, got dressed, and went down to the sitting room together for breakfast. Mrs. Berry had had hers earlier and gave me my breakfast about ten o'clock, but Edith said she felt ill and couldn't eat anything. Not long after this she was sick on the hearth rug and kept on vomiting. She couldn't stop,"

"Did you see Mrs. Berry give her anything at that time?", she was asked.

"Yes, she gave her a powder."

"Where did she get this powder from?"

"I don't know. I didn't see her get it."

"What happened next?"

"After the doctor had been Edith was taken to the bedroom. I stayed with her all day. That night Mrs. Berry told me to sleep downstairs in the sitting room, but after I was undressed I went back up to the bedroom and told her I was feared of sleeping down there on my own. Edith patted the pillow and said, 'come and sleep here then', and I did. When we woke up she seemed a bit better, but later on that day she started being sick again."

Mr. Cottingham asked her what they had eaten, apart from their meals at the Workhouse, and was told that they had bought biscuits, chocolate and coconut chips on the Thursday, while on the following day, when visiting Oldham market, they had bought some fish.

"It was Finnan Haddock", said Beatrice. "We had it to our tea on the Friday."

"Is it possible that the fish could have made Edith sick do you think?"

"I don't know."

"How did you find the fish?"

"It was nice. Mrs. Berry had some too."

"And it did not disagree with either of you?"

"No,"

"You spent a great deal of time with Edith while she was ill, didn't you?", went on Mr. Cottingham.

"Yes. I was with her nearly all the time."

"Did you talk?"

"I read to her a lot."

"Oh you read to her."

"'Yes, she was very intelligent and she seemed pleased at what I was reading."

"But did you talk also?"

"Yes."

"Did Edith tell you that she had been given anything which had burnt her lips?"

"No."

"Had you known her long?"

"Yes, quite a long time."

"Do you ever remember her being ill before?"

"No."

"Be sure now."

"No I don't think so."

"Did Edith seem strong to you?"

"No, not strong really."

"You remember Dr. Patterson coming in on the Sunday don't you?"

"Yes, it was about dinnertime."

"Did you see him give any medicine to Edith?"

"No."

"Do you remember seeing any medicine in the room?"

"No."

"Perhaps a black medicine?"

"No."

Before Beatrice Hall left the stand Mr. Cottingham again established that she had not been separated from Edith Annie at any time between their coming downstairs together and the deceased being taken ill.

As she stepped down Mr. McConnell said that as the case would obviously not be concluded that day it would perhaps be a good idea if members of the jury were allowed a few minutes to make arrangements for 'spending the night in custody', as he put it. The judge agreed to this, and several of the jurymen wrote out messages to be sent to their homes.

The next witness, Ann Dillan, told the court; "I have been an inmate of the Oldham Workhouse since my husband deserted me three years ago, and while the prisoner has been there I've been employed under her."

"You also knew her daughter, Edith Annie?" Mr. McConnell asked her.

"Oh yes. She was a merry little girl."

"Did you see her on Saturday morning January 1st?"

"Yes. It was sometime after nine o'clock. She was coming down the stairs with her companion."

"Did she appear to be in good health?"

"Yes, as far as I could see."

"When did you first see the prisoner that morning?"

"About a-quarter-to-ten. She was in the surgery."

"Alone?"

"No, Edith Annie was with her."

"Did the deceased appear ill at that time?"

"Not that I recall."

"How long were you in the surgery?"

"A few minutes. I went in to get the dinner note, as it was my duty to do every day. Mrs. Berry asked me if I was going out. It was News Years Day, and a lot of the inmates were having liberty. I told her I wasn't bothering. After that I took the dinner note and left the room."

"When did you next see Mrs. Berry and Edith?"

"About a-quarter-to-eleven. They were in the sitting room then. Beatrice Hall was there too. Edith had just been sick and was leaning against her mother's breast. Mrs. Berry said to me "the child is sick", and I replied "Indeed she is". The mother had a glass in her hand which seemed to have a white liquid in it. She was trying to get the child to swallow it, but she would not. I saw the little girl that night, and she didn't seem quite as poorly, but she kept rubbing her stomach and saying 'Oh my belly'.

"After the child died", prosecuting counsel asked her, "did a certain conversation take place between yourself and the accused?"

"Yes." replied the witness. "It was on the 11th of January. I'd been told to keep an eye on her. I went into her room and found her walking up and down. She seemed to be crying, and I asked what was the matter. She said she was weeping over it being said that the child had been poisoned. I asked her if she thought it was true."

"And what did she reply?"

"She just said "Well they say so". I then asked if she'd given the child anything by mistake, and she said, 'No I never gave her anything except the Seidlitz Powder you saw me give her."

Mr. Cottingham now proceeded to cross-examine and straight away took up the question of Ann Dillan having been detailed to keep Mrs. Berry under surveillance. "Who told you to keep an eye on her?"

"I was doing it at the direction of a police constable. I didn't tell her I was watching her, but I think she knew. Inspector Purser had told her I was there to keep her company."

"And were you to report anything she said to the police?"

"No."

"I see. You were just there to keep her spirits up."

"She did not say that". interrupted Mr. Justice Hawkins. "She said she was there to keep her company."

"You have just said", continued Mr. Cottingham, "that you first saw Mrs. Berry and her daughter alone in the surgery at a-quarter-to-ten that morning?"

"Yes."

"Did anyone see you go into the surgery on that occasion?"

"I don't know."

"Alice Alcroft was in the kitchen during the whole of that morning and the kitchen door was open. Yet she did not see you go into the surgery, although she does recall seeing you pass along the corridor to go to the linen cupboard."

"Yes, but that was later on in the morning, at a-quarter-to-eleven. I said it was a-quarter-to-ten when I went into the surgery."

"Did you ever alter that time?"

"No."

Mr. Cottingham now asked to see the witnesses depositions as taken down at the magistrates court, and these were handed to him. After scrutinizing them, he asked the witness; "When you were before the Magistrates, did you not say that _____

"No", cut in Mr. Justice Hawkins. "I cannot allow you to read that."

"Very well", countered Mr. Cottingham. "I will ask the witness whether she ever said it was a-quarter-*past*-ten when she saw Mrs. Berry and her child in the surgery?"

"Never."

"You did not say that when you were before the magistrates?"

"No."

"But you had your depositions read over to you."

"No. I only signed my name to them."

"So you now swear it was *not* a-quarter-past-ten when you were in the surgery?"

"Yes."

"Mr. Cottingham", said the judge, "Magistrates clerks are not infallible. In fact, in those very depositions I have found two or three quite obvious errors. Because what the witness says now differs somewhat from what is stated in the depositions, it does not follow that she is telling an untruth."

"No, not necessarily", answered Mr. Cottingham, not wishing to fully conceed the point.

Mr. Hesketh Booth, Magistrates Clerk to the Justices for the Borough of Oldham, was now called to the witness box, but not for the purpose of explaining any discrepancies in the depositions. As Chief Constable Charles Hodgkinson could not be present due to illness, his depositions would have to read out and sworn to by Mr. Booth, who stated that he had taken them down at the Magistrates Court and that Hodgkinson had read them before signing.

The Magistrates Clerk, who must have been more than a little embarrassed following earlier references to his work, made his statement under cross-examination by Mr. Cottingham, and concluded by saying, no doubt as explanation of his errors, that he had had the difficult task of taking down a great many depositions during the Oldham hearing, whereupon Mr. Cottingham remarked; "And the prisoner was dismissed."

Mr. Justice Hawkins took exception to this. "I don't think that has anything to do with the case here. And I might add Mr. Cottingham, that you are treading on very dangerous ground."

The depositions of the missing chemist were now handed in and sworn to by Frederick Nassau Molesworth, Coroner for the Rochdale Division of the County of Lancaster.

The next witness was Ellen Thompson, who told of having seen the deceased vomit matter streaked with blood. She had emptied most of it away she said, and Alice Alcroft had wiped up the rest from the floor on Mrs. Berry's instructions. She herself had carried Edith up to the mother's bedroom on the first day of her illness, and on the following day had first noticed a blister on the child's mouth. She was asked about a bottle of black medicine, and said; "Mrs. Berry gave it her on a teaspoon, but it ran out of the side of her mouth." She also told the court; "When Mrs. Berry heard that Dr. Patterson intended bringing Dr. Robertson to see Edith, she said she feared the worst. 'The child is weak to begin with', she said. 'I know she will not recover.' I was in the sickroom on the Monday night when Mrs. Sanderson was with her. It was the last time I saw her alive."

The court was then adjourned until 10-30 the following morning, when Mr. Cottingham would begin his cross-examination of the witness. Mrs. Berry had a quiet word with her counsel through the bars of the dock before being led away.

From the prosecutions point of view the first day had gone exactly according to plan, although the question of motive still remained. Much had been made of the insurance money, and although the amount involved had now considerably increased, there was still plenty of room for doubt here. For one thing Mrs. Berry might not have been informed that the £100 proposal had been rejected, but then again she had not received a policy acknowledging acceptance either. Therefore, the suggestion that she would blindly proceed with a plan to commit murder on the strength of it appeared very unlikely to say the least. It seemed painfully obvious that the prosecution had been forced to stick with the insurance money as a motive in the apparent absence of an alternative.

Mr. Cottingham had tried hard to show that the deceased might conceivably have suffered from an inherent disease which had taken its toll on other members of her family, and had done his best to get Ann Sanderson to agree with him, going beyond the bounds of normal courtroom procedure to do it. His main purpose that day, however, had been to cast doubt on Ann Dillans claim that she had seen the dead girl alone in the surgery with Mrs. Berry on that first morning of her illness. With the assistance of Mr. Justice Hawkins, however, she had stuck to her story, refusing to be shaken by the defence counsels badgering tactics.

On the following evening the Oldham Chronicle referred to the question of the errors in Ann Dillans depositions, saying; 'We have to come from home to learn news regarding our own concerns. For instance, no one in Oldham would ever have supposed that the Magistrates Clerk is less than immaculate, and yet Mr. Justice Hawkins found serious fault yesterday with the way in which the depositions were taken down when the case was before the magistrates.'

....

The jurymen filed back into court for the second day of the trial, having spent the night at the Grand Hotel Liverpool. They were followed shortly afterwards by the prisoner who was dressed as on the previous day and appeared just as composed, leaning back confortably in her chair, hands folded daintily across her knees, a stance she was to adopt throughout the trial.

Also in attendance were the Chaplain of Walton Gaol, attired in a black robe with red binding, and Mr. Anderson, Governor of the prison. The number of females present, most of whom were very fashionably dressed, was again quite remarkable, and was referred to by one newspaper as nothing less than morbid curiosity. There were also quite a few Oldhamers amongst the spectators, many of whom had no doubt followed the drama from the beginning and were determined not to miss the final instalment.

And there in the full glare of the spotlight sat Mrs. Berry. 'The observed of all the observers', as the Oldham Standard put it. So calm and apparently unconcerned under their concentrated gaze.

Two men, one from a waxworks, worked away earnestly sketching the defendant. One of the two, obviously unaccustomed to the position of a prisoner in the dock, asked a reporter which was Mrs. Berry. On her being pointed out he was heard to exclaim "Oh, I thought it was the other one", referring to the female warder. Apparently he had spent quite some time sketching the wrong woman.

On the court being called to order Ellen Thompson again took the stand. By todays standards she would be regarded as comparatively young. But in 1887 a woman in her forties was considered to be rather more than mature. In any case Ellen Thompson had led a very hard life. Born into extreme poverty and marrying young, she had soon found herself with a fast multiplying brood which she could not hope to support on her husband's meagre and irregular earnings. Finally Mr. Thompson had given up the struggle and departed for Australia and a new life, leaving his wife and six children almost destitute and with little hope for the future. In this sort of situation there was only one place to go ____ the Workhouse. It is therefore not surprising perhaps that Ellen Thompson had the appearance of a much older woman as she stood in the witness box and waited for Mr. Cottingham to fire his questions at her.

He was well aware that there were only two points worth

persuing as far as this particular witness was concerned. The question of Ann Dillan having seen the prisoner and deceased alone together in the surgery, and the medicine containing creosote, which, it was alleged by the prosecution, had not been administered anyway.

In a further attempt to discredit Dillans story he did manage to elicit from Ellen Thompson that in addition to several visits to the sitting room that morning she had also gone into the kitchen more than once and had seen Alice Alcroft there. While this clearly showed that the old woman had been in a position to have observed Ann Dillan enter the surgery if she had in fact done so, it did not rule out the possibility that Dillan had gone in and out while Alice Alcroft's back was turned, or while she was perhaps absorbed in her work. After all, she had not been looking out for Dillan at the time..

As regards the medicine, it was the defences intention to attempt to show that the creosote contained in it might well have caused the blistering on the child's lips, but Ellen Thompson said she could not remember seeing the bottle shaken before being opened.

Next on the scene came Alice Alcroft, who described herself as a widow and an inmate of the Workhouse for a good number of years. Questioned by Mr. Mellor, she told the court of having mopped up vomit and then being sent for the mineral powder by Mrs. Berry.

"When was the next time you saw the deceased?" Mellor asked her.

"When she was being carried up to the bedroom."

"Who was carrying her?"

"What is the issue here?" asked the judge impatiently.

"The fact that the child was carried up to the bedroom has not been questioned as far as I can recollect."

"There is no question about that", said Mr. Cottingham.

"Nor about the child being sick."

"It seems to be a repetition which does not carry us any further", said the judge.

"Well", said Mr. Cottingham, getting in a dig wherever he could, "if they think they can strengthen their case by repetition, I cannot object to them doing so."

"Perhaps if some of these questions are not put", answered Mr. McConnell for the prosecution, "we might not learn something which we ought to hear."

"I wish it to be understood that I do not want to hurry anyone", said Mr. Justice Hawkins, "but if other witnesses have been examined on the same point and are in agreement, I think we can take it that what this witness states is true, without going into details as to how the deceased was carried up to bed and by whom. This sort of thing might well result in taking the attention of the jury away from what is really material."

"Very well my lord". said McConnell. "I will shorten the case as much as possible.

Before leaving the witness box Alice Alcroft was asked by Mr. McConnell if she had in fact seen Ann Dillan at all on the morning in question, and replied that she had, when Dillan had gone down to the stores. "I have the key to the stores and she came to me for it."

"Where were you at that time?" she was asked.

"In the kitchen."

"Was that after you went into the sitting room with the mineral powder?"

"It was quite a while after."

"And you're very sure of that?"

"Yes, I'm certain of it," replied the old woman.

While Mr. Cottingham continued to question the witness a telegram was handed to Mr. J.W. Mellor, which he read before passing it on to McConnell, who in turn handed it to Mr. Cottingham. A whispered conversation then took place between the two leading barristers which caused the judge to ask; "Have you finished with this witness or not?"

"We have received a telegram my lord", replied Mr. McConnell. "It appears that some of the witnesses from the Workhouse are wanted at home."

The telegram was handed up to the judge who read it and then announced that there had been an outbreak of scarlet fever at the Oldham Workhouse. As several of the witnesses were nurses, their presence was urgently requested, as was that of all the Workhouse staff involved in the case. However, Mr. Justice Hawkins made it clear that he could not release a single witness at this stage of the proceedings and remarked rather irritably that the message was very vague indeed and did not even state who had sent it.

"Probably it was the porter", volunteered Mr. J.W. Mellor.

"You ought surely to know who sent such a message, containing the request it does", the judge snapped back at him.

After some deliberation Mr. Justice Hawkins informed counsel that he would allow the Oldham witnesses to return to the Workhouse only when it had been ascertained that they would no longer be required, and not before. He was desirous, he said, that once they had left the Assizes they should not come back again, a remark which created some laughter in the court.

After this, Sarah Anderson, head nurse of the female imbecile ward, Lydia Evett, head nurse in the children's hospital, and Ann Partland, a Workhouse servant, all gave evidence to the effect that each had visited the sickroom during the child's illness and had observed marks on her mouth. William Henry Thorpe of Yorkshire Street Oldham, photographer, also gave evidence, in the course of which photographs of the girl's face, taken after death, were shown to the judge and jury.

Charles Purser, Detective Inspector in the Oldham Borough Police, came next and stated that he had been present when the photographs were taken, along with the Chief Constable. He told the court that he had also accompanied his superior on his initial visit to the Workhouse to interview Mrs. Berry, but had not taken any notes as this had been done by Mr. Hodgkinson. The judge then asked Mr. McConnell if he intended calling the Chief Constable.

"We are going to put his depositions in", replied McConnell.

"Why isn't Mr. Hodgkinson present?" asked the judge. He was told that the Chief Constable had met with an accident some weeks previously and had injured his back.

Dr. Patterson was called to the stand to verify this and stated that he had examined Hodgkinson several days earlier. "He is suffering from an injury to the spine caused by a fall during the late frost and is not in a fit state to travel to Liverpool."

Mr. Cottingham was not satisfied and asked Dr. Patterson if he would be prepared to swear to this. The doctor, however, declined to do so and further discussion on this point was cut short by Mr. McConnell, who said he did not intend to tender the Chief Constables depositions unless it became necessary later in the case.

No doubt the doctor's story was true, but it did seem strange that he was not prepared to swear to it. Of course he may have realised that Hodgkinson might now be much better than he had been when examined. If so it could mean one of two things. Either the Chief Constable felt that the prosecution could get along quite well without him, or he was none too anxious to face Mr. Cottingham again.

The question of the insurance money now cropped up once

more, the prosecution calling James Pickford, Chief Secretary of the Rational Sick and Burial Society, who stated that he had paid Mrs. Berry £10 following the death of her daughter, the money being drawn at his companies head office in Devonshire Street Manchester.

He was followed by Henry Jackson of Whitworth Road Rochdale, whose evidence was expected to have a great bearing on the case. It will be recalled that Jackson had given evidence at the inquest on Mary Ann Finley, stating on that occasion that his company, the Prudential, had paid to Elizabeth Berry the sum of £27.6s. on the death of her mother. He now told the court; "I know the prisoner and remember her coming to my house in April of last year. She proposed to insure her own life and that of her daughter Edith Annie. The insurance was to be mutual."

"What is the meaning of mutual?" asked Mr. Mellor.

"I object to that question", interrupted Mr. Cottingham. "The proposal was not in writing and I submit that such proposals usually are."

"It is not for the purpose of going into the question of the proposal", answered the judge, overuling him, "but simply to show the conduct of the prisoner at the time."

"The term mutual means that two persons are insured on one policy", explained the agent. "and at the death of either of them the survivor gets the insurance money. Mrs. Berry said that she wished to effect such a policy for the sum of £100 and I told her this would cost her a little over £4 per year. She said she intended getting married and wanted the insurance for safety, which I agreed was a good idea."

Cross-examined by Mr. Cottingham, the witness stated that he had not had any communication with Mrs. Berry since, regarding the proposed insurance. "I did not send her the results of the proposals because ____"

"Had Mrs. Berry paid any premiums?" Mr. Cottingham asked, cutting him short.

"No", admitted the agent.

The defence appeared to have scored a point, although this was slightly nullified when Jackson revealed that the proposals were in fact in writing.

"Where are they?" asked the judge.

"At our office."

"Are they signed?"

"Yes my lord."

"By whom?"

"By the prisoner", replied Jackson.

As it was getting on to one-thirty Mr. McConnell suggested that it might be better to adjourn, as his next witness was a medical man whose evidence would occupy a considerable amount of time. This was agreed and the Workhouse witnesses were then informed that they were free to return to Oldham. They quickly left the court.

The paupers among them had been allowed to travel to Liverpool in ordinary clothes, instead of the regulation 'Union' garb which they normally wore at all times and in which they had attended the magistrates court.

CHAPTER 10
THE DOCTORS DILEMMA

On the resumption Dr. Patterson entered the witness box and told his story in great detail, mentioning that on his first visit to the deceased he had made up a mixture containing tincture of iron and cinchona which he left with the mother. When he called later that night after being sent for again he was told that despite having received two doses of the medicine the patient had continued to vomit throughout the day.

"I noticed a towel stained with blood in the room and I told the mother to stop using the medicine."

"When you saw the towel and was told that the vomiting had been continuous, didn't this make a deep impression on you?" the judge asked him.

"No my lord", replied the doctor, "it did not."

"On the Saturday, did you form any opinion as to what the girl was suffering from?"

"I did not my lord. But I did form the opinion that it was no ordinary disease. Well it was not really an opinion _____ rather an impression."

"Did the symptoms on Saturday suggest to you any known disease?" asked Mr. Mellor.

"On the Saturday evening they did not. Nor was I certain on the Sunday morning."

"Why did you discontinue the medicine?"

"For two reasons. In the first place I was told that it had been rejected, and in the second place I came to the conclusion that the opinion I had first formed was wrong."

"What was that opinion?"

"That the bleeding might be due to an ulceration of the stomach."

"Then in the evening you thought you were wrong?" the judge

asked.

"I did my lord."

"What was your opinion then?"

"That the symptoms did not point to any disease with which I was acquainted."

Dr. Patterson then told the court that on the Sunday morning he had made up a second mixture _____ bicarbonate of soda and the rinsings of a creosote bottle. "For acidity of the stomach and to allay the vomiting."

He had then made out a note for a further supply of creosote to be sent for, leaving dosage instructions with Mrs. Berry.

"There would not be any colour to the mixture", he added. "It would be quite clear, like water."

He had been sent for again that night and found the patient much worse, her eyes sunken and her lips red and swollen. At that point he informed Mrs. Berry that the child was dangerously ill.

"On that visit I formed the opinion that she was suffering from corrosive poison."

It was then that he had brought his friend Dr. Robertson into the case, and during their visit together, late on the Sunday night, the mixture of bismuth and morphia had been made up in the surgery and handed to Alice Alcroft.

He had seen the child again on the Monday morning and on examining the inside of her mouth found that the gums and tongue were coated white and the redness around the mouth had now formed a large blister.

"That same night I again visited the child. Her feet were cold and she was very restless. The medicine bottle at that time was not quite full. I poured some onto a spoon and gave it to her but she immediately vomited it back. I then gave an injection of morphia and she rested. This would be between nine and ten on the

Monday night. The next morning I saw her dead body."

"In your opinion doctor", asked Mr. Mellor, "what did the child die from?"

"It died from corrosive poisoning."

"Did you form an opinion as to when the poison was administered?"

"I could not say, but the child had poison in her on the Saturday morning and again on Sunday evening."

Mr. Mellor now took the doctor through his evidence regarding his dealings with Mrs. Berry after her child's death. He explained that he had delayed making out a death certificate until after a partial post mortem had been performed. He was asked by the judge if he had brought his notes with him and replied that he had.

"Have you ever been asked for them?"

"No."

"Nor even for a copy?

"No my lord."

"That's a pity." said Mr. Hawkins. "It might not make any difference to the case, but it compels me to write the full details down."

"I may say my lord ____ ", began the doctor.

"You may not say anything until you are asked". the judge interrupted him rather rudely. "You may now read us your notes from the post mortem examination."

Somewhat put out by this rebuff, Dr. Patterson began to read the notes but stuck at a word in the very first paragraph, which did not help to alter the judge's mood.

"I'm sorry my lord", said the doctor. "There is a word here which I cannot make out. Perhaps Dr. Robertson can read it, as it is in his writing."

"Then they are not your notes at all."

"No my lord. They are Dr. Robertson's."

He then went on to explain to the judge that it was the usual practice at post mortems for one doctor to make the examination while another took down the details.

Mr. Mellor, in an attempt to get things moving again, asked the witness; "What were the conclusions you came to following the post mortem?"

Mr. Cottingham was on his feet in a flash; "I object to that. Let him state the facts first and give his conclusions afterwards."

Mr. Justice Hawkins supported the defence in this instance, but before letting the doctor continue he asked to see the notes, which were handed to him. After a vain attempt to read them he passed them back to the doctor and told him to carry on as best he could. Giving details of the examination, Dr. Patterson told the court; "On opening the abdomen we found the stomach and intestines heavily congested and of a dark blue black colour. The blood vessels were also congested. On opening the stomach we found that the lining membrane was congested in different parts."

"What did you state to be the cause of death on the certificate?" Mr. Mellor asked him.

"Acute inflamation of the lining membrane of the stomach and bowels."

It was now the turn of the defence, and the Oldham medical man must have known he was in for a rough ride as Mr. Cottingham rose slowly from his seat and fixed the doctor with a cold deliberate stare.

"Dr. Patterson", be began. "what made you form the opinion that the deceased had had poison given to her?"

"The sudden violent illness, the vomiting again and again, the character of the matter vomited and the condition of the stomach."

"How came you to the conclusion that poison had been administered on the Saturday morning? Was it before you made the post mortem examination?"

"No."

"Oh, then you took the post mortem appearances into consideration?"

"I did."

"Now tell me doctor, did not the symptoms you describe suggest to you the action of poison?"

"Not on the Saturday morning."

"Did you not think the patient was attacked by some unusual malady?"

"Yes, and one which would require very careful treatment."

"Will you swear now that you told the mother her child was suffering from ulceration of the stomach?"

"Yes I did say that, but on thinking the matter over I began to suspect poison might be the cause of the illness."

"When did you alter your opinion?"

"During the Sunday evening and before I saw the patient a second time. On the way up to Dr. Robertsons in fact."

"Was it from observation or on reflection?"

"On reflection."

"What did you think of the case on the Saturday?"

"I thought it was serious."

"When you found her better on the Sunday morning were you of the opinion then that she had had poison.?"

"Yes."

"Then what made you say that you thought she would get

better?"

"Because many people in cases of poisoning have been known to recover from the effects."

"Now when you came to the conclusion that poison had been given to the child on the Saturday morning _____"

"I did not say that I came to that conclusion on the Saturday morning."

"He said he thought at first that the child was suffering from an ulcerated stomach", corrected the judge, "but after thinking the matter over all day he came to the conclusion that poison had been administered."

"What kind of poison was it that you thought the child was suffering from?" asked Mr. Cottingham.

"An irritant poison."

"Did you administer a counter irritant?"

"I did not."

"Do you mean to say that it was then no use to give a counter irritant?"

"I do". replied the doctor. "I used ice, which I ordered to be sucked. Ice is not a counter irritant. It was prescribed for the vomiting and also to stay the bleeding."

"Was what you did, assuming that poison had been taken, done with a view to counteracting the effects of poison?"

"You make a mistake", said the doctor very confidently. "I did not assume that poison had been administered. I said I had a suspicion of it."

"Well", said Mr Cottingham, rather cryptically, "we all know what a doctors suspicions are."

"The illness was not a natural one", went on the doctor. "that much was quite clear. It was the sort of illness which might be

Elizabeth Berry and Edith Annie - An artist's impression.

The original parish poorhouse near Cross Street and Lees Road, Oldham.

The old Workhouse entrance at Boundary Park as it appeared in more recent times, before the demolishers moved in.

Oldham Workhouse - courtyard and entrance to main building.

Workhouse staff pose for group photograph- Photo courtesy of Local Interest Centre, Oldham.

Workhouse nurses enjoying various recreational pursuits in their staff room - Photo courtesy of Local Interest Centre, Oldham.

Workhouse infirmary - Though conditions were somewhat spartan the wards were kept scrupulously clean. - Photo courtesy of Local Interest Centre, Oldham.

Workhouse inmates at work in the institutions wash-house. - Photo courtesy of Local Interest Centre, Oldham.

Back Albion Street, Castleton, where Mary Ann Finley died in suspicious circumstances in 1886.

The Blue Pitts Inn, Castleton - scene of the inquest on Mary Ann Finley. Though the front has been re-built the old brickwork can still be seen along gable end.

Close-up of the grave where Mary Ann Finley lies buried along with eleven other poor people. As relatives could not always afford the small cost of an inscription only nine names appear on the headstone.

Public or inscription graves at Moston Cemetery. Scene of the exhumation of the body of Mary Ann Finley.

James Berry - Public Executioner from 1884 to 1892. A sternly religous man, Berry took his work very seriously and even carried a business card stating his profession.

The forgotten grave of Edith Annie at Chadderton Cemetery - There is nothing to mark the spot, but grave number 14-39 is now partly covered by a bench.

The old Tommyfield market, Oldham, where 'Colonel' William Wrigley entertained as he sold his watches and jewellery.

The author stands amongst rubble as the old Workhouse is demolished - 1986.

caused by an irritant poison."

"So because there are certain symptoms which you cannot attribute to natural causes you come to the conclusion that an irritant poison has been given?"

"I did not say that."

"How is it that you did not prescribe an antidote?"

"It would have been useless ten hours after the poison had been administered."

This was a point which had not come up at the magistral hearing, and the doctor's words caused Mr. Cottingham to ask incredulously; "Do you mean to tell us that when an irritant poison has been administered and a few hours have elapsed, and vomiting has taken place in the meantime, that it would be useless to give an antidote?"

"Yes, it would do no good at all."

"Did you still believe on the Sunday morning that poison had been given to the child?"

"I had a suspicion."

"Was your suspicion more or less when you found the patient better?"

"I cannot answer that. ____ The suspicion remained."

"Did you then do anything?"

"Yes, I thought the child would be better if the vomiting could be checked, and I prescribed accordingly."

"What did you prescribe?"

"Creosote and bicarbonate of soda."

"Knowing it was to deal with an irritant poison?"

"No, it was to deal with the results of it."

Mr. Cottingham now left the question of Dr. Pattersons failure to deal effectively with the poison to pursue another line, and one which was to place the doctor in a very uncomfortable position indeed. Having got him on the rack he would then return to his original theme regarding the poison, and this method of continually switching his attack, at which the Manchester barrister was very adept, was to have a very unsettling effect on Dr. Patterson and later on his colleague Dr. Robertson also.

"When you left the patient on the Sunday morning", asked Mr. Cottingham, after a slight pause, "did you make any arrangements regarding your next visit?"

"No. There was no necessity for it. I told the mother that the child was so much better that I would not come to see her again, but that she must let me know how she got on."

"Now, it is rather an alarming thing when a doctor goes away under these circumstances, for him to get a message to come back almost at once, is it not?"

"Yes it is rather a strange thing", the doctor agreed, not realising that Cottingham was setting a trap for him.

"At what time did you receive this message?"

"It would be about seven in the evening."

"And you had no doubt that the message came from the mother?"

"None at all."

"How is it then that you did not go immediately?"

"I had one or two urgent matters to attend to."

"What were they?" Mr. Cottingham wanted to know.

"First of all I had to stay during surgery hours at my own house. Secondly all my people had gone to church and I had no one to leave in the house until they came back."

"So you would not go to visit a child after receiving an urgent request from the mother because you had no one to leave in the house."

"He gave two reasons", chipped in Mr. Justice Hawkins, coming to the doctors aid again.

"What time *did* you get to the Workhouse that evening?" asked Mr. Cottingham, ignoring the judge's interruption.

"At about a-quarter-to-nine."

"Really?....but you did not see the patient until nine-thirty."

"No, I had several calls to make in other parts of the Workhouse first."

"Were they urgent calls doctor?"

"One or two were, yes."

"But what could have been more urgent than the call you received from Mrs. Berry?"

"Well I had to visit the lunatic asylum for one thing."

"Was it vital that you go there as soon as you arrived at the Workhouse?"

"Well I wouldn't say vital, no. But ____"

"Then why did you not postpone your visit to that part of the house where the lunatics are and go to the child?"

"Because I did not consider that the case was so urgent."

"When you left her in the morning the patient was making rapid strides towards recovery, yet when you got there that night she was dangerously ill. Did you reproach the mother?"

"Not in the slightest."

"Did you consider it a pity that you had delayed so long?"

"No."

"Your suspicions were then absolutely confirmed?"

"Yes."

"That being so, did you ask the mother what the child had been given between your visits?"

"I don't recollect that I did?"

"You had access to the child in the mother's presence?"

"Yes."

"Did you ask her to leave you alone with the patient?"

"No I did not, and would not if I had it to do over again."

"Did it cross your mind then that the mother might have administered the poison?"

"I have not said so."

"Did it! I ask you?"

"I decline to answer that question."

"You will have to answer it!" insisted Mr. Cottingham.

"If my lord says so, then I will."

The judge, however, did not say so. Instead Mr. Justice Hawkins said he did not feel that it affected the case materially. Mr. Cottingham, none too happy about this, then asked; "Will you give a reason for refusing to answer?"

"No", replied the doctor.

"Very well then. Did you form an opinion as to who had administered the poison on the Sunday afternoon?"

"No I did not."

"Have you not said more than once that you believed poison had been given to the child on the Sunday afternoon by the mother?"

"I did not form that opinion on the Sunday."

"Now sir, on your oath. Did you?"

"I will swear I did not. I have said I had a suspicion that it was the mother, but I did not say I formed that suspicion on the Sunday."

"Did you believe it was the mother on the Sunday?" asked Mr. Cottingham doggedly.

"I did not say so."

"I did not say that you said it at the time, but have you not stated since that on the Sunday you came to the conclusion that the mother did it?"

"I do not believe I have. No I don't recollect having said that."

The doctor now appeared a little hot under the collar, and the judge asked him; "Doctor, did you form the opinion positively on the Sunday night that the child had been poisoned?"

"I did my lord. I formed that opinion while in the bedroom in the presence of the mother."

"Did you communicate your suspicions to Dr. Robertson that night?" Mr. Cottingham asked.

"Yes."

"When?"

"When I went up to King Street for him."

Mr. Cottingham now returned to the line of questioning which had proved so telling for the defence at the Magistral hearing.

"When you returned to the Workhouse with Dr. Robertson, why did you not prescribe an antidote or an alleviate. Some treatment of the poison which you believed was in the girl?"

"I did prescribe an alleviate ____ morphia."

"But not an antidote."

"I did not prescribe an antidote for two reasons. First I did not know what the poison was, and secondly an antidote for a corrosive poison is useless after the lapse of an hour as I've already stated."

"Are you telling us then that any treatment for corrosive poison is useless after one hour?"

"Practically useless, yes."

"Do you mean to say that you would not give a patient a

chance of life?"

"I would if I knew what the poison was, but it is pointless prescribing after an hour has elapsed from the time the poison is administered. That night we prescribed for what was killing the patient. The vomiting and the purging."

"Do you say", asked the judge. "that it is impossible to save life after the lapse of an hour, or that the chances are against it?"

"I would give the patient a chance if I knew what the poison was, but if I did not know then it would be unsafe to prescribe."

"On Sunday there were new symptoms", said Mr. Cottingham, "including purging and blistering of the mouth?"

"That's correct."

"You are indebted to the prisoner, are you not doctor, for the statement she made to you about the whole affair. I mean regarding the child's illness. It was voluntary wasn't it?"

"Yes, quite so."

"Which is the most important symptom in your diagnosis. The state of her mouth and lips, or her general appearance at the time she was ill?"

"I cannot say", replied the doctor, refusing to be caught out in this way.

"Assuming the child was suffering from inflamation of the stomach on the Saturday, is it not likely that the illness would be much more noticeable and dangerous on the Sunday?"

"It might have been."

"When did you take the temperature of the patient?" asked Mr. Cottingham casually, very neatly switching his line of attack again.

"I never took it."

"You did not take her temperature at all?"

"No, not that I remember."

"If corrosive poison had been given to the child would not the pain have been so severe as to be apparent to any person who was with her at the time or shortly afterwards?"

"Well ... I should say so, yes."

"Now, when did sulphuric acid suggest itself?"

"Never."

"Will you swear to that?"

"Not until I heard ____"

"Never mind what you heard. Did you suspect sulphuric acid?"

"No I did not."

"Did you not believe that the deceased had been given oxalic or sulphuric acid? snapped Mr. Cottingham, firing the questions at him with the rapidity of machine gun bullets.

"No."

"Can you suggest what poison it was then?"

"No."

"Did you tell the mother that the child was suffering from poisoning?"

"No, I did not think it wise to do so?"

"Oh you did not think it wise to tell the mother that?"

"No."

"You suspected the child was being poisoned, and that the mother was poisoning her?"

"I never said so."

"You left the child in the care of the mother the whole of Sunday night. And was she not in the mother's bedroom, attended by the woman whom you believed was poisoning her?"

"She was in the mother's bedroom yes ____"

"And you had your suspicions?"

"Yes I had."

"Then why did you not bring another nurse in to attend to her?"

"Because the moment I had done so the mother's character would have gone."

"What!" Mr. Cottingham was astounded. "Do you mean to say that you put the character of the mother in competition with the life of the child, when you believed that the child was suffering from the effects of poison?"

"No, that is not so", replied Dr. Patterson, squirming now. "After all I had no conviction. I only *thought* the girl had been poisoned."

"On Sunday night", asked the judge, "did you believe that the child was being poisoned, and that the mother was giving her the poison?"

"I had those suspicions, but it would not have been fair to myself to have expressed those suspicions at the time."

"Did you ask who had been in to visit the child?"

"No my lord."

"You made no inquiries regarding what persons had had admittance to the sickroom?"

"No not then", replied the doctor, rather lamely, "but I did afterwards."

Mr. Cottingham now took up the questioning again. "Dr. Patterson, why did you leave the mother alone with the child?"

"Because the child was fatally ill and it would have done no good whatsoever to have left her in charge of anyone else."

"Do you mean to tell the jury that you saw no harm in leaving the child under the care of a woman whom you suspected was giving her poison?"

"I did not say so."

"But that is exactly what you did. You left the deceased alone with the mother, did you not?"

"Yes I may have done so", replied the doctor awkwardly.

"May have done so? That's precisely what you did. You left this woman, whom you suspected was poisoning her child, alone with the patient and with the key to the surgery in her possession. With access to the various poisons."

"Yes, but I locked up the poisons cupboard."

Mr. Cottingham now turned his cross-examination in another direction. "When you handed over to Dr. Harris the intestines for analysis, did you tell him your suspicions?"

"Very likely I did, but I'm not sure."

"You had already seen Mrs. Berry and got a statement from her."

"Yes."

"Did you tell her it was quite safe for her to tell you everything?"

"No, I told her not to tell me anything she didn't want to."

"Why did you want a statement from her?"

"It was merely curiosity."

"Merely curiosity! Was your curiosity so unsatisfied that you asked her to sign it?"

Dr. Patterson made no reply to the question and the judge took advantage of the slight pause to ask how many more medical witnesses were still to be called. On being informed by Mr. McConnell that there were at least three, the impatient Mr. Hawkins enquired of Mr. Cottingham if he was anywhere near finishing with the witness. The defence barrister, never one to be rushed, was in fact close to completing his cross-examination of Dr. Patterson and replied that he had only one further question, which he said he would prefer the judge to put to the witness.

"It is with regard to the the coco chips deceased had eaten on the day before her illness. I would like to know if it is possible that they could have caused the child to become ill."

"What are coco chips? asked the judge. "Do you know doctor?"

"No I do not." replied Dr. Patterson.

After a brief consultation at the solicitors bench, Mr. Cottingham told the judge; "They are parts of a coconut."

"I do not see the point Mr. Cottingham."

"I would be interested to find out what quantity of these the child ate and who saw her eating them", said Mr. Cottingham.

"Well it seems a very vague and useless question to me", grumbled the judge. "But still if you insist I will put the question....Doctor, would coco chips have produced the appearances you saw?"

"No." was the emphatic reply. "Decidedly not."

Dr. Patterson was then told that the cross-examination was at an end and thankfully stepped down from the witness box. Mr. Cottingham might not have furthered his case very much by asking that apparently futile question regarding the coconut chips, for apart from irritating the judge it had proved a rather tame finale after such a devastating piece of cross-examination.

There was no denying though that he had made things extremely uncomfortable for the doctor, whose answers had not always been convincing. If he had suspected poison as early in the case as he claimed he had it seems very surprising indeed that he failed to take more positive action. If he had felt for one moment that the child had poison in her system then surely the best course would have been to rush her into hospital and have the stomachs contents drained without delay. There does not seem to have been the sense of urgency one would expect in such a case. On the Sunday night for example he had been in no great hurry to get to the patient, even visiting apparently less urgent cases in the same building first, for if any of these cases had been really pressing he would surely have mentioned that fact in court. Taking into account that he prescribed three different medicines within the space of two days it would certainly appear that the doctor was a very puzzled man, rather than one in control of the situation.

According to his evidence, which we have touched on only briefly here, he saw such a dramatic change in the patient between his Sunday morning visit and his next call on the same evening, he became convinced that some poisonous substance was being administered to her. Before deciding on his next move he had brought his friend Dr. Robertson into the case, and although the two of them were of the opinion that the child had poison in her body at the time of their visit late on the Sunday night, they had taken no positive steps to combat it, but had merely prescribed to relieve the pain, having apparently given up the fight to save the child's life. And although supposedly convinced that poison was being administered between his visits, Dr. Patterson had made no effort at the time to discover who might be responsible, nor even made it his business to enquire as to what persons had been left alone with the patient. As he had allowed open access to the sickroom it was clear that if he suspected anyone it could only have been the mother. In those circumstances it seems astonishing that he was still prepared to leave her in charge of the sick child. Not that these facts could have any bearing on Mrs. Berry's guilt or innocence, but the apparent inconsistency of some of Dr. Pattersons actions was hardly likely to prove helpful to the prosecution. He had undergone a severe grilling at the hands of

Mr. Cottingham and must have been very relieved to get out of the witness box and back to the safety of his seat. His near neighbour, Dr. Kershaw, was no doubt well satisfied with the way in which his arch enemy had been put through the mangle. Throughout the whole of the time Dr. Patterson was on the stand, the former Royton Medical Officer had appeared very active indeed, taking copious notes and even at times appearing to prompt Mr. Cottingham in his cross-examination of the witness.

In view of what had gone before it would certainly be interesting to see what transpired when Dr. Robertson gave evidence, but first another medical man, Dr. Abraham Leach junior of Manchester Street Oldham, was called. As he took his place in the witness box Mrs. Berry rose and whispered something to the female warder, who, after a brief word with her male colleague, descended the dock steps and returned shortly afterwards with a cup of water which she gave to the prisoner. Handling it very daintily, Mrs. Berry no more than wet her lips before placing it on the floor beside her chair and resuming her usual position.

Dr. Leach, who had travelled from Oldham that same afternoon, stated; "I am a surgeon and have attended Charles Hodgkinson for about six weeks past. He is suffering from the results of a fall. I saw him earlier today and he was still in bed. If he had to travel today I should anticipate a recurrence of the paralysis from which he has recently suffered."

The Chief Constable's depositions were therefore read over and were not questioned by the defence. Ann Sanderson was then briefly recalled and was followed into the witness box by Dr. Robertson, who had only just begun to give his evidence when court was adjourned for the day.

Dr. Leach had arrived in Liverpool after being telegraphed for, so that no doubt would remain as to the Chief Constable's indisposition, while Ann Sanderson's fleeting return to the witness box had been merely to deny Mrs. Berry's alleged statement, mentioned in the Chief Constables depositions, that her daughter had previously suffered ill-health.

The prisoner had listened attentively and with apparent calmness to the evidence, and had not found it necessary even once to communicate with her counsel throughout the entire days proceedings.

As regards the Castleton affair, it was reported in that evenings newspapers that the investigation had now been taken over by the Scotland Yard authorities, which did not bode well for the accused woman.

....

The examination-in-chief of Dr. Robertson was resumed by Mr. McConnell at 10-35 the following morning. The courtroom was not quite so packed as it had been on the preceeding two days, but there was still quite a large attendance, including many females of course, a fact which prompted a prominent member of the Liverpool bar to write a letter to a local newspaper expressing his disgust at all women who attended murder trials. This did not appear to give anyone a guilt complex, however, for the ladies continued to turn up in droves.

Dr. Robertson told the court; "When I first saw the deceased on the Sunday night she was complaining of pains in the abdomen. I pressed her stomach and various parts and found indications of the pain. I asked to see the vomit and was shown a towel stained with fresh blood in an excessively tenacious condition. I have never seen mucus like that. When I saw the redness around the child's mouth I asked Mrs. Berry when this had commenced but she did not reply. Dr. Patterson said it had not been there that morning and she did not deny this. I came to the opinion then that corrosive or irritant poison had been administered."

"You have stated", said Mr. McConnell, "that you could not give an antidote because you did not know what poison was inside the girl, is that not so?"

"If he did not know what he had to treat", interjected the judge impatiently, "it would be quite impossible to prescribe an antidote, wouldn't it?"

"At the time I saw the deceased it was quite impossible to tell what had been given to her."

Asked about the post mortem, Dr. Robertson told the court; "The greater part of the smaller and lower intestines were removed, as were also the stomach, part of the right kidney and spleen. I put these parts in four bottles and labelled them 'Edith Annie Berry'. They were corked and sealed by Dr. Patterson in my presence and I took them to my home and put them in my desk, which I then locked up. On the following day I handed them over to Dr. Harris. The same day I was present when Dr. Harris and Dr. Patterson made a further examination, the results of which are in the documents produced.

"From the post mortem examination, what do you say was the cause of death?"

"Corrosive poison", replied Dr. Robertson.

"From the post mortem alone?" queried Mr. Justice Hawkins.

"No my lord. From the symptoms during life as well as the post mortem appearances. The symptoms I saw were not consistent with any form of ordinary disease. The signs and marks I saw pointed to death from corrosive poisoning."

"Now then doctor .....", said Mr. Cottingham, commencing the cross-examination. "May we take it that you made a very thorough examination on the occasion of the post mortem?"

"We did", replied Dr. Robertson, very sure of himself. "Extremely thorough."

"Could you not, by treating parts of the body chemically, have ascertained the presence of alkali or acid?"

"We might or might not", answered the doctor rather negatively.

"Now going back to the time when the child was dying and you visited her. Did I understand you to say that you prescribed no antidote because the poison was unknown to you?"

"That is correct."

"You had no idea what it might be?"

"No."

"Have you never suggested any particular poison?"

"Yes I have."

"What?"

"Oxalic acid."

"When did you suggest that?"

"After the post mortem."

"Not before?"

"No."

"Do you mean to say that you have not already stated elsewhere that you gave bismuth as an antidote to oxalic acid, which you thought was in the child?"

"No", replied the doctor uncomfortably. "At least I did not mean to say that."

"What *did* you say?" the judge asked him.

"I may have said that the proper treatment for acid is bismuth."

"How do you mean that?" asked Mr. Cottingham. "Do you mean that it will not neutralize the poison, but will counteract the effects of it?"

"Yes."

"What are the effects produced by the poison which bismuth would counteract?"

"It would counteract the immediate action."

"But what is the immediate action?"

"Inflamation."

"Then you gave bismuth to allay the inflamation?"

"Yes."

"But wasn't bismuth and morphia prescribed to stay the vomiting and allay the pain?"

"Partly for that – and also for subduing the inflamation."

"Did you not state before the magistrates that you know of no antidote for oxalic acid poisoning?"

"I do not remember quite what I said at that time", replied Dr. Robertson.

"Did you state it?" Mr. Cottingham pressed him.

"I think I did", admitted the doctor after a slight pause.

"Have you since the post mortem, come to any conclusion as regards another poison?"

"I have come to no conclusions."

"Have you given any opinion as to the poison you believe was used?"

"I have."

"What was it?"

"Sulphuric acid."

"Have you altered that opinion since?"

"I have not."

"Did you communicate this opinion to anyone, or was it an opinion expressed by anyone with which you agreed?"

"I believe it was suggested by Dr. Harris."

"Thank you", said Mr. Cottingham, no doubt satisfied he had shown that Dr. Robertson was merely echoing the opinion of Dr. Harris.

"Now, there is a skin affection of the lip known as harbes labiatia went on Mr. Cottingham, who had obviously done a great deal of homework. "The disease is common in both children and grown-ups, and may be accompanied by inflamatory action of the stomach. Are the appearances you saw after death those which you would expect to find, supposing that the redness of the lip you saw before death had been caused by this disease?"

"I cannot answer that. I would like to explain that my experience of post mortem examinations is not sufficient to warrant my expressing an opinion on this."

"Dr. Robertson, have you ever previously dealt with a case of sulphuric or oxalic acid poisoning?"

"No", admitted the doctor. "I have not."

"Was the post mortem made by daylight?"

"Yes."

"You examined the stomach and intestines?"

"Only cursorily."

"And the misentary?" *

"Yes, in the same way."

"Is the misentary a seat of tubercular deposits?"

"It is often found to be so."

"Which is likely to elude observation if the examination is not

*Tissue attaching the intestinal canal to posterior wall of abdomen.

made with great care?"

"Yes ... you could say that."

"Did you find any of these deposits on the first examination?"

"No."

"But of course your examination was only a cursory one."

"Yes."

"At the second post mortem, was there any examination of the misentary?"

"I cannot answer that. I did not make any further particular examination."

"Did Dr. Harris?"

"I cannot say what Dr. Harris saw."

"What are the other seats of tubercular deposits apart from the misentary?"

"The lungs, the brain ....."

"Is any caseous formation found in the lungs indicative of tuberculosis?"

"Not necessarily."

"I believe a formation of that kind was found in the second post mortem examination. Is that not so?"

"I'm not sure."

"I refer you then to the notes of that examination which state that a cheesy nebule the size of a pea was found. Is this appearance not sometimes associated with T.B.?"

"Yes it is."

"When you saw the child on that Sunday evening you came to the conclusion that she was suffering from an irritant poison."

"My suspicion was simply a guess. That's why it did not warrant treatment."

"Did you come to any conclusions as to when the poison was administered?"

"Well yes, in a general way."

"What do you mean by that?"

"From ten to twelve hours."

"Did you say on another occasion that it might have been administered at any time within the previous two or three days?"

"It is possible that I might have said so. Dr. Patterson told me what the symptoms had been on his previous visits. When I saw the child myself on the Sunday night I was told that there had been vomiting and purging all that day. Also, there was this redness on the lip which had shown itself since Dr. Pattersons visit earlier in the day. I therefore came to the conclusion that poison had been administered between his visit that morning and my seeing the child the same night."

"Do you think that the amount of poison supposed to have been given would be sufficient to corrode any surface to which it was applied?"

"Yes. In my opinion the spots on the lip were caused by some corrosive poison. Probably sulphuric acid."

"The child was eleven years of age. May we take it that the length of her gullet would be about 12 to 13 inches in the general way?"

"Yes, about that."

"How many of these spots you mention were on the gullet?"

"I only noticed one spot at the top of the gullet, but there were other marks of corrosion, including black streaks, along the whole length of the upper surface of the gullet."

"Supposing", said Mr. Cottingham "that sulphuric acid, an irritant, had been administered. Although affecting the lip it apparently missed the mouth and the mucus membrane, leaving only the marks on the gullet you mention. Now how did it do so?"

"I did not say that it did so."

"Well you found no corrosion in the stomach, nor in the duodenum."

"It is often so in cases of corrosive poison."

"But you have no experience of corrosive poison have you doctor?" said Mr. Cottingham, trapping him very neatly. Dr. Robertson was stumped for a moment but managed to gather himself enough to reply rather awkwardly; "No, but I have read about such cases."

"If the poison passed downwards from the mouth to the stomach", went on Mr. Cottingham, "how is it that the duodenum was not affected?"

"It does sometimes happen that such a poison passes through without leaving any traces in the duodenum."

Mr. Cottingham, keen to argue this point out, now produced a medical book, and was about to refer to it when the judge interrupted him, saying that he found the defence counsels method of questioning rather irregular and suggesting that he should read from the book and then ask the witness 'Do you agree with that?'

Though Mr. Cottingham thanked him for the suggestion he was obviously unimpressed by it, for he immediately put down the book and did not refer to it again.

Re-examined by Mr. McConnell, Dr. Robertson explained; "I have told Mr. Cottingham that there was no corrosion on the duodenum because the bile, which is alkaline in character, affords a protection against the action of the acid. On the entrance of a poison the gullet would try to close itself against it, so that the poison would be momentarily arrested. I should expect to find a corrosive mark at the spot where that arrest took place."

Mr. Cottingham now rose again and addressed the witness; "You have told us just now that the poison might go down without leaving any traces on the mouth. Supposing it was ejected – vomited. Would it not then have the effect of throwing the acid upwards and back into the mouth?"

"I cannot say."

"And would it not also have an effect upon the lining of the mouth?"

"Yes, it might on second contact."

"And now, supposing it did not come back. Where would it go to?"

"The stomach."

"Would you not therefore expect to find some corrosive appearances in the stomach?"

"No."

"Why not?"

"Well the first reason is that it might be vomited."

"Yes but I'm asking you. Supposing it was not vomited?"

"Then its action would depend upon the contents of the stomach."

"Doctor, what action would it have on the stomach?"

"It would have the same corrosive effect."

"Thank you", said Mr. Cottingham, and indicated that he was finished with the witness. The court was then adjourned for lunch.

First on the stand following the half-hour break was Edward March, a doctor practicing in Rochdale, who had been called for the purpose of testifying as to the indisposition of John Taylor. Dr. March stated that he had been attending the Rochdale chemist for the past week as he was suffering from 'excitement of the brain'. "I saw him this morning", said the doctor, "and he was bordering on acute mania. He is certainly not in a fit state to travel to Liverpool."

"Do you apprehend danger if he does so?" Mr. McConnell asked.

"I object to that", cut in Mr. Cottingham.

The witness was then questioned by the judge and said that if Taylor were to travel it might bring on another attack of 'mania'. "He has to be watched day and night", said the doctor. He did admit, however, that the chemist was physically capable of travelling and able to understand any questions put to him.

Mr. Justice Hawkins then told the court that this evidence raised a new point, as it appeared that Taylor was both physically able to travel and also sane. His lordship now deliberated whether the chemist's evidence, given at Rochdale, could be admitted. Mr. McConnell maintained that it could, but after taking into account that although represented by a solicitor at Castleton, the prisoner had not been present in person, the judge decided that the chemist's depositions could not be admitted in evidence. In this instance he was very fair to the defence and the decision must have come as quite a relief to Mrs. Berry and her counsel.

Dr. Thomas Harris, whose evidence was expected to be crucial to the outcome of the case, now took the stand. In referring to the dry red patch around the child's mouth he was quite emphatic in stating that in his opinion the marks were not consistent with having been caused by a lemon, as had been claimed by the defendant.

Dr. Harris's evidence supported that of the two Oldham doctors, although given in much greater detail. He finished by stating; "There is no evidence that the child was suffering from any ordinary disease. It appears she was poisoned."

"Are you able to give an opinion as to what the poison was?" Mr. Mellor asked him.

"An opinion, that is all."

"What is it doctor?"

"Probably sulphuric acid."

"Would you alter your opinion if you were told that on analysis no trace of poison could be discovered?"

"No, I would not."

"Could corrosive poison be worked out of the system by vomiting?"

"Yes. Twenty-four hours vomiting and violent purging, would, I should say, be sufficient to do it."

Mr. Cottingham now began his cross-examination; "Supposing sulphuric acid had been given to the child. Would the effects of it be immediate?"

"Yes."

"And accompanied by a considerable amount of pain I would think?"

"It would depend on the patient", replied Dr. Harris, who was to prove a much more formidable witness then the two medical men who had preceeded him.

"But would you expect the patient to have pain?" Mr. Cottingham persisted.

"Yes, I should think so."

"Do you mean considerable pain?"

"Yes."

"Supposing the poison had been taken by the mouth. Would you expect to find after death some marks in the mouth where the poison had come into contact with the surface?"

"Not necessarily", replied Dr. Harris. "It is a fact that the change caused by a poison of this kind is not a continuous one along the whole line upon which it has travelled."

"But can you explain how a corrosive poison, which had had an effect on the outer lip and on the gullet, could pass through the mouth without leaving even a trace?"

This seemed to be a very good question, but Dr. Harris was equal to it. "I did not say that it left no trace", he replied. "I said the mouth presented no abnormal appearances. However, I did not state that there were no abnormal appearances during life."

"I did not ask you that", Mr. Cottingham corrected him. "Would a corrosive of sufficient quantity and strength to mark the lips and gullet, leave any change in the mouth?"

"It would in all probability, yes. But usually sulphuric acid does not produce changes in the mouth."

"Did you find any direct corrosion in the stomach?"

"No, simply signs of an irritant."

"You examined the lungs?"

"Yes. the left one was quite healthy."

"But in the right lung you found a cheesy nebule."

"Yes."

"Is that not a tubercular manifestation?"

"In the majority of cases it is, but not always."

"Having found that indication, did you not make a more thorough examination of the lungs for tuberculosis?"

"I did, but the examination was not a special one."

"At what point in the examination did you look at the lungs?"

"In the early part of it. The entire examination took me two and a half hours and was done by gaslight, but the light was a good one and I used a microscope to examine some parts of the body."

"Did you examine the misentary with the microscope for indications of tuberculosis?"

"No."

"How is that, when it was most likely that you would have found them there?"

"I did examine the misentary."

"But not under the microscope?"

"No."

"But tubercular manifestations are sometimes so minute that they may elude the examiner."

"Not if he is careful."

"Why did you not continue to search for indications of tuberculosis in other parts where they were most likely to be found?"

"I did. I examined the whole of the body. I found no indications of tuberculosis."

"Then how do you explain the presence of this cheesy nebule?"

The doctor could not explain it, except tc say that is is caused in the majority of cases by the drying up of the tube.

"Now then", went on Mr. Cottingham, "how do you explain the fact that there were no traces of poison in the duodenum? I understood you to say previously that such a state of things was not possible."

"At the time I made that statement", said Dr. Harris, "I was not aware that it is possible for the duodenum to be free from traces of poison in the case of sulphuric acid having been administered. But on looking it up, and consulting with persons who have had considerable experience of cases of this kind, I find it is a very common thing for the duodenum to be free from traces of the acid."

"Can you say how the poison was got into the girl?"

"No, I cannot."

Questioned again by Mr. McConnell, Dr. Harris said that in his opinion the redness on the lips might have been caused by an accident during administeration.

"Could the appearances on the lips have been produced by creosote?" Mr. Cottingham asked.

"In my opinion they could not."

"Would the rinsings of a creosote bottle, in which there was not a drop of creosote remaining, cause the marks on the lip?"

"I can answer that for you", said the judge, quickly spotting the incongruous way in which Mr. Cottingham had inadvertantly worded his question. His remark was greeted with some laughter in the court. When it had quietened down the witness answered rather unnecessarily; "It would not."

Dr. Harris was then dismissed, having been in the witness box for more than two hours.

Prior to the next witness being called Inspector Purser was asked to return to the stand and told the court that he was present when the Chief Constable had taken a statement from the prisoner.

"I saw the deceased on the bed in which she died, and I saw a piece of carpet in the sitting room taken up by Alice Alcroft. I took this to Mr. Estcourt the analyst, and also a bottle, a cup, a towel and a pocket handkerchief.

Mr. Charles Estcourt, of Talbot Road, Old Trafford, Manchester, following him into the witness box, stated; "I received the articles referred to by the last witness. I also received from my son the bottles previously referred to, and made a chemical analysis of the contents. However, I found no poisonous matter whatsoever, either organic or inorganic. In my opinion though, the charred patch I saw on the gullet could have been caused by sulphuric acid."

Mr. Byrne, for the defence, asked him; "What effect would sulphuric acid have on the flesh?"

"It would carbonise it."

"So if sulphuric acid had been used the lips would be charred, wouldn't they?"

"Yes, that is supposing the acid was not washed off immediately afterwards."

"We do not propose to call any further witnesses" Mr. McConnell now informed the court. "I wish only to question briefly one or two who have already given evidence."

"Then you had better call them at once", said Mr. Justice Hawkins.

Ann Sanderson, recalled to the stand, stated that she herself had not given anything to the deceased "except for a little milk". Beatrice Hall said that she had given her friend nothing either to eat or drink. After insurance agent Harry Jackson had made a brief re-appearance, Mr. McConnell announced; "That my lord, is the case for the prosecution."

Mr. Cottingham asked if he would be called upon to put the case for the defence that evening, as he was "not equal to the task". The judge assured him that he had not intended to go any further that day. The court was then adjourned.

As the spectators began to file out some of the jurors enquired of the judge as to how long the case was now likely to take before completion. Mr. Justice Hawkins declined to hazard a guess, but said he would do his best to ensure that they were 'liberated' as soon as possible. One juryman asked if they might be afforded a little more freedom, as they had been closely confined since Monday morning, having been locked up in their hotel with little opportunity of getting any fresh air or exercise. His lordship said he would arrange for them to be taken out for a drive before coming into court on the following morning. They seemed more satisfied on hearing this and raised no further queries or complaints.

CHAPTER 11
VERDICT

At a quarter-past-eleven on Friday, February 25th, 1887, Mr. Justice Hawkins took his seat for what would be the final day in the long drawn out trial of Elizabeth Berry.

Before Mr. Cottingham opened the case for the defence Dr. Patterson was recalled to the witness box by the judge, who questioned him regarding poisons kept in his surgery at the Workhouse. He replied that he had made out a list of these. At the time they had been either locked in the cupboard or lying on the counter. He would swear that the list was a true one he said, and not from memory. It was a copy of a similar list he had given to the Coroner. In answer to a question by Mr. Cottingham, Dr. Patterson admitted that he did not check the drugs until the 9th of January, when the list was compiled.

"Are you able to say though, that these drugs were all in the surgery on January 1st?" the judge asked him.

"They were my lord."

"Among them, was there sulphuric acid?"

"Not the strongest kind, but there was some sulphuric acid there."

The first witness for the defence was now called. He was William Thompson, Fellow of the Royal Institute of Edinburgh, who stated that he had a long experience of practical chemistry, particularly in the action of sulphuric acid. Mr. Thompson told the court that if such a poison had been administered there would be marks of a very different nature than those found on the lips of the girl. If a strong acid was put on and rubbed off quickly he would expect to find no mark at all, but if it was allowed to remain there for three or four minutes say, then a white mark or blister would be produced.

"If a strong acid was administered by the mouth", Mr. Byrne

asked him, "what would you expect to find?"

"Indications of abnormal appearances wherever the acid came into contact with the tissue", was the reply.

Dr. Thompson went on to tell the court that if sulphuric acid had been used he would expect to find traces of it after death. He had heard the black patch on the gullet described. If this had been caused by acid there should have been traces of it for weeks afterwards. Sulphuric acid when leaving the stomach would be ejected in the vomit, and would retain its corrosive properties. If the vomit came in contact with any textile surface, such as a carpet, a great many of the colours of the carpet would be injured and more or less charred. On a towel he would expect to find sulphuric acid if the vomit on the towel had contained that acid, and if strong it would destroy the texture of the towel. Sulphuric acid would cause great and immediate pain if applied to the skin or any other parts of the body. He knew of the substance called creosote. It was of an oily nature and was made up of a number of chemical substances, some of which could cause blistering on the skin. Therefore a dose of creosote might produce the same effect on the gullet if swallowed. A certain amount of creosote always adheres to the bottle, so a little could be obtained from any bottle which had contained the substance.

Cross-examined by Mr. McConnell, he said that he had experience of examining the viscera of persons who had died from sulphuric acid poisoning, and he had found marks on the gullet in only one case. That case had occurred some sixteen years before, but as far as he could remember the whole of the tissues were marked. "I base the opinion that sulphuric acid, had it been present, could have been found, by analysis from experiments I have made in the past week using a piece of meat. As regards the creosote, it is partially soluable in water. But if a bottle were emptied to the utmost drop then filled with water, I believe that the remains would either float on the top or be found at the bottom of the bottle. The addition of bicarbonate of soda would have no effect on its solubility."

"Supposing", said Mr. Cottingham, "that some creosote got onto the lips of a patient. What would be its effect?"

"I should think it would produce an eruption. Although I cannot positively say that it would."

After much questioning of the witness by both factions on the most minute points, Mr. Justice Hawkins decided to examine the doctor himself. The idea was to get things moving, but as it turned out his questioning of the witness proved to be very much in the prosecutions favour.

"What would be the immediate effect of sulphuric acid taken into the stomach? asked the judge.

"It would act as an irritant."

"And produce vomiting?"

"Yes."

"What would be the next result? I mean if the contents of the stomach were discharged."

"It would produce inflammation."

"And would it produce something like phlegm?"

"Yes."

"Streaked with blood?"

"Yes, I should think so."

"Would you say that some of the poisons on Dr. Pattersons list would have the same effect?"

"Yes they would."

"You have heard about the corroded appearance of the gullet. Would you expect to find these appearances if a corrosive poison had been given?

"I should say so."

"Would it be difficult to administer anything through the mouth after that. If you wanted to give poison for example?"

"Yes, I would think so."

Finally the dead girl's photograph was handed to the witness and the judge asked him if a drop or two of creosote would produce the marks above the mouth.

"I should say not", was his reply.

Coming from his star witness this was quite a blow to Mr. Cottingham, who now attempted to re-examine, only to be cut short by Mr. Justice Hawkins, who pointed out that the witness had been called by Mr. Cottingham and had been examined and re-examined by both he and Mr. Byrne, also by Mr. McConnell, none of whom had seen fit to put the questions that he himself had put, and he now felt that if there were any more to be asked they should be put through him. As neither of the leading barristers offered to take him up on this the witness was told to stand down.

Dr. Thompson had proved to be a great disappointment as far as the defence was concerned, thanks largely to the interference of Mr. Justice Hawkins. No further witnesses were called by Mr. Cottingham, perhaps because of the attitude of the judge, or simply because he felt that they could now be of no possible help to his case, taking into account what had gone before.

There now only remained the final summing up, and there can have been little doubt in Cottinghams mind at this point that his client's life still hung by a very slender thread. Unfortunately for Mrs. Berry things had not quite gone according to plan, the chief cause of course being William Thompson, who had taken the stand as a witness for the defence and finished up testifying in the prosecutions favour. On the credit side Alice Alcroft had proved to be a gem of a witness, while Drs. Patterson and Robertson had been given a very rough time of it by Mr. Cottingham, who was to lambast them still further in his summing up. They had been asked some very awkward questions by the defence barrister and had not come over as convincingly as the prosecution would have hoped. Ann Sanderson too had been thrown off balance by Mr. Cottinghams attempt to establish that tuberculosis might have been the root cause of the child's fatal illness. In following this up through Dr. Harris though, he had run into a dead end, yet the pathologist had been forced to admit that he had made no special examination to ascertain whether or not tuberculosis was present in the child's body, despite having found what could well have been an indication of it.

With the shadow of the Castleton affair looming large in the background the dice were now very heavily loaded against the prisoner. Mrs. Berry must have been fully aware of this as she sat in the dock and watched her counsel as he prepared to address the jury, her expression as inscrutable as it had been on the first day of the trial.

Mr. Cottingham remained as determined as ever, for he felt very strongly that the prosecution had failed to prove its case. He now proceeded to let the jury know it.

"Gentlemen of the jury ....", be began. "the prisoner is charged, not only with murder, but with the most detestable species of murder possible. In the whole history of the ages murder by poison has been looked upon as the most diabolical, for it involves great cruelty, premeditation and cold-bloodedness; and you must remember that Mrs. Berry is not only charged with poisoning a fellow creature, but with causing the death of her own child.

'Now I wish you to pause and ask yourselves. What was the motive for such an act?

'The evidence of the prosecution divides itself into two parts. The death of the child by poison and the question of administration; whether by Mrs. Berry or by anyone else. And you must be satisfied on these points before coming to a verdict. Has the prosecution made out a case of death by poisoning or not? They have called evidence, but is that evidence conclusive enough?

'Now you will recall the testimony given by those two medical men from Oldham, Drs. Patterson and Robertson. Again this evidence is in two parts. The symptoms during life and the appearances after death. For the first we have to rely almost solely on the evidence of Dr. Patterson. I must ask you to look at it very carefully, and also to consider his conduct during the case, whilst taking his evidence with the utmost possible caution. Remember you depend entirely on him for the whole of the symptoms. What you must ask yourselves is this. Did he conclude from the symptoms he saw that it was a case of poisoning, or did he come to that conclusion only subsequently? Is he to be judged from his acts rather than from his words?

'If his account is to be taken as correct, what does it come to? He was called in by the mother and he diagnosed ulceration of the stomach, but later on he tells us that he had suspected poisoning. The child became better that night and on the Sunday morning he said she was in a fair way of recovery. He prescribed bicarbonate of soda and creosote, but this was not to deal with any poison or the effects of poison. That night, after he had been sent for, if he suspected foul play, why did he allow two hours to elapse before visiting the patient? When he did arrive that night he says he came to the conclusion that the child had been given a second dose of poison since his previous visit. How then did he come to leave the mother in charge, not only of the child, but also of these poisonous medicines? Why did he not take any precautions to prevent the life of the child being endangered further? Did he really have the conviction that the child was dying from poison?

'Now I don't wish to be hard on Dr. Patterson, but I'm afraid he is in a dilemma out of which he cannot escape. I do not wish you to look at Dr. Patterson as a man who has perjured himself, but as one who has been mistaken in his way of dealing with the case. He had a very difficult and obscure case to deal with. So obscure in fact that he could not find one like it in all his experience.

'I ask the jury to judge Dr. Patterson by his acts, and you must also judge Dr. Robertson in the same way. Was any one of those acts consistent with the suspicions which they claim they had? They prescribed a mixture – morphia and bismuth. Neither of these drugs are ever given as an antidote to poison.

'I would also like to point out that never at any time was there any concealment of the vomit on the part of the mother. And if these two doctors had any suspicions it is surely very singular that neither of them examined the vomit for the purpose of finding traces of poison, and there would have been traces if sulphuric acid had been given to the child. Dr. Robertson of course said he suspected the poison was oxalic acid. How is it then that nothing was given to counteract that poison? Throughout the whole of his attendence in the case Dr. Patterson never gave a medicine consistent with the fact that the illness was due to poisoning. The treatment was directed at another disease altogether. Confirmatory of this is the fact that a certificate was given stating death to be due to gastro enteritis. I leave it to the jury as practical men to say whether these two doctors have the right to come here and charge this woman with having administered poison, when the whole course of their own conduct is antagonistic to the hypothesis that poison was administered by anyone, let alone by the prisoner.

'So much for the symptoms during life. The same uncertainty seems to have followed Dr. Patterson even after death. What was his conduct towards the prisoner? What business had he, as a medical man, to go to anyone, much less Mrs. Berry, whom he says he suspected, and consult her about the post mortem? If he and his colleague came to the conclusion that the child was being slowly poisoned, was it not their duty to go to the police and place the matter in their hands? Instead of that they took a most extraordinary course. They waited until the child was dead, then went and consulted as to the certificate Dr. Patterson was to give. As a matter of fact he had no right to give one at all under the circumstances, and yet he wrote out a certificate to the effect that death was due to natural causes.

'I am not charging either of these men with any offence. They could not of course have had any design on the life of the child. But they were in a difficulty and they were anxious to get out of it in the best way they could. The prisoner offered no opposition to a post mortem, and then some appearances were found which they thought indicated poisoning. The whole of the symptoms during life had been opposed to poisoning, and it was not until after they had held their examination that they came to the conclusion that poison had been administered. Unless this is so how can we reconcile the conduct of these medical men? Is it not surprising that neither of these men could hit upon the real cause of death? Even Dr. Harris, with all his skill, could not tell us with any certainty what the actual poison was, and it is very surprising that the two Oldham doctors can adopt opinions when both acknowledge their ignorance as to the poison used. They say they did not give any antidote because they did not know what had been administered. Dr. Harris suggested sulphuric acid and now they say they believe it was the same thing."

"They say it was *probably* sulphuric acid", the judge corrected him.

"I would call the attention of the jury", continued Mr. Cottingham, ignoring the interruption, "to the fact that the lips of the patient presented no abnormal appearance until sometime between 2 and 5 o'clock on the Sunday afternoon. Yet we have had clear evidence of the fact that the action of sulphuric acid is immediate and not progressive; and although all the medical witnesses have agreed that it had been administered through the mouth, this extraordinary poison apparently passed through the gullet and into the stomach without having the effect which, it is asserted by the medical witnesses for the other side, it ought to have had.

'Now you will recall Mr. Estcourt saying that chemically speaking his analysis showed nothing that might not be found after death from natural causes. I ask you gentlemen. Have you ever heard of a case of poisoning where poison in some form or other has not been found on analysis? We also have the evidence of Dr. Thompson, who has told us positively that he would expect to find traces of sulphuric acid after death. Remember the towel and the piece of carpet which had vomit on them? These were sent for analysis, yet no trace of sulphuric acid was found on either of these articles.

'I submit that you the jury really will have to consider very carefully the possibility that the child's sickness might well have been due to inflammation of the bowels rather than poisoning."

As Mr. Cottingham was still not finished it was decided to break for lunch, and on resuming the defence barrister again addressed the jury.

"I have suggested that the death of this child might be due to natural causes, and tuberculosis has been mentioned, but the jury must not suppose for an instant that I attribute death to the direct action of this disease. What I do say is that beyond a doubt the child was or had been a tubercular subject, and it is very important to look to the family history here. Her father died after a long illness, of emaciation, and one of her brothers died from an affection of the bowels. The girl was admitted by the prosecution to have been fairly well nourished, *but not robust*. Is it not possible that coconut chips, which are exceedingly indigestable, could have caused the illness initially?

Mr. Justice Hawkins now decided to interrupt again and must

have regretted it almost at once, for in answer to his question; "Do you say that as an expert?" Mr. Cottingham turned on him with a pained expression, and replied; "No my lord, from common sense; and may I remind your lordship that I am not giving evidence."

An embarrassed Mr., Hawkins had no reply to this, and the intrepid Manchester barrister continued: "Now passing on to the symptoms manifested by the girl. The first thing she complained of was feeling sick. She did not complain of any pain. The sickness continued and the doctor prescribed for it, but there was no pain until late on the Sunday afternoon."

"You are wrong in saying that", cut in the judge, seizing his chance. "She complained of pain as early as the Saturday morning."

"I am much obliged to his lordship for the correction", replied Mr. Cottingham icily, "but when she first had pain it was in the stomach only. Now please consider this gentlemen. Sulphuric acid is a poison which would pass down the throat like liquid fire. Yet she made no complaint of pain in the throat until near her death.

'On the Saturday evening, we are told by Dr. Patterson that there was a return to the vomiting and appearances of sinking and general collapse. Is that unusual in cases of inflammation? Might it be that the treatment given was not particularly skilful? Dr. Patterson has admitted that his first diagnosis of the case was incorrect. When you consider his conduct you will not be far wrong if you come to the conclusion that he treated the child ignorantly for the malady from which she was suffering.

'Gentlemen, there is no evidence to show that the child ever took this poison at all, for if she had it would have been physically impossible to disguise that fact. Surely she would have screamed out in agony on swallowing the acid.

'But just suppose for a moment that the prosecution had proved beyond doubt that death was due to poison. The question remains, did this woman, whose conduct has always been that of a loving and devoted mother, administer that poison? Could she have done so in fact? Beatrice Hall said she came downstairs with the deceased on the Saturday morning and never left her for a single moment until the time she was taken ill. True, the mother gave her a powder, but this was after the commencement of the illness. The evidence of Ann Dillan should be very carefully considered. It was not corroborated by anyone, but it was contradicted by Beatrice Hall and up to a point by Alice Alcroft. Anything given to the child by the mother was given in the presence of others. In fact there were people going in and out of the sickroom most of the time and Mrs. Berry accepted the offers of various people to sit with the girl whilst she herself went about her duties. Now would she have done this if she had been in the process of poisoning the child?

'As to the motive, there is just no evidence of any. There was a proposal for insurance on the child, but it was never accepted and no premium was ever paid.

"What motive ....", said Mr. Cottingham, building up towards his final assault on the jury. "what motive could Mrs. Berry possibly have for committing such a foul deed? What motive could transform a mother into a monster? A monster so horrid, so detestable, that the crowd of common criminals would move aside and allow her to pass with a shudder of reprehension. I personally cannot conceive of a woman so loathsome as to accomplish the death of her own child under such circumstances as those suggested by the prosecution..

"If that poor child", concluded Mr. Cottingham, "could return here from the grave; would she come as an accuser calling down vengence upon this woman. Or would she come as a ministering angel. Proclaiming the innocence of a mother who had always been so solicitous, so loving and so anxious for her welfare?"

Mr. Cottingham's closing remarks, which may seem rather melodramatic these days, drew applause from a good number of those in court, and order had to be restored before Mr. McConnell could begin his summing up for the prosecution, which was to be comparatively brief.

Once again Mr. Cottingham's closing speech had been a very compelling one and extremely sound in its logic. Also, he had taken the jury through the evidence step by step, cutting through a tangled mass of evidence and leaving only the material facts to be considered.

It was now Mr. McConnell's turn to address the jury, and he began by pointing out that, as he felt he had already laid the evidence before them, he would simply confine himself to remarking on the issues raised by his learned friend and leave the rest to them. This was typical of the Liverpool barrister, who was certainly not given to over elaboration, and who possessed the commendable quality of always remaining within his brief.

"Mr. Cottingham challenged the prosecution", he went on, "to show a motive for the alleged crime. But I say that no motive could possibly be commensurate with a crime such as this. In any case it is not the duty of the prosecution to prove motive. Our duty is to lay before the court the facts alone. It is up to you the jury to decide whether there was a motive or not.

'As regards the issues raised by my learned friend concerning the claim that death was due to poisoning, I can only say that if you do not believe the evidence of the two Oldham doctors you should remember that it was followed by that of Dr. Harris, whose evidence as to the post mortem appearances, coupled with his own credibility, should go a long way. There is, I submit, sufficient proof to show that death was not due to any disease, but to an irritant poison.

'If that is so the question arises as to who administered it, and if I have proved that the prisoner had ample opportunity to do it, then I think it must weigh heavily in the consideration of your verdict. She was seen in the surgery with her daughter at a quarter-to-ten on the Saturday morning, and shortly after that the child was taken ill. We have evidence that the deceased said to the prisoner "No Mamma, I cannot take it", on being given a glass of something by the mother. There was every opportunity for Mrs. Berry, in her position as a nurse and as the mother, to have given almost anything to the patient. She merely had to say it was for the childs own good. The only person with constant access to the deceased was the prisoner. Also, the vomit was not preserved, and I say that she should have preserved it so that it might have been examined in order to discover what was actually the matter with the child, so that steps could be taken to cure her.

'The prisoner had full access to the drugs and poisons in the surgery and she knew to a great extent their uses. I ask you first of all to decide whether it has been proved that the child came to its death by poison. If you agree that it did and you are of the opinion that no one else could have done it but the prisoner, even if the evidence is only circumstancial, then it is for you to say so.

'I ask you to give this your most careful consideration; and unless you have any reasonable doubt, you are bound by your oath to do your duty."

Mr. McConnell now resumed his seat and waited for Mr. Justice Hawkins to have the final word. The prosecuting barrister had added very little weight to his case, in fact it is possible that he actually weakened it. Is it so unusual for a child to refuse medicine? To complain that it tastes bad? And surely it is asking a lot to expect any mother, even a nurse, to preserve vomit when a child is being constantly sick. On the contrary, as a nurse Mrs. Berry would at all times be insistent on absolute hygene and cleanliness. So the fact that she had the vomit washed away and the carpet cleaned was surely no indication that she was anxious to expunge any evidence. It is something any mother does when a child is suffering from sickness, otherwise the room remains filled with the unpleasant stench of vomit. Also, it had been clearly shown that the prisoner was not the only person with access to the drugs and poisons. Dr. Patterson had stated they were not all locked away in the cupboard, but were sometimes left lying about in the surgery. That being the case almost anyone could have given the child poison, especially as the prosecution appeared to place so little importance in the necessity to show motive. This is always assuming of course that death by poisoning had been proven. In conclusion Mr. McConnell had all but admitted that the case against the prisoner was based purely on circumstantial evidence. Knowing this, would the jury return a verdict of guilty?

A great deal would depend on what Mr. Justice Hawkins had to say, that much was plainly obvious. As it turned out his speech was not a particularly lengthy one, and although it was of course intended to be impartial there were certain passages which seemed to indicate quite clearly which way the judge was leaning. Certainly there can be little doubt that Mr. Cottingham must have longed to intervene in the same way the judge had interrupted him, for on at least one occasion during his speech the defence's case was misrepresented by His Lordship.

"You have had laid before you in a calm manner", he told the jury, "the case for the prosecution; and on the other hand the impassioned plea of Mr. Cottingham, whose duty it is to use all the ingenuity and ability he possesses on behalf of his client, for he has no obligation to society as does counsel for the prosecution."

Mr. Hawkins said he would not go into details of the evidence, but there were one or two points he wished to bring up. "I do not think it necessary to travel over all the eloquent language which Mr. Cottingham has addressed to you touching on every portion of the evidence given here. I do not think it will help you in coming to a judgement.

'Referring to the question of Mrs. Berry having been seen to give the deceased a drink from a glass containing a white liquid, it is not suggested that this was anything other than a mineral powder, but this incident, not having been seen by Beatrice Hall, goes to show that she was not in the room all the time, and that the prisoner was therefore alone with the child on at least one occasion."

After telling the jury that he saw no reason to doubt the integrity of the medical witnesses, Mr. Hawkins quite rightly pointed out that they would have to ask themselves how the black corroded patch on the gullet and streaks of corrosion had come to be there. He also mentioned that Mr. Cottingham had endeavoured to prove that the child was suffering from tuberculosis, and added; "But there is not one particle of evidence to justify the suspicion that she died from this disease. She was as healthy as a girl could be."

Now it will be recalled that Mr. Cottingham had stressed in his closing speech that he did not wish the jury to suppose for an instant that he attributed death to tuberculosis. Also, the judge did not comment on the fact that Dr. Harris had made no attempt to delve further into the possibility that tuberculosis might have been a contributary factor, despite his discovery of the cheesy nebule.

"As to whether the prisoners conduct warrants the founding of this charge I will say nothing. It has been stated that she had no motive. But it is quite impossible ever to expect to find adequate motive for a crime so diabolical as this", said the judge, echoing the opinion of Mr. McConnell. "And though in some cases there appears to be no motive at all, you may depend on it that in all great crimes committed by people in their senses, there is always a motive."

He then reviewed Mrs. Berry's financial position and followed this up by mentioning the proposed insurance of £100, which was refused. "The prisoner, however, was unaware of this fact, or at all events had not been informed by the insurance company of the refusal."

The weakness in this argument has already been dealt with. The judge now went on to discuss the depositions of the Chief Constable, referring to a conversation between he and Mrs. Berry in which she was alleged to have stated that Mrs. Sanderson had informed her that the child was in the habit of being constipated, Mrs. Sanderson on the other hand having denied this assertion.

"That being so", said Mr. Hawkins. "it is for the jury to decide why the prisoner made such false statements."

Here the judge was telling the jury that Mrs. Berry was a liar and that her sister-in-law was telling the truth. But was there any proof of this? "Why attribute to Mrs. Sanderson something which she did not say?" he continued. "and why did the prisoner want to make people believe that the child was ill when she left Mrs. Sanderson's charge?

'Unhappily it has occurred before now that people have been wicked enough, forgetting all maternal instinct and every tie that ought to bind a mother to her child, to take life for the most paltry consideration. It is not the supposed maternal affection which you must look at, but the facts as they are, and ask yourselves whether the prisoner at the bar is one of those inhuman people who many a time in your recollections have been guilty of this most hideous crime."

Coming to the end of his summing up, Mr. Hawkins told the jury that whatever he had omitted they must supply from their own memories, or he would be only too glad to read it over to them, but he felt he had gone into the evidence at sufficient length. In conclusion, he told them; "If you feel the prisoner is innocent, or if the evidence does not satisfy you as to her guilt, then she is entitled to be acquitted. But if you are satisfied that this dreadful crime imputed to the prisoner can be attributed to her, then the interests of justice demand that you should say so in your verdict; and let not your verdict be the result of either passion prejudice or sympathy."

So the jury filed silently out to consider their verdict, leaving behind them a packed courtroom and an atmosphere charged with tension.

Mr. Cottingham had again turned in a remarkable performance, fighting over every minute point raised, at times to the extreme irritation of Mr. Justice Hawkins. Whether Mrs. Berry was guilty or not, there had been a great many flaws in the prosecutions case, and Cottingham had exposed them to the full.

The jury members did not take very long to make up their minds. Only twelve minutes in fact. On returning to the courtroom their names were formally called over, before the Clerk of the Assize asked;

"Gentlemen of the jury, have you agreed upon your verdict?"

"We have", replied the foreman.

"Do you find the defendant guilty or not guilty of wilful murder?"

There was a momentary pause, then cutting like a knife through the hushed silence of the courtroom, came the answer.

"GUILTY"

At this a sensation ran through the court, and Mrs. Berry's composure finally gave way. For on hearing the verdict she threw up her hands in dispair. The female warder standing behind moved in and took hold of Mrs. Berry by her shoulders, thinking she might faint. The distressed prisoner quickly recovered herself however, as the babble of excited conversation in the courtroom was cut short by the booming voice of the Clerk;

"Prisoner at the bar. Have you anything to say why the court should not proceed to pass sentence of death upon you according to law?"

All eyes were now on the prisoner. For a moment she hesitated, then slowly rose from her seat and stepped to the front of the dock. In a voice quite loud and firm, yet filled with emotion, she replied; "I may be found guilty. But the whole world cannot make me guilty."

For a few moments there was silence in the court as Mrs. Berry's words, delivered with what appeared to be absolute sincerity, sank home. Mr. Justice Hawkins now solemnly donned the black cap and addressed the prisoner.

"Elizabeth Berry ... the law of this country knows but one punishment for the crime of murder, the crime of which the jury has found you guilty. A murder so cold-blooded, so merciless and so cruel, in causing a poor child, to whom you gave birth, to suffer so much pain and agony as to surpass all belief. The law demands of me that I should pass on you sentence of death. I hope that during the few days that remain to you, you will forget this world and all the wrongs you have done and prepare yourself to meet Almighty God, from whom alone you can hope for pardon for your sin.

'The sentence of the court is that you be taken to the place from whence you came, and from thence to a lawful place of execution, that there you be hung by your neck until dead, and that your body be then buried within the precincts of the prison in which you shall be confined until you are executed .... and may the Lord God Almighty have mercy on your soul."

With that the prisoner was led from the dock down to the cells, and the Assizes formally closed.

. . . .

Throughout the trial the defendant had maintained the same

calm demeanour, never appearing restless but always sitting in the same posture. One veteran court official afterwards remarked that of all the thirty or so persons he had seen tried for murder he had "never come across a cooler customer than Mrs. Berry."

In fact, apart from the momentary lapse when the verdict was announced, one would never have guessed from her attitude that she was on trial for her life. On being returned to Walton Gaol, where, as a condemned person, she was now placed under the closest surveillance, she still managed to retain her remarkable composure.

Those nerves of steel, however, were about to crack. Even the sphinx-like Mrs. Berry had a breaking point, as would become apparent during the course of the next two weeks. For the moment though, as she waited for the inevitable, she still held a firm grip on her emotions.

It was a long held custom to allow three Sundays to go by between passing of sentence and execution. The hanging was therefore set for the middle of March, and would take place, not at Kirkdale Prison as was usual at that time, but at Walton Gaol. It was a wierd twist of fate that the hangman's name was also Berry.

CHAPTER 12
'NO OFFICIAL KNOWLEDGE'

The trial was over, but the great interest shown by the public was by no means at an end, the newspapers being packed with comment, not only on the proceedings, with strong criticism of certain of the principals involved, but also of the impending resumption of the Castleton inquest, talk of appeals against the death sentence and wild rumours regarding Mrs. Berry's past, allegedly substantiated by the statements of various people claiming to have known her intimately.

The statement made by Mrs. Berry on leaving the sickroom, namely; "I cannot bear to see the last", was regarded by the Oldham Chronicle as 'very significant in the light of later disclosures.' The same newspaper mentioned that Mrs. Sanderson had been the most affected of all the witnesses, being so overcome by her feelings that she had wept while giving her evidence.

> 'But this was only natural', ran the article. 'From her the poor girl received a wealth of affection which her mother ought to have, but never did, bestow, though she maybe simulated it.'

This assertion was of course purely retrospective and would probably never have been made had the verdict gone the other way, for even after her arrest Mrs. Berry was described by many people at the Workhouse as a genuinely devoted and loving mother, who always had the greatest affection for all children, including her own.

The Manchester Guardian felt that the public would be extremely reluctant to accept the theory that any woman would deliberately inflict upon her own child such a lingering and agonising death.

> That she should stand by with an impassive countenance whilst her victim, whom she was bound by every tie of nature to cherish and protect, slowly

succumbed to the effects of the poison she administered, and that this atrocity should be perpetrated for the sake of a paltry sum of money—these are charges which on the face of it seem wild and incredible, and are such as ought not to be believed except upon the clearest and most convincing evidence.

The Guardian felt, however, that such evidence had been forthcoming, and went on to state that;

It has been found again and again that women are ready to assume the role of secret poisoner for the greed of gain.

Another newspaper followed this up by saying;

Unfortunately there is a terrible suspicion present in the public mind that these awful poisionings are more frequent than the comparatively rare discoveries of them would suggest, and that the undetected and often unsuspected crimes of this sort are far more numerous than those found out. In the majority of these cases the criminals are women, whilst their victims are often trusting, affectionate and helpless dependants.

As regards Mr. Justice Hawkins, the Oldham Chronicle felt that his summing up was:-

... not at all favourable to the prisoner. For His Lordship seemed to close, one by one, each avenue of escape which the prisoner's counsel had endeavoured to provide for her.

The Oldham Standard also felt that the judge's closing address had been 'strongly against the prisoner', whilst the Liverpool Mercury remarked;

Mr. Justice Hawkins seemed loath to prejudice the case for the Crown by any comment upon the conduct of Dr. Patterson, except to say; "We are not trying Dr. Patterson, but the prisoner." No doubt the Oldham medical man may have his reasons for the course he persued, but the public will nevertheless regret that a gentleman who suspected foul play from the commencement did not take effective steps to prevent the fatal denouement. By the simple expedient of locking up all the poisons in the surgery on the Saturday morning, the public would have been saved from the perpetration of a crime which is appalling to humanity.

Thus, while the newspapers gave their opinions and the public avidly discussed the many intriguing facets of the case, the spotlight was turned once more on the tiny township of Castleton, where the Blue Pitts Inn would again be the scene of the action.

....

It was stated in one newspaper that Mrs. Berry sat in her cell at Walton Gaol totally ignorant of all that was going on at Castleton, not even being aware of the exhumation of her mother's body, a claim which seems hardly credible. The report also mentioned that 'of course the Coroners jury will have no official knowledge of the conviction at Liverpool.'

No 'official knowledge' perhaps, but as the Castleton jurymen filed into the clubroom of the Blue Pitts Inn at 2 o'clock on February 28th, 1887, there could have been only one thought uppermost in their minds. They were being asked to decide on the cause of death of a woman whose daughter had only two days previously been found guilty of wilful murder; a woman whose death had been so similar to that of the murder victim. They would obviously have followed the newspaper reports with much more than the ordinary laymans interest. It was impossible for them not to be biased.

The subject of the inquest was of course Mary Ann Finley, but the name of Elizabeth Berry was soon brought up, and from the evidence of the first witness called it became quite clear that her story of having turned up at Castleton only because her appointment at Birmingham Workhouse had been put back a week was nothing less than a tissue of lies.

Mr. George Shaw of Springbank, Cobden Road, Chesterfield, told the court; "I am Clerk to the Guardians of the Poor for the Chesterfield Union. Elizabeth Berry was appointed as nurse to that Workhouse on January 22nd, 1886 and entered upon her duties on the first of February. However, on the following morning at eleven-thirty she left the Workhouse, saying that her mother was seriously ill. I received a letter from her three days later stating that the mother was sinking fast and that it would be impossible for Mrs. Berry to leave her. She enclosed a letter of resignation which was dated February 3rd."

So apart from the story of her ficticious appointment at Birmingham, as told to the neighbours in Castleton, she was now shown to have clearly stated in a letter that her mother was dangerously ill at a time when Mrs. Finley was in fact in reasonably good health.

Frank Thomas Paul, Fellow of the Royal College of Surgeons and lecturer at the University of Liverpool, told the court that he had received five bottles from Dr. Harris, four of them containing parts of the deceased, the other earth from the grave. "I have submitted these to chemical analysis, the result of which shows that no mineral poison was present in the body. However, I have extracted a substance from the stomach and intestines which has the same effect on animals as atropa, and I believe it to be atropa.

'I ought to explain that the presence of this poison cannot be discovered in the same way as other poisons. It can only be told by its effect on animals, and it is for this reason that I cannot say positively that it is atropa."

He went on to state that a small quantity of atropa would be fatal, and when asked by a juror what effect such a poison would have on the system, replied that it would cause dilation of the pupils of the eyes.

"You have perhaps been to a chemists and had something dropped into your eyes. That would be atropa. It does not act on the system in the same way as an irritant poison. It simply acts on the nerves as a poison."

Mrs. Finley's local doctor, William Henry Sharples of Castleton, now gave evidence, stating that he had attended the deceased woman for nose bleeds around the 22nd of January 1886. She had more or less recovered from this illness, but on February 6th he had again been called to her house.

"It struck me at the time," he said, "that she was subject to nervousness and that she might adopt anything suggested to her. On that occasion she complained of sleeplessness. After that I saw her every day until the 12th. She had some symptoms of paralysis that day and seemed very hoarse. I then considered the case more serious and felt that there was evidence of brain mischief. She complained of feeling loss of sensation and I was told that she had had a fit. There was a person in attendance. I think it must have been her daughter, Mrs. Berry. I told this person that I thought the illness might be an affection of the brain. When I left her on the Friday I thought the woman was seriously ill, but I did not expect her immediate death. However, on the following morning the daughter came to tell me that her mother had passed away. I questioned her and was told that Mrs. Finley had had several convulsive attacks during the night and had died in one of them.

'After talking to Mrs. Berry for about ten minutes I gave her a certificate to the effect that the deceased had died from cerebral hemorrhage. I gave it not only from what Mrs. Berry told me, but from what I saw of Mrs. Finley during her illness. On the day before she died I noticed that the pupils of her eyes were dilated and unequal. Also the face was flushed, the pulse quick and irregular and there was a tremulous motion of the muscles all over her. When I tried to examine her eyes she pushed me away. I gave the certificate because I saw no reasonable doubt that the cause of death was not a natural one."

Dr. Paul, recalled, said; "I have heard the evidence of Dr. Sharples and am of the opinion that the symptoms he has described are consistent with poisoning by atropa."

Dr. Harris, who appears to have spent a great deal of his time in courtrooms, had a grim story to tell.

"I made a post mortem examination of the exhumed body on February 3rd of this year at Moston Cemetery. It was very much decomposed, the hands being nearly separated by masceration from the body. The abdominal cavity, however, was not open, the walls of it not having been destroyed. The body was that of a well nourished woman somewhat beyond middle age. The heart was in a good state of preservation, the bowels were healthy and the brain presented no abnormal appearance, apart from being softened by decomposition."

"Can you tell us from your examination," asked the Coroner, "what the cause of death was?"

"No I cannot."

"But there was no disease?"

"No, there was not sufficient disease found to account for death."

"After hearing the symptoms described by Dr. Sharples, do you corroborate Dr. Paul's view that they are consistent with poisoning by atropa?"

"Quite so", replied Dr. Harris. "They are not only consistent, but from the facts of the case they are suspicious of atropa poisoning. One of the strongest symptoms described was the excited state of the patient. Poisoning by atropa can be mistaken for delirium tremens."

"Would these symptoms be consistent with a disease called cerebral hemorrhage?" asked a juror.

"Very improbable," replied the doctor. "but could be mistaken for it."

The next witness was Mrs. Finley's sister, Mrs. Pemberton, of East View, Burslem, who told of receiving a telegram from Mrs. Berry on the 11th of February. It read; 'Mrs. Welsh is dangerously ill. If you wish to see her come at once ____ E. BERRY.'

She had caught the next train north and had helped nurse the patient until her death, but had never given her any medicine, as this was always done by Mrs. Berry. Mrs. Pemberton told of a visit to the house by Mrs. Finley's grand-daughter Edith Annie, who had afterwards returned by train to Manchester, being seen off by Mrs. Berry.

"On the Friday night," said Mrs. Pemberton. "I told Lizzie that in my opinion her mother seemed better. She replied that she was not, but was sinking fast. I had no suspicion though that anything was wrong. I thought my sister died a natural death."

Joseph Chadderton, district manager of the Wesleyan and General Assurance Society, stated that Mrs. Finley had been insured with his company for £100.

"On March 22nd 1886 Mrs. Berry came to our office and said that she wanted the money as she was going to Australia. She mentioned the name of the ship, but I forget it now. She also volunteered the information that she was going as companion to an invalid, who was making the trip for her health. She wanted the money at once she said, so I let her have it. We paid her £100, less 16s 8d, the amount of interest charged for paying the money before it was due."

Chadderton went on to explain that the insurance policy had been effected by Mrs. Finley herself in 1882, and transferred to

Elizabeth Berry just a few days later. Another insurance man, George Coombs of the Rational Sick and Burial Society, Manchester, told of Mrs. Berry having insured her mother with his company, and of having drawn the money, £13.4s., on February 15th, 1886, two days after Mrs. Finley's death.

So after establishing what the doctors present considered to be the real cause of death, the Coroners court had even gone so far as to show motive.

It will be recalled that at their previous sitting on February 14th the jury had heard the evidence of John Taylor, the chemist, who spoke of a small dark person visiting his shop with a prescription for atropa. Also, William Lawson, the Oldham Workhouse Master, had sworn that the signature 'Ellen Saunders, Freehold, Castleton' was without doubt the handwriting of Elizabeth Berry. To further prove that 'Ellen Saunders' did not exist, William Taylor of High Street, Castleton, described as a 'letter carrier', was called to the witness box, and stated; "I have known the Freehold, Castleton, for thirteen and a half years. I never knew of an Ellen Saunders living there, and had there been such a person I should have been aware of it. I've made inquiries recently, but nobody in the Freehold has ever heard of the woman."

The whole of the evidence now having been heard, the jury was asked to give a verdict. It came as no surprise when the foreman rose and announced that they were unanimously of the opinion that Mrs. Berry was guilty of the wilful murder of her mother.

The trim little nurse was indeed beginning to emerge as something of a monster. Yet until the events at Castleton had come to light she was generally regarded as someone who had been rather shabbily treated. The case had aroused considerable interest, mainly because it had proved to be a controversial one.

Many people believed that Dr. Patterson's suspicions and subsequent actions had been fully justified, while others were amazed that the prosecution had gone into court armed with what amounted to no more than circumstantial evidence, yet had still managed to get a conviction, in spite of the fact that not a trace of poison was ever found in the child's body.

The two factions were very sharply divided, and as the newspapers continued to give the case daily coverage the arguments raged in public houses, reform clubs and even in the streets. The name Elizabeth Berry was on everyones lips. Yet in a sense she remained a somethat nebulous figure; so very little was really known about her. This, however, would very soon be rectified ____ and with a vengence.

CHAPTER 13

MRS. BERRY'S PAST

A great number of people who claimed to have known the condemned woman were now coming forward with stories of her past life, some of which were quite obviously gross distortions of the truth. Others, however, appeared to have some foundation in fact, and give an interesting insight into the mind and character of this strange woman.

Her father Joseph Welsh was a former soldier who fought in the Crimean War of 1854-56. Soon after his release from the army he married her mother, Mary Ann, at St. Joseph's Roman Catholic church Goulden Street, New Cross, Manchester, and within a short time twins were born to the couple. One child, however, died in infancy. The survivor was named Elizabeth, and not too much is known about her early life apart from the fact that very little of it was spent with the father, who apparently disappeared from the scene when she was quite young.

The mother and daughter moved house several times during this period and neighbours who enquired about the missing husband were usually told by Mary Ann that he had been killed at Sebastopol in the Crimea.

The truth of the matter was that Welsh, becoming restless after his years in the armed forces, had left his family soon after the birth of the twins and gone off to America, his whereabouts only becoming known when Mary Ann received a letter containing money some six months later. Following this rather unexpected communication, however, she did not hear another word for several years, apart from one brief note informing her that he had joined the U.S. army.

Elizabeth meanwhile was living a most difficult and impoverished life with her mother. A life to which she felt strangely alien, unlike Mary Ann, who seemed to accept her downtrodden role as readily as the rest of their neighbours. The

New Cross, Ancoats and Miles Platting areas of Manchester, where Elizabeth grew up, were somewhat over-populated with Irish families and Catholic churches. It was an environment of which she did not feel a part, and although born a Catholic, she certainly broke all ties with that religion at some later date, for while in prison she was attended by a minister of the Church of England.

She received the barest minimum of formal education, but having an agile enquiring mind and an eagerness to learn, she rapidly increased her knowledge, mainly through reading, so that by the time she reached her teens she felt confident enough to be able to pass herself off as an 'educated person'. In those days this really meant something, and would, Elizabeth felt sure, be the passport to a higher station in life.

Unfortunately, due to the family's very poor circumstances, she was forced to enter the cotton trade to earn a living and was employed, along with her mother, at various mills in the Manchester area. Such work, however, was not always readily available, and like many others at that time the Welshes were obliged to travel to wherever they could find it. At sometime in the late 1860's the mother and daughter turned up in Royton near Oldham and were taken on at the Springhill Mill, owned by Thomas Saville and Sons. It was here that Mrs. Welsh met William Finley, who was to become her second husband. A shiftless man of roving disposition, he was known as 'the tramp weaver', and was something of a character as we shall see. A Manchester man, he found himself in difficult circumstances when his wife died, leaving him with five children to bring up. Callously he had abandoned them and taken to wandering around the country in search of work. What money he earned always went the same way _____ across the bar of the nearest tavern. The children were taken to the Workhouse and he does not appear to have given them another thought.

After a time, Finley, along with Mrs. Welsh and her daughter, left Royton and moved to Hollinwood Oldham, where they occupied a house in Hollins Road. All three found employment at the weaving shed run by a Mr. Shaw on the premises of the Oldham Twist Company and subsequently moved to a larger house in Millbrook, quite near to their work.

At some time previously Mrs. Welsh had contacted the American War Office regarding her long lost husband and received a reply stating that Welsh had been discharged in 1867 after fighting in the civil war and had gone to live in Louisiana. Now contemplating marriage to Finley, she made further inquiries and was duly informed that Joseph Welsh had died some time before. So, on July 22nd 1871, Mary Ann became Mrs. Finley, when the couple were married at St. Margarets Church Hollinwood. Soon after this the family left the weaving shed, all three going to work at Butterworth and Murgatroyds Glebe Mills, also in Hollinwood. They now found a house to rent in Drury Lane and settled down to what Mary Ann hoped would be a happy life together.

The marriage, however, was to be a short-lived and extremely turbulent one, and the fly in the ointment appears to have been Mary Ann's daughter Elizabeth, then known as Lizzie, who had resented the presence of Finley from the very beginning and was adamant in her refusal to accept him as a stepfather. She set out from the start to make things awkward for him, often sitting in his company for an entire evening without speaking to him and frequently causing friction between Finley and her mother.

Things finally came to a head only five weeks after the wedding. It had been a week of quarrels and general unpleasantness, and Finley was feeling somewhat disillusioned with married life as he prepared to leave for work one Saturday morning. As he reached the door his wife called after him; "And come straight home with your wages."

"That's all you ever think about, money!" he shouted back,

and slammed the door.

William Finley did not go straight home that day but made for the nearest pub, which was not unusual in any case. When he eventually did turn up several hours later there was an angry scene. Faced by two contemptuous sneering women Finley flew into a temper and smashed several windows. With his wife in tears and Lizzie threatening revenge, the erring weaver staggered off upstairs, where he soon fell into a drunken stuper. But if he imagined that to be the end of the affair he was very much mistaken, for Lizzie was quite determined not only to pay him back, but to get rid of him altogether.

The following day, Sunday, passed without incident, but on the Monday morning Finley noticed that Lizzie was absent from her work, and wondered why. He did not know that she was on her way to Manchester to visit the Guardians of the Poor of that city for the purpose of informing them that a certain William Finley, wanted by the authorities for deserting his children, was living in Oldham. Before the day was out Finley was under arrest and on his way to Belle Vue Gaol, where he served a three months sentence.

On his release he made his way back to Hollinwood. Knowing he would not be made welcome he did not go directly to the house, but sent a woman to collect his belongings while he waited in a public house nearby. He was most annoyed when she returned empty-handed to inform him that his possessions had been pawned by the two woman for twenty-eight shillings, which they had no intention of passing on to him. After spending the rest of the day drowning his sorrows Finley made up his mind to leave the district for good, and set out once again for Royton, where he got a start at the Union Mill. However, his constantly itchy feet would not allow him to settle there and it was not long before he was off again on his travels.

Five years passed and Finley did not see or communicate with his wife during that time, but contact was somehow eventually made, and the couple agreed to try again, no doubt feeling that they were now a little older and wiser. In any event the two women joined Finley in Royton where they all lived together at a lodging house known as 'Owd Betty's' in Chapel Lane. But the re-union was not destined to last for very long. Finley came downstairs one morning after a particularly heavy night of drinking to find his things tied up in a bundle. He asked an old woman named Matty, also a resident, who was responsible, and was told that the bundle had been put there by his wife. She had then gone to work, leaving word that he was to 'flit'. This caused Finley to lose control of his temper, and bellowing; I'll take ____ good care that she's the one who flits", he rushed upstairs in a fit of blind rage and seized a box containing some of his wife's possessions. Still shouting and swearing he hurled it out of a bedroom window into the street below. As far as is known no one was walking past at the time. After collecting his bundle Finley very wisely made himself scarce, setting off once more to roam the countryside and not being seen again in Royton for some years.

With the drunken weaver out of the way, the mother and daughter, who were at that time working as weavers themselves at John Buckleys Mill, moved into an unpretentious but neat little house in Sandy Lane. Buckleys Mill was later burnt down and subsequently re-built, being afterwards run as a spinning mill by the Park and Sandy Lane Spinning Company.

Mrs. Finley was described later by her neighbours in Sandy Lane as a hard working, cleanly-clad, quiet and domesticated woman whose house was always very well cared for. Although not a particularly good mixer she seems to have gained the respect both of her neighbours and workmates. Her daughter on the other hand was not nearly so well thought of, Lizzie's manner being considered rather superior for a humble mill girl. Also, she exhibited a love of finery which was quite out of keeping with her position, being only too eager to get out of her working clothes and dress up in the evenings. This may seem like normal behavior today, but in Victorian times it was considered quite wrong to attempt to live above one's station in life. A labourer always dressed as a labourer, and even if he put on his best clothes on a Sunday he merely exchanged his grimy cap for a cleaner one and his muffler for a silk scarf. He would still wear the same sort of roughly cut suit, and to go beyond this and try to dress like a gentleman would be construed as aping one's betters. Therefore Lizzie's conduct was very much frowned upon by the sober hard working villagers of Royton.

After the fire at Buckleys the mother and daughter both found work at the Springhill Mill again. Lizzie had now developed into an extremely attractive young woman, but although apparently keen to encourage the attentions of the opposite sex, she was most reserved in her relations with the mill hands and remained quite aloof from them.

It was about this time that a young man named Thomas Berry, whom the family had known in Manchester, began to take a serious interest in Lizzie. His visits, which had been infrequent up to then, now became regular each weekend, and in due course the couple were married, after which they remained in Royton, living with the mother.

About a year later Lizzie gave birth to her first child, a boy, and was attended by none other than Dr. John Kershaw, who was then in practice in the town. Whether the Royton doctor remembered this when he later became involved in the poisoning case is not known, but it seems extremely unlikely, as it would have been just one of many confinements he must have attended during his long career. The child was named Harold.

Before the christening a most startling incident occurred, which, had it not been for the timely intervention of Mrs. Finley, would almost certainly have ended in tragedy. Going into her daughter's bedroom one day, not long after the child was born, the older woman was horrified to find Lizzie in the act of putting the baby on the fire. Another second or two and she would have been too late to prevent its being burnt to death. As it was she managed to snatch the child away from its mother, and afterwards took great care never to leave her alone with the baby again during the first few months of its life. The incident was kept as quiet as possible, but Mrs. Finley did mention it to the wife of a Royton tradesman, which is how the story came out at a later date.

The child's safety, however, was taken out of Mrs. Finley's hands some six months after this when Lizzie and her husband decided to move back to Manchester. In any case the young mother now appeared much better balanced mentally than she had been soon after the confinement, so Mrs. Finley's mind was easier. The couple found a house to rent in Saville Street, Miles Platting, where a second child, Edith Annie, was born two years later.

Thomas Berry, a quietly spoken, rather pale faced young man, was well liked by most of those who knew him. He was very much wrapped up in his young wife, whose every whim he attempted to fulfil, even to the point of denying himself some of the ordinary requirements of life. Lizzie, or Elizabeth, as she now preferred to be known, did not take kindly to the idea of having to live in a working class community. Although never having known anything better, she had at least received some sort of formal education, and in her eyes this in itself placed her on a much higher plane than her neighbours, the majority of whom could neither read nor write. In addition to this she possessed a built-in superiority complex which seemed to instill in her the belief that she was entitled to something more from life than a modest existence in Saville Street. At first the idea of being mistress of her own house had held a certain appeal, but once the novelty of it wore off she became moody and difficult to live with.

Such a situation was bound to place Thomas Berry in a rather difficult position. For though he worked long hours in his job as a pointsman at Victoria Station Manchester, his wages were very meagre indeed, even with overtime, which he was always prepared to undertake, as it meant a few extra shillings with which to mollify his restless wife. He was a member of the choir at the local church of St. Lukes, and though he enjoyed this very much his increasing Sunday duties eventually forced him to give it up. To add to his worries another child was born during this period, a boy, which died however, after only four months.

Mrs. Berry meanwhile continued to strut around the neighbourhood as if she were the wife of the local squire, much to the irritation of the other residents, to whom she seldom condescended to speak. As one of them later remarked; "She was a proud haughty woman, who strode along this street as if she was everybody and we were 'nowt.'"

It was not long before Thomas Berry's health began to fail and after several periods of illness he was moved onto lighter work. After a time though, even this became too much for him and he was forced to give up altogether.

According to one neighbour, his death, in July 1881, was startlingly sudden, and his burial carried out with equal dispatch. This statement, however, is most certainly a wild exaggeration, for it is a fact that after taking to his bed the unfortunate railwayman lived for another two years, although apparently in great pain for most of that time. Under these circumstances of course there was no inquest, and the emaciated body was duly interred in Harpurhey Cemetery, where the baby had been buried. He was thirty-one years old.

Mrs. Berry, who received an insurance payment of £70, plus another for £18.4s, did not allow her grief to weigh too heavily on her. She now moved to a slightly better house in Jackson Street, close by, where she remained for only four weeks before selling up and going to live with her in-laws, the Sandersons, in Albion

Street, also in Miles Platting. Though it now became necessary for her to go out and earn a living for herself and her family she had no intention of returning to the cotton mills. Instead she managed to get herself engaged as housekeeper to a local G.P., Dr. Shaw. The appointment, however, lasted no more than one day, the doctor dismissing her without being specific as to why she was unsuitable. One theory is that she acted more like the woman of the house than an employee, and there could well be some truth in this. The unexpected rebuff must have been something of a blow to her pride, but does not appear to have resulted in a loss of confidence, for she very quickly found another situation, this time as a trainee nurse at the Manchester Royal Infirmary.

At about this time she became very friendly with the Curate of St. Lukes, even offering to help him with some of his social work. Quite innocently the Curate gladly accepted and found Mrs. Berry's energy and drive a great asset over the next few months, during which time the recently bereaved widow made sure that the relationship grew progressively more intimate. At some point, however, the Curate became aware of what was in Mrs. Berry's mind and made it quite clear that he had no intention of marrying her. He now discovered to his cost that the widow was not nearly so sweet as she had appeared, for on realising that her ambition was to be frustrated she immediately turned nasty and informed the startled young man that she would sue him for breach of promise. It was no empty threat she told him, for she fully intended to take the matter to court. The curate in fact had not proposed to her and would no doubt have won his case without too much difficulty, but the crafty Mrs. Berry reasoned that he would much prefer to hush the matter up rather than face a scandal. She guessed right, for when it became clear that she was quite prepared to start proceedings she received a visit from the Curate's mother, who told her in no uncertain terms exactly what she thought of her conduct. It made no difference and the meeting ended with the mother reluctantly handing over the sum of £150, a transaction that amounted to nothing less than blackmail.

There is no record of what Mrs. Berry did with the money, but she does not appear to have been particularly thrifty, and no doubt the bulk of it was spent in the best fashion shops of Manchester, for when seen out she was always very smartly attired, favouring elegant well-cut garments rather than cheap flashy ones.

Despite her recent windfall the purposeful Mrs. Berry was still determined to gain some sort of status and continued with her training at the Infirmary. After a time she managed to get an appointment at Prestwich Asylum, Manchester. This lasted only a short time, however, before she was summarily dismissed. Again the reason is not known.

She now left the district for a period, the children remaining in the care of their aunt and uncle in Miles Platting. She was said to have gone to the South of England to find work, but precisely where is not clear. She did, however, find employment sometime after this at Wellington Infirmary Shropshire, where she stayed for about nine months.

It was during her time at Wellington that the death of her son Harold occurred. While on a visit to Miles Platting Mrs. Berry took the children on a trip to Blackpool. During the journey home both children became ill. Edith Annie recovered, but the boy died a few days later, his mother collecting the £5 insurance money before returning to Wellington. She was not there for very long after this, giving up her job and applying for a vacancy at the Rochdale Workhouse. In her letter of application she described herself as having 'considerable experience', and closed with the words;

> If given the situation it is my earnest desire, under the
> Divine Blessing, to do my duty truly and well.

But the Guardians of Rochdale were obviously unimpressed by this very profound declaration and appointed another applicant.

Mrs. Berry continued to send off her eloquently phrased letters and soon succeeded in getting herself taken on at Burton-on-Trent Workhouse, where she remained from April 1883 until October 1885, a lengthy spell for one so restless. After Burton it was Henley-on-Thames, but according to reports she showed so little respect for the Master there that she was told to pack her things and leave, having been on the premises only a matter of hours. Her next appointment, at Chesterfield, was just as short-lived, although on this occasion she apparently left of her own accord. It was from Chesterfield that she made her way to Castleton to stay with the unfortunate Mrs. Finley at the beginning of February 1886.

After her mother's death Mrs. Berry does not appear to have worked for some months. From Castleton she moved to Manchester, but did not go to live with the Sandersons. Instead she obtained lodgings with a Mrs. Pyott, a widow, in Wilmot Street off Stretford Road. From this address she sent off a stream of applications for jobs, but did not meet with any success at first. After quite a lengthy period of unemployment, however, a letter arrived from the Oldham Guardians informing her that her application for the post of head nurse in the female infirmary there had been successful. On receiving the letter she hurried to the house of a friend, Miss. Bennett, who later said that Mrs. Berry had been extremely pleased at the news.

Following her daughter's marriage and subsequent removal to Miles Platting Mary Ann Finley had left Royton and gone to live in Rochdale, where she was joined in 1880 by her wandering husband, whom she had not laid eyes on for some years. They were glad to see each other and decided that there was little point in both of them living alone. They therefore decided to get together and set up house in New Street Rochdale. Finley jokingly told his wife; "Well Mary Ann, I've lived wi' thee five week one time and then again for six week. I'll try three month this time."

He was two days out in his prediction, his departure coinciding with the arrival of Lizzie on a visit to her mother. She was not pleased to find Finley in attendance and the meeting was not a particulary friendly one. After Lizzie had gone there was a row over a family bible which Mary Ann had given to her daughter against Finley's wishes. Forgetting all their resolutions the pugnacious pair set about each other with a vengeance. It was just like old times and ended as always with Finley grabbing his bundle and storming out of the house, "For good this time!" He never saw his wife again, although he later heard that she had moved to Castleton.

This episode quite probably throws some light on Lizzie's reasons for 'not owning' her mother for some time after. However, once she was satisfied that Mrs. Finley would never again take up with her husband she apparently relented and their friendship was resumed.

Finley himself now became an itinerant pedler, his wanderings taking him all over the North of England during the next six years. One day, while travelling from Rishton to Blackburn, he happened to meet a former acquaintance who told him that his wife had died. This was about eight months after the event and Finley said he was very sorry to hear of it. He continued on his travels and some months after this was shocked to learn of the exhumation. Finley was in Manchester at the time and immediately made his way to Royton to remain in that vicinity and "see it out" as he put it. Characteristically he made the Blue Bell Inn his headquarters, where he no doubt regaled the customers with much inside information on the notorious Mrs. Berry. He was now in his fifties but looked older. Above average height, he wore a straggly beard and dressed rather shabbily. "I'd be far better off now," he told a reporter, "had I not seen so many empty gill pots."

Not surprisingly the wandering pedler had very little to say in Mrs. Berry's favour. She had always treated him like dirt, even on his wedding day, when, at a celebration party, a friend of his had said to Lizzie; "This is your father now you know." She had glared at him and replied arrogantly. "I'll never call him that."

"No, she never liked me", said Finley. "In fact I'll tell you straight. If I'd lived under the same roof as her much longer I reckon I'd have been a goner for sure."

CHAPTER 14
UNDER SENTENCE OF DEATH

On the Saturday following the trial, George Robinson, the young man from Joseph Whittaker's office, was handed a letter from the Governor of Walton Gaol, asking him to visit Mrs. Berry at her request. As he was still in Liverpool, he went immediately to the prison, and on producing the letter was admitted and shown into an inner room, divided in the usual way by a partition with chairs on either side.

Robinson had been in constant touch with Mrs. Berry from the day of her arrest and had come to know her quite intimately. With a feeling of apprehension he sat and waited, hoping that the interview would not prove too painful and that the prisoner would be able to retain control of her emotions. After waiting for some minutes he heard footsteps and the sound of a door just opposite him being unlocked. There was a slight pause, then the door swung open and Mrs. Berry entered, flanked by two warders. Robinson was shocked at her appearance. Though only two days had passed since the close of the trial a great change had already taken place. The once pretty face was now as pale as death, the cheeks sunken and the eyes red-rimmed and puffy. The shapeless blue serge frock with white collar and the little white prison cap seemed wholly out of character after the fashionable attire worn in court.

Wearily Elizabeth Berry stepped forward, greeted Robinson with a flat 'good morning', then collapsed in a dead faint. The two female warders made a grab at her, but were too late to catch the prisoner as she fell backwards, her head hitting the bare stone flags with a sickening crack. A very shaken Mr. Robinson could do nothing to help, being obliged to remain on his side of the division and watch anxiously as the warders knelt down beside Mrs. Berry and attempted to revive her. Though unconscious, she appeared to be crying, and seemed to Robinson to be in a very serious condition. One of the warders ran to get a doctor who was very quickly on the scene followed by a second medical man. Robinson saw the prisoner lifted up and carried from the visitors room, but would not leave until some word had been relayed to him from within. After a while a warder appeared with the news that Mrs. Berry was in such a critical state that it was feared she might cheat the hangman. Still Robinson remained, and some two hours later was told that his client had been given an injection and now seemed to be recovering. If he could come back later there was every possibility that she would be in a fit condition to see him. With that Robinson left the prison and returned later that evening when he was again admitted to the visitors room. Not long afterwards Mrs. Berry was brought in. She appeared to be in a very sorry state indeed. Slowly she dragged herself forward, and reaching through the grating, gripped Robinson's hand almost in desperation. The two of them then settled down and Mrs. Berry began to talk of her trial, saying that she felt the judge's summing up had been very harsh. Apart from that she made some rather uncomplimentary remarks about one of the witnesses, and though Robinson would not divulge which one, the name would not be too difficult to guess at.

Following these prelimineries they got down to the business about which Mrs. Berry had asked Robinson to come – the disposal of her possessions, among which were certain pieces of furniture at the Sandersons house. As she gave her instructions she would from time to time be overcome with emotion and break down, sobbing bitterly.

The scene, played out in the eerie dimness of a room illuminated only by the light of a flickering candle, had its effect on young Robinson, who was very relieved when the interview at last came to an end. When he left it was with the distinct impression that Mrs. Berry was now resigned to her fate.

She was by now extremely low in spirits, and though she had not admitted her guilt, it was felt that she might now confess to the crime, particularly as she was spending a great deal of her time with the prison chaplain.

On the Monday, two days later, Mrs. Sanderson arrived at the prison, having received a letter from Mrs. Berry begging her to come. The two women did not talk together for very long, however, the interview coming to an abrupt end when Mrs. Berry broke down completely and had to be led away.

Another visitor that week was Mrs. Pemberton, who travelled up from Burslem to see her niece for the last time. She had been very surprised at receiving the request to visit, for after attending each day at the Oldham Police Court she had stayed behind at the close of the hearing and sent a message through to the prisoner asking if she might be allowed to see her for a few moments. The request had been refused, Mrs. Berry having asked indignantly; "What is she doing here anyway?"

. . . .

The prisoner was by now in a very poor state of health and was said to be 'simply wasting away'. Her condition, widely reported at the time, did not, however, induce in her former neighbours at Miles Platting any feelings of sympathy. The general belief in that locality in fact, was that the former nurse was guilty of at least two other murders in addition to the two already attributed to her.

"Mister," said one old fellow, addressing a visiting reporter, "in the space of about five years she buried a husband, a mother, two sons and a daughter that we know of. And each and every one of them died sudden like. Now how do you explain that eh?"

The feeling in Miles Platting at that time seemed to be that if Mrs. Berry had been allowed to walk along Saville Street there would have been no need for the services of the hangman.

In the village of Castleton feelings ran just as high and everyone there who had known the condemned woman agreed that she was an excessively vain and completely heartless person. One woman told the story that the nurse had once visited Castleton to find her mother out of work and in distressed circumstances. Mrs. Berry had flaunted the contents of her purse – £11 in gold, but had declined to give her mother a penny of it. All this of course might have been pure fiction, but on the other hand one could now believe almost anything about a woman convicted of murdering her own child in cold blood.

And so inevitably the stories and anecdotes alluding to Mrs. Berry's past, some of which would doubtless never have been told had she been acquitted, continued to appear in the press, as former friends and acquaintances recalled various incidents involving the now infamous head nurse.

At the time of her arrest quite a number of people at the Oldham Workhouse had spoken up on her behalf, insisting that she could not possibly be guilty of the alleged crime. As well as being a dedicated nurse she was also very well liked and a great lover of children they had said. However, since her subsequent trial and conviction most of the statements issuing from the Workhouse were in total contradiction to all this. It was now claimed that her conduct in respect of some of the hospital patients had been callous, even cruel, and her general behaviour extremely odd to say the least. One could never take her word for anything they said, her conversation being invariably laced with exaggerations, half-truths and downright lies. One example given was that on arriving at the Workhouse she had given out the story that her mother had died the previous year leaving her the sum of £1500.

Although much of what was now being attributed to the prisoner was quite obviously inaccurate, there is without doubt a certain amount of substance in some of these allegations, which makes them worth relating.

Apparently Mrs. Berry's strange behaviour had been in evidence almost from the moment of her appointment to the position of head nurse at Oldham, for after arrangements had been made for her to arrive at the Workhouse to take up her duties on July 12th 1886, a telegram had been received by the Governor informing him that she would not after all be able to come to Oldham on that date, as her child had fallen downstairs and injured herself. This statement was certainly quite untrue, as the child was at that time living with Mrs. Sanderson, who, when asked about it later, could not recall any such incident. The next communication received from Mrs. Berry was on the 16th July. It was a letter stating that after further consideration she had decided not to accept the appointment. The Governor made his way to Oldham that morning for the purpose of passing on the letter to Mr. Mellor, Clerk to the Guardians. On arriving in the town centre Mr. Lawson was very surprised indeed to bump into none other than the recently appointed head nurse, who said she had just got off the train. He asked her what she was doing in Oldham and was told that she was on her way to the Workhouse.

"But I just received your letter informing me that you had decided not to accept the situation", said Lawson.

"I know nothing about any letter", replied Mrs. Berry. "I've been travelling all night and I'm very tired."

A very puzzled Mr. Lawson returned with her to the Workhouse, where Mrs. Berry commenced her duties, the incident not being referred to again by either of them.

At first the newcomer appeared to be a very agreeable sort of woman; intelligent, well-read and a good conversationalist, but at times she was seen to exhibit another side of her character. She could be very moody and it was stated that her treatment of some of the Workhouse servants was often quite violent. If one of them offended her in any way she was not above throwing some handy object at the unfortunate culprit, such as a boot or a bottle. One strange story, told later, would appear to support the theory that she was far from being a mentally normal person.

One morning Mrs. Berry entered a ward where several woman lay bedfast. After walking up and down for several minutes she suddenly seized one startled patient by the shoulders and began to shake her, afterwards going to another bed and slapping the occupant across the face. This outrage was repeated as she passed from bed to bed, the frightened patients being too helpless to defend themselves. Several Workhouse servants are said to have witnessed this disgraceful exhibition, but being afraid to intervene themselves they sent for Dr. Paterson who was in another part of the Workhouse at the time. On entering the ward he attempted to reason with the apparently demented head nurse, but it was some time before she could be brought under control, threatening to kill the first person who came near her. Eventually, however, she became quieter and was walked up and down for a while in an effort to calm her. After a time she seemed normal again, her moment of madness probably being attributed to nervous strain.

The crises had not passed, however, for during the night she again became violent and had to be held down, with great difficulty, by two of the strongest women. After much screaming and struggling she seemed to go limp, breathing very heavily as she lay there. Eventually she lapsed into a deep sleep.

Next morning she appeared much better and was given a draught with instructions to take half then and the remainder on going to bed that night. When left alone, however, she took the whole mixture at once. A moment later one of the servants entered the room and narrowly missed being hit by a flying glass, aimed at her by Mrs. Berry. The doctor was again sent for, but before he could be contacted the rampaging head nurse had smashed several ornaments and locked herself inside the surgery, the door of which had to be broken open before she could be placed under restraint. After further struggling the draught began to have its effect and before long she was lying on her bed sleeping soundly. On waking she found herself surrounded by a number of the staff, all peering down anxiously at her. At once she became very indignant, wanting to know what they were all staring at. When questioned about the attack she would not reply and refused to acknowledge that it had ever taken place.

Following this very disturbing and unsavoury incident, after which Mrs. Berry was extremely fortunate to retain her position, she seemed to settle down to the routine of Workhouse life quite well again. Though her work entailed long hours she found time for other things. She was said to be very interested in physiology and claimed to have studied many books on the subject. More than one person, however, remarked that she was much more inclined towards other types of literature, such as sensational novels.

A woman who occupied a room directly below the one in which Mrs. Berry slept mentioned that she was often awakened late at night by the sound of footsteps overhead and concluded that the head nurse found great difficulty in sleeping. The story was put out that she had been in the habit of taking opium while at Burton-on-Trent and had not managed to break herself of it after her arrival at Oldham. This claim, however, was never substantiated. There is no doubt though that Mrs. Berry was something of an insomniac, and on nights when she could not get to sleep at all she would gather a number of the Workhouse servants in her room, among them Ellen Thompson, Ann Dillan, Sarah Jane Knight and old Alice Alcroft, asking them to keep her company. On one of these occasions, while several people were in the room, Mrs. Berry, who had been dozing, suddenly leapt to her feet, saying that she could hear someone walking about outside her door with only one step. Although everyone remained silent and listened for the mysterious sound nothing could be heard except the ticking of the clock. Yet Mrs. Berry insisted that she could still hear it distinctly "as if someone were moving about outside the window". Such fancies it was stated, she often indulged in, while at other times she was afraid of nothing.

On the mantlepiece in Mrs. Berry's sitting room stood two photographs. One was of Thomas Berry, her late husband, whom, she told everyone, had been a clerk in Rylands offices Manchester, a statement which was quite untrue. The other picture she said, was that of a young man from Derby whom she had known while working in the Midlands. According to her he had wanted to marry her but had died before any wedding plans could be finalised. His premature demise, she told people, had prevented her reaching the very highest strata of society, as he had been extremely well-to-do. His photograph, which she constantly admired, was still there at the time she was placed under house arrest, as was that of her deceased husband. But one night shortly afterwards Ellen Thompson saw Mrs. Berry going up to her bedroom and noticed that she appeared to be concealing something under her gown.

"I thought she intended cutting her throat or something", the servant told someone later. She followed Mrs. Berry upstairs a few minutes later and found her already in bed. Before extinguishing the gaslight Thompson noticed something lying on the floor and on picking it up found that it was the two photographs screwed up together. After leaving the room she straightened them out and returned them to their place on the mantlepiece, where Mrs. Berry found them next morning. As soon as she saw them she snatched them down and threw them into the fire. Then, with a strange smile on her face, she stood and watched until the last fragments had disappeared into the flames.

During this period she was very bitter indeed and resented being kept under the observation of the servants. Several times she swore that she would make them suffer, along with Dr. Patterson, against whom she felt very strongly.

She was just as fastidious about the tidiness of her rooms as she had always been, and severely reprimanded one of the servants for leaving a piece of coal on the carpet, threatening what she would do to her when she returned later from the hearing. She did not return, however, for after that days proceedings she was taken to the Oldham Town Hall.

On being brought back to the Workhouse for the resumed inquest a week later she was allowed into her rooms and noticed that some pictures had been removed from the walls. She became quite angry and demanded to know what had been done with them.

"They're mine," she told the Governor, "and I shall want them in a few days." At the same time she helped herself to some lavender water from the mantlepiece which belonged to a nurse who had been put in charge following her arrest. Several days later Mrs. Berry asked for the bottle to be sent to her in her cell at the Town Hall, but of course her request was ignored.

When asked why she did not go in black after her mother's death, she replied that it did not suit her. She was certainly very particular about her clothes and was said to have made a special trip to Manchester and paid four guineas for the evening gown in which she attended the Christmas Ball, a tidy sum in those days, particularly when viewed in relation to her salary.

While residing at the Workhouse she was never heard to mention her previous connections with the town and few if any knew that she had lived in Oldham previously. Also, when leaving the Workhouse, she was never seen to proceed in the direction of nearby Royton, where she had been well known, but would always go the other way, towards Oldham town centre.

It was said that the Miles Platting curate was not the only man from whom Mrs. Berry attempted to extort money. Apparently a young man employed at the Workhouse also fell into her trap, but somehow managed to extricate himself without paying up. Perhaps he had insufficient funds with which to meet her demands or else he simply ignored them. In either event the threats were not carried out. It is claimed, however, that the would-be victim was violently sick after taking a powder, allegedly given him by Mrs. Berry, and that the vomit contained blood. The name of the man was never made public, so the story may well be untrue. Mrs. Berry was often heard to remark though that "those who loved her best died the soonest", an assertion not entirely without foundation when viewed in the light of subsequent events.

CHAPTER 15

UNEXPECTED VISITORS

Of the nine hundred prisoners in Walton Gaol at that time Mrs. Berry was by far the best known, arousing the greatest interest even among the prison staff, who, accustomed as they were to coming into contact with criminals of all kinds, nonetheless found the idea of being in close proximity to a woman found guilty of murdering her child and her mother somewhat awe inspiring. Only a handful of staff were allowed to see her however, so closely was she now confined.

Most of her time was spent in either praying, reading, being read to by a female warder or writing letters. Quite a number of people had received requests to visit her and most of them had duly turned up, no doubt feeling some apprehension as the interviews were not calculated to be pleasant, considering Mrs. Berry's position. At least one person though was quite anxious to visit her of his own accord. He was Joseph Emmot of Hollinwood Oldham, who claimed to have known the prisoner in her younger days. At that time, he told friends, he had lived only a few doors away from Mrs. Berry and her mother in Drury Lane Hollinwood. She was then in her teens and he knew her of course as Lizzie Welsh. She was at times he said, a very gay sort of person, but at others could be just the reverse, and her temper, even in those days, could never be depended upon. After the Welshes left Hollinwood Emmot lost track of them completely, until one day some twelve or thirteen years later when he suddenly encountered Lizzie in Blackpool. She was being driven along the promenade in a carriage accompanied by a little girl. Emmot stopped the carriage and shook hands with Mrs. Berry, who seemed very pleased to see him he said, after all that time. The girl she introduced as her daughter and they talked for some minutes before the carriage drove on. After that Emmot heard no more of her until he read about the poisoning case in the newspapers. Even then he did not connect the accused woman with the Lizzie

Welsh he had known in Hollinwood. It had suddenly come to him one night as he lay in bed he told someone, after having seen a picture of the defendant in a newspaper. About a week after Mrs. Berry was sentenced Emmot told his wife that he intended travelling to Liverpool as he had to meet someone there. He did not say who that someone was, but it is possible that his wife guessed, for she pleaded with him not to go. He was not to be dissuaded, however, and set off that same night, although he did not possess any invitation to visit the prisoner, and had no idea how he would go about getting into the prison.

On the following morning he made the necessary inquiries and was told that he would have to apply to the Governor. He therefore made his way to the prison and after explaining his business at the entrance was admitted into the lodge, where he was allowed to wait while his request was passed on to the Governor. It was some considerable time before the officer who had taken the message returned to say that the request had been granted. Mr Emmot was told; "Follow me, and don't lets have any nonsense with her. We've had enough already."

The visitor was led into a room where Mrs. Berry was seated alone. On seeing him she rose and said simply; "Joe ....."

She was obviously very moved, not because Joe Emmot was anyone special to her, but more probably because he was a figure from the past who at this moment represented to her a link with happier times.

As for Emmot, he was very shocked at her appearance and later said that she had aged terribly. Of course having seen her only once before in fifteen years he remembered her as a pretty vivacious girl in her teens with a clear bright complexion and dark bushy fringe. Now, standing before him in her sombre prison garb, she looked "the very picture of misery" as he put it.

The two of them sat down and talked, the conversation

naturally enough turning to the times they had spent together in Hollinwood and the people they had known there. For just a little while the prisoner seemed to forget the terrible position she was in and even laughed as they recalled incidents of years before. Then inevitably the conversation turned to more recent events and Mrs. Berry appeared about to break down. She managed somehow though to retain control of her emotions and went on to tell Emmot that the judge at her trial had been against her and that she could not see that any motive had been shown, as she had received so little insurance money on the child's death. Also, she pointed out, she had had over £70 in the bank at the time.

After an interview lasting nearly two hours Emmot rose and shook hands with the prisoner for the last time and asked her if there was anything at all he could do for her. She replied that he might pay a visit to Chadderton Cemetery and plant a few flowers on her little girl's grave. At this, Joe Emmot, very much affected, took his leave of her and left the prison.

. . . .

Apart from Emmot there was at least one other Oldhamer who planned to favour the condemned woman with an unsolicited visit, though not until the day of her execution. His name was William Wrigley and he was a man well known in the town as something of a character, who rejoiced in the title of the 'Colonel'. A member of the local Board of Guardians, he was also an extremely active town councillor, representing St. Marys Ward, and earned his living as a travelling auctioneer. A fast talking and highly entertaining showman, the 'Colonel' was known in practically every town in the North West, but more especially on his home territory, to which he returned regularly to sell his watches jewellery and similar odds and ends on Oldham's Tommyfield market ground.

Like everyone else in the town Wrigley had taken a considerable interest in the poisoning case, but, characteristically, had decided to take steps to secure for himself a major role in the drama – or at least in the final act. He had sworn that he would attend the execution and had even taken bets on it. Also he constantly exhibited a letter, allegedly written to him by James Berry, the Executioner, in public houses around the town centre. Wrigleys conduct, though regarded as humourous by some, was considered most offensive as far as others were concerned, and none more so than the prisoners legal representative, Joseph Whittaker. The Oldham solicitor, extremely upset at what he felt was a public outrage, wrote a letter to the Under Sheriff, enclosing a newspaper cutting giving details of the 'Colonels' exploits. The letter ran:

> As solicitor for Mrs. Berry, the prisoner under sentence of death at Walton Gaol, I respectfully draw your attention to the fact that a man residing here named William Wrigley, a noted character, has, even before the poor woman was sentenced, boasted that he would attend her execution, and has attempted to take bets in public houses that he will be present. If he is allowed to be there I am sure the people of Oldham will feel that the dignity of the law will suffer and the decency of its administration be outraged. As solicitor for Mrs. Berry I respectfully ask you to save her from this infliction.

Had William Wrigley known about Whittaker's letter it is doubtful that it would have deterred him very much. This was too meaty a situation to let go by without extracting full value from it, and the 'Colonel', who thrived on all publicity, good or bad, remained as enthusiastic as ever in anticipation of the forthcoming event. He continued to hold court in the local taverns, claiming that he and James Berry were very close friends and stating that the hangman had previously made him a promise that if he were ever called upon to hang anyone from Oldham the 'Colonel' would have the honour of assisting him in his gruesome work. Whether there was any truth in the tale remained to be seen.

....

Joseph Whittaker meanwhile, in consequence of Mr Robinsons' visit to Liverpool, had other business to attend to. On the following Thursday he presented the Oldham Magistrates with an application to the effect that he be appointed curator of his clients effects, most of which were still at the Workhouse, and which he proposed to take possession of. Formerly, a prisoner sentenced to death or convicted of a felony forfeited his or her goods to the Crown, but since the passing of the Act 33 and 34 Victoria this was no longer the case and Whittaker said he believed the magistrates had it in their power to grant him custody of the goods.

"Under what authority?" asked the Magistrates Clerk.

"It is in the 21st section", replied the solicitor, going on to quote the whole section.

"But that is in the case of death. You are asking to be appointed while the prisoner is still alive."

Whittaker pointed out that a curator could be appointed by any justice of the peace, and went on to explain that what money Mrs. Berry possessed had been quickly swallowed up due to the length and complexity of the case. Despite this he felt it his duty to stick with his client to the very end, although he could expect no fee. She had therefore told him that since she had no money she would give him a share of her effects which were in the possession of the Governor of the Workhouse. Application had been made for them he said, but the Workhouse people had refused to give them up. After hearing all this the Clerk informed him; "I'm afraid I cannot advise the magistrates to grant your application. I suggest you write to the Home Office."

Two days later Whittaker saw his client and told her the result of his visit to the magistrates. A letter was subsequently received at the Workhouse dated March 7th in which Mrs. Berry asked the Governor to release her possessions. It ran;

> Dear Sir
>
> I presume you are aware of the terrible fate that awaits me, and in the short time that is left to me there are several matters I wish to arrange. You will know that my clothes, together with other articles, are still at the Workhouse. These things Mr. Whittaker wishes me to give to him on the plea that he has not been sufficiently paid for my defence. He has received £64 and in addition he has my watch and chain, valued at £14. I have left every article I possess to Mr. George H. Robinson, to dispose of according to my instructions, and I appeal to you not to allow anyone else to remove a single item.
>
> Mr. Robinson has promised to erect a stone on the grave of my darling, and for this I am exceedingly grateful.
>
> E. Berry.

As well as his concern over the money due to his office Whittaker was anxious to take charge of his clients tangible assets for another reason. Her aunt, Mrs. Pemberton, had also tendered an application to take possession of the articles, the Guardians quite rightly refusing to release them to her. The issue was finally settled several days later when a letter arrived from the Home Office confirming George Robinson's appointment as sole administrator.

On his visit to Walton Gaol Whittaker undertook to organise a petition for reprieve, to be forwarded to the Home Secretary. He told Mrs. Berry that he had no intention of exhibiting it in a public place for the purpose of getting signatures. Possibly it was his intention to approach people directly. On the other hand it may well have been that he had very little confidence in the probability of many people signing it unless solicited to do so.

Whittaker was accompanied on his visit that day by Mr. Sanderson, and as they entered the prison they met two Workhouse officials who were just leaving. Their names were Fletcher and Minahan and they had gone to Liverpool at Mrs. Berry's request. They had spent over two hours with the prisoner, but before being admitted had been cautioned by the matron not to mention anything regarding what had happened in the outside world since her trial, a precaution aimed no doubt at keeping her on a reasonably even keel. They were also informed that they might shake hands with her if they would show their open hand to the warder before doing so. The visitors were taken through a door and across a corridor. A second door was then unlocked and they were told to enter. They were now in the condemned cell. Mrs. Berry looked up from a letter she was reading, then rose and stood looking across at them for several seconds without speaking. She seemed very happy to see them and could not hide her feelings, large tears rolling slowly down her cheeks and dropping onto the coarse blue dress.

After shaking hands with her the two men enquired about her health and were told that she was feeling much better than she had been earlier in the week. The visitors now sat down to talk to the prisoner, a male and a female warder remaining in the cell, which was warm and quite comfortably furnished. As well as a fireplace there were three high windows, a clean bed, two small tables and a couple of armchairs. A fire burned in the grate and on one table lay the remains of a meal. On the other was a bible and several books of poetry, while the bed was strewn with recently opened letters. "You see", said Mrs. Berry. "I have had a great many letters, both from friends and from people I've never even met. All sympathising with me."

Fletcher, who acted as schoolmaster at the Workhouse, asked if she had expected the verdict to go against her, and she replied; "Not until the last day of the trial. Looking at the faces of the jury then I could read my fate in their expressions."

She was asked by Minahan, a hospital attendant in the Workhouse Infirmary, if she held out any hope of a reprieve, and although her reply indicated that she did, she told him that she was prepared for the worst. Crossing the room, she picked up one of the books and began to read aloud Longfellows poem 'Resignation', ploughing her way through all thirteen verses of it. As she read her voice was calm and clear and neither visitors nor warders made any sound until she had finished. After this she read out extracts from some of her letters, including one from a lady in Brighton and another from a man in Ireland. They both expressed their sympathy and this seemed to please her very much.

The matron then entered and asked if the interview was almost at an end, but Mrs. Berry asked if her visitors might remain for a further half-hour and the matron agreed to this.

The condemned woman said she had decided to give a few of her closest friends a small gift and asked if her two former colleagues would accept something from her. Each one named a small article and she said she would instruct her solicitor to deal with it when he had taken possession of her belongings.

At this point there was a further interruption, Her Majesty's Inspector of prisons entering the cell during the course of his monthly inspection. He asked if the prisoner had any complaints or if she needed anything and was told that all was satisfactory.

After he had gone some mention was made of her mother's death, but Mrs. Berry seemed loathe to discuss it. The warder, however, immediately cut the conversation short by raising his hand to signify that any such discussion would be likely to contravene the prison regulations.

Before Fletcher and Minahan left Mrs. Berry told them that though she had a longing to be visited by her friends each meeting was an ordeal.

"I listen to the striking of the clock", she said, "and count the hours upon it. And I know that one morning very soon I shall hear it strike seven for the last time.

CHAPTER 16

THE EXECUTIONER

The fateful day, March 14th, was drawing near, and the residents of Walton, a fashionable suburb of Liverpool, did not take kindly to the idea of a hanging taking place in their midst. Apart from the horror of it all they were none too happy about the notoriety which they felt such an event would bring with it. Up to that time not one single execution had taken place at Walton Gaol, although some six months previously a man had narrowly escaped the noose, when, at almost the very last moment, with the scaffold erected and the hangman in attendence, word had been received from the Home Office that the murderer had been granted a reprieve.

The possibility of a repeat performance, however, was very remote, and preparations for the coming event were now well advanced. The hole into which the body would fall and over which the scaffold would be erected had already been dug out by the convicts. It was around 6ft wide and after a good depth had been reached the sides were bricked up and work commenced on the scaffold itself. This macabre scene was not played out in the open, but under cover of a shed known as 'the coach-house', normally used for housing the prison vans.

During the course of the scaffolds erection Mrs. Berry asked a warder what was the cause of all the noise and was told that structural alterations were being carried out in another part of the prison. This incident was brought to the notice of the Governor, who immediately ordered Mrs. Berry's removal to a different cell, where the disturbing sounds could not be heard.

It is interesting to note that about the time preparations were being made to hang Mrs. Berry a new mode of execution was being discussed in America – electrocution. It was said to be a much more humane method, the heavily charged battery causing instantaneous death. It was also stated to be quite painless, although how proof of this was ever obtained was not made clear.

By 1887, death by hanging, while still an extremely unpleasant way to go, was not quite the unsavoury spectacle it had been in earlier times, and the man who held the office of public executioner was no longer regarded as a barbarous savage. For although remaining a somewhat awe-inspiring figure to most people, the hangman now enjoyed a certain amount of respectability and was without doubt a skilled and dedicated professional.

William Calcroft, who performed the last public execution in England in 1868 could certainly not be described as a skilful craftsman. A rough and ready sort of individual, his only concern was to get the job done, regardless of how much suffering was caused in the process. Although holding the post for over forty years he made not the slightest attempt to improve his method of hanging criminals, but persisted throughout his career with the 'short drop', which did not break the neck, but simply choked the unfortunate victim to death, and it was not uncommon to see a man struggle and kick for quite a while before finally becoming limp.

Calcraft was succeeded by William Marwood, who was his opposite in almost every sense. A quietly spoken, serious minded man, Marwood's arrival on the scene brought a certain dignity to the position. His paramount aim was to place the business of hanging on a much more scientific basis, his theory being that the weight of a condemned persons body should be taken into account before deciding on the length of rope to be used. The size of the drop required could then be calculated with reasonable accuracy. In other words, the lighter the man, the longer the rope needed to hang him. Marwood believed that a correctly measured drop would result in the neck being broken instantly, thereby despatching the victim in a quicker and more humane manner.

Subsequent executions proved him correct, and from then on hanging was carried out with far greater proficiency than had previously been the case.

Marwood numbered among his customers the notorious Charlie Peace, who went to his death at Armley Gaol Leeds in 1879 as bravely as any man before or since.

James Berry, who followed Marwood, was born in Heckmondwyke Yorkshire, and held the job from 1884 until 1892. Berry first became interested in the gruesome trade when he was introduced to Marwood while serving as a young man in the Bradford Borough Police Force.* He later claimed that although very impressed by the hangman, whom he described as a quiet unassuming sort of man, he certainly had no thoughts then of taking up the profession himself. After Marwood's death, however, Berry, at that time working hard as a boot salesman to support a rapidly increasing family, applied for the post, being one of several hundred to do so. Though he failed to secure the job he must have come very close, for when the successful applicant, Bartholemew Binns, tendered his resignation after only four months, James Berry was the man they sent for.

Having come strongly under the influence of Marwood, with whom he had conversed several times following their first meeting, Berry was keen to perfect his methods. He was not without a few ideas of his own and carried out repeated experiments at his house in Bradford, using bags of sand.

In March 1884 he was given his first assignment ____ the execution of Robert Vickers and William Innes, two poachers who had committed murder after being caught in the act.

The hangings were to be carried out at Calton Gaol Edinburgh, on the morning of March 29th, and Berry travelled by train to Scotland two days earlier, giving himself ample time to inspect the

* My Experiences As An Executioner ____ David & Charles.

scaffold, test the trapdoor and make sure that everything was satisfactorily prepared. After this he set about determining the length of drop he was to give each man and finally decided that Vickers, who weighed 10 stone 4lbs, should be given 8ft 6ins, while Innes, at 9 stone 6lbs, would need 10ft of rope.* In each case Berry's calculations proved to be accurate, for both men died quickly, the prison doctor writing out a testimonial to the effect that the executions had been carried out in a highly satisfactory manner.

Berry was naturally pleased at the success of his debut, but felt that there was still room for improvement, and subsequently worked out a table of weights and measures, giving a 14 stone man an 8ft drop, while at the other end of the scale, a man weighing only 8 stone was allowed a drop of 10 feet.

This table he used as a guide, amending it as he gained greater experience and always taking into account the height and build of a condemned man as well as his weight.

After the double event in Edinburgh Berry continued to excel at his new profession, but early in 1885 he had a rather disturbing experience while carrying out the sentence at Exeter of John Lee, convicted of the murder of the woman for whom he had worked as a servant in Babbacombe, Devon.*

Lee was very calm as the noose was placed around his neck and everything appeared to be going exactly according to plan. But when Berry pulled the lever nothing happened. Although the sound of the bolts could be clearly heard as they slid from their sockets the trapdoor failed to spring open. While the prisoner still stood silently awaiting the end, the white cap completely covering his head, Berry and several warders rushed forward and stamped frantically on the trap but could not force it downwards. Lee was then removed from the scaffold and escorted to an adjoining room, while Berry closely examined the trapdoors. The hangman, who

* My Experiences As An Executioner _____ David & Charles.

had thoroughly tested the trapdoors previously, now did so again and found that they worked perfectly. The prisoner was returned to the scaffold and placed in position, but when the lever was pulled the trapdoors again refused to open. The bewildered Lee was finally returned to his cell and never again mounted the scaffold. He had gone through a terrible ordeal and because of this his sentence was ultimately commuted to life imprisonment.

One theory put forward as a possible explanation of why the trap had failed to function properly was that heavy rain during the night had caused the wood to swell, but Berry refuted this suggestion and gave it as his opinion that the contraption was not up to standard, and in fact he had only the day previously advised the Governor that it should be re-built at some time in the near future.

As an executioner Berry was reasonably competent, but far from infallable, as was shown all too clearly in November 1885 when he travelled to Norwich Castle to hang Robert Goodale, sentenced to death for the murder of his wife.*

On finding that the condemned man tipped the scales at more than 15 stone, Berry calculated that according to his table a drop of 7ft 8ins should be given, but after seeing the prisoner and taking into account that the man appeared somewhat fleshy, particularly around the neck, he decided to play safe and worked out a drop of only 5ft 9in, his one great fear being that if given too much rope a victim might well be decapitated.

The Governor of the prison was most anxious that the execution should go smoothly and with the minimum amount of suffering to the prisoner. But it was not to be, for Berry's shortened drop did not prove short enough. When the hangman pulled back the lever and Goodale fell out of sight through the trapdoors the rope did not become taut but jerked upwards then dropped loosely back into the hole. White as a sheet, Berry stepped forward

* My Experiences As An Executioner _____ David & Charles.

and peered down into the pit. He was horrified to see that Goodales head had been completely torn off. The Governer was so overcome by the incident that he broke down and wept. Of course there was an inquiry to discover whether or not the accident had occurred due to negligence, but, supported by the evidence of the prison doctor, Berry was exonerated and the matter dropped.

Now realising that his table of weights and measures required a drastic overhaul, Berry gave it much thought over the ensuing weeks and finally came to the conclusion that a drop of only 2ft 1in would have been sufficient to hang Robert Goodale. The table was then reconstructed and adequately served its purpose over the next few years.

After this rather eventful period Berry settled down well to his job. He was prepared to go anywhere in the British Isles to perform an execution and in time became quite prosperous due to the fact that there was plenty of work to be had if one went about it in the right way. Whenever he learned of a sentence of death being passed he would send one of his specially printed forms along to the Sheriff concerned, offering to do the job and stating his terms. He also had business cards printed, which read:

JAMES BERRY
executioner
1 BILTON PLACE
BRADFORD, YORKS.*

A religious man, Berry always concerned himself with the spiritual well-being of his victims and got into the habit of sending a copy of a poem entitled 'FOR ONE UNDER SENTENCE OF DEATH' to the chaplain of each prison at which he was engaged to carry out a hanging. This practice was curtailed, however, when one prison Governor suggested to Berry that he would do well to stick to his own business and leave the religious side of it to the chaplain.

* My Experiences As An Executioner _____ David & Charles.

Though necessarily a hard man, Berry did not particularly relish the idea of hanging a woman, but he was called upon to do so several times during his career, and as the date of Elizabeth Berry's execution drew closer it is just possible that he experienced a certain amount of apprehension. For only seven months before he had gone through a rather harrowing time while carrying out the execution of Mary Ann Britland at Strangeways Gaol Manchester, the condemned woman shrieking and wailing from the moment he entered her cell until being placed on the drop, where she was held until the last possible moment by two warders, who then stepped smartly out of the way before the trap fell. Mrs. Britlands heart-rending cries had unnerved even the ice cool Berry, and would haunt him for the rest of his life.

How would Elizabeth Berry stand up to the terror of the gallows when her time came? That was a question Berry must have asked himself over and over again as he checked his equipment and prepared to make the journey to Liverpool.

CHAPTER 17
ENTER THE 'COLONEL'

There is no doubt that 'Colonel' William Wrigley was quite a fascinating character, even if the title was a somewhat flattering one. For although Wrigley was in fact a former military man he had never attained that exalted rank nor any approaching it.

As a young man he joined the Duke of Lancasters Own Yeomanry Cavalry, but apparently did not see the army as his ultimate destiny, and after a while returned to civilian life, having progressed no higher than Corporal. Back in Oldham Wrigley joined the local police force, but finding the wages low the prospects poor and the routine monotonous and restricting he soon gave it up to start his own business, a photographers shop in Yorkshire Street. This did not last long either, for although moderately successful, Wrigley found the photographic business even less stimulating than the police force. He became thoroughly bored with it and sold out at the first opportunity.

The venture, however, did prove fruitful in one respect, for it revealed the fact that Wrigley was a born salesman. It was therefore not surprising that he should next turn up on Oldham market behind a clog stall, where he did quite a thriving business for a time. The life was much more to his liking, and in addition to disposing of his wares at a good profit he was now gaining a reputation as a witty orator and something of a local personality. His stall was invariably thronged with far more spectators than customers, and Wrigley, always in a good humour whatever the state of trade, somehow managed to keep up an almost non-stop spiel from opening to packing-up time. Politics was always one of his favourite topics of conversation, though he never allowed this to interfere with business, but somehow contrived to intertwine the two in such a way as to be preaching entertaining and selling all at the same time.

It was around this period that people first began to refer to him as the 'Colonel', and although the precise reason for this is not clear there can be no denying the fact that with his proud and erect military bearing he was eminently suited to the role in which he had cast himself. By this time he was making a reasonable living and decided to branch out a little. Buying a horse-drawn caravan, he began to travel all over the North. He had now abandoned clogs in favour of watches and jewellery, a game he was to dabble in off and on for the rest of his life. He was in his element and highly successful. With his hat perched jauntily on the side of his head and a carnation always in his buttonhole, the 'Colonel' could woo an audience with the best of them. When there were hecklers in the crowd he was at his sharpest and wittiest and any man who dared tangle with him was sure to come a poor second. For a man of humble background with almost no formal education he possessed an astonishing vocabulary and could more than hold his own in any company. Of course he loved to be the centre of attention, and the sound of his own voice with its rich Lancashire accent was sweet music to the 'Colonel's' ears. Though a fast talking slick salesman Wrigley had about him a basic warmth and honesty which somehow communicated itself to his audience, and it was this as much as anything which made him such a favourite wherever he appeared. To the 'Colonel', the people who frequented the market grounds were much more than just potential customers. They were an audience. And an audience was the one thing he craved in life above all else. Some might say that here was a gifted man who had wasted his talents, but the 'Colonel' was happy enough. He had at last found the perfect platform from which to project his very colourful image. It measured some thirty feet in length and stood a good deal of the time on Oldham's Tommyfield Market surrounded by scores of people, very few of whom had come to buy jewellery or watches. Upstage of the platform a brightly painted wooden structure acted as backcloth, being lit by a battery of gas jets.

Each evening around seven the jets would be lit, and, knowing that the appearance of the 'Mayor of Tommyfield' was imminent, people of all age groups would begin to gather round the 'Colonel's' pitch. As the shops and stalls remained open until midnight at that time, Wrigley could always be sure that a good number of folk would be about, especially at weekends, and this suited him down to the ground, for he loved to make his entrance to a hearty round of applause.

At a few minutes after seven our hero would step forth onto the brilliantly lit stage to an enthusiastic response from the admiring populace. Though the crowd was usually a large one it was never quite large enough for the 'Colonel', and he would immediately set about haranguing the multitude in such a loud and urgent manner that any stray passers-by would be almost certain to join those already assembled.

After exchanging a few wisecracks with acquaintances among the crowd the great man would go into his act.

"My dear friends", he usually began. "Softened by the hardships sorrows and difficulties experienced by my fellow men, I stand before you this evening prepared to sacrifice ____ yes I said sacrifice ____ my own comfort and happiness for the benefit of those who have a weakness for jewellery but lack that very necessary commodity ____ brass."

After inviting his rapt listeners to feast their eyes upon the extensive collection of shimmering articles on display, he would offer for sale the first piece. A necklace "fit to grace the noble neck of Queen Victoria herself", or a 'timekeeper' for which he would "not expect a King's ransom, nor embarrass his audience by talking in terms of pennies, but would suggest that the bidding be commenced at the very modest figure of .... half a crown say.,"

Having warmed up he would now discourse on just about every subject under the sun. For not only was 'Colonel' Wrigley well read and well informed on most things, he was also full of opinions and a great bluffer when it came to touching upon subjects of which he knew very little, though these were admittedly few and far between. While cash, watches and jewellery changed hands at a steady rate the 'Colonel' would air his knowledge on the state of the share market, the Premier's latest speech in Parliament, the crime rate in America, the hostility and hardships encountered by our troops in India, the failure of the grain crop in Belgium, the difficulties and complexities surrounding the Irish question, the price of grass skirts in Hawaii, the futility of strikes, the technicalities and anomalies of the legal profession, the inflated cost of top hats in Singapore, the administration of outdoor relief to the poor, the value of an alliance with the Far Eastern Countries, the number of arrests for drunkeness in Liverpool, the privations experienced by expeditions to the North Pole, the saddening depravity of human nature and the quality of Dublin stout. All of these diverse subjects and many more would be dealt with during the course of the evening, and as the 'Colonel' was also well equipped with a seemingly endless stock of humourous stories and jokes the spectators were treated to as good a nights entertainment as could be bought at the local theatre or music hall. And although Wrigley's main objective was of course to dispose of his watches and trinkets, there can be no doubt that he got just as much pleasure out of his auctioneering as he did from the money it put into his pocket.

Even when off duty he was never content to enter a public house merely to enjoy a quiet drink. For after downing his first pint he would be sure to produce a cluster of glittering timepieces, and spreading them out on the bar, would ask the customers to name a price for any on view.

One of the many stories told about him concerns a visit to a local tavern where men of means congregated. After placing his timepieces on the bar top Wrigley stood back and watched as the company examined his wares. There happened to be one or two clever fellows present, and amid much laughter and joking several good-natured if somewhat uncomplimentary remarks were passed regarding the quality of the merchandise. The 'Colonel', who had remained uncharacteristically silent up to this point, now stepped forward. "Come along gentlemen, don't dither. Make your selection and name your price."

One man, a local mill owner who was reputed to be as tight as a drum when it came to parting with his 'brass', examined several of the watches very closely, then, determined to put one over on the 'Colonel' by bidding excessively low for what appeared to be one of the best watches on the bar, he winked at his cronies and announced rather smugly: "I'll give thee five bob for that one."

"Aye righto then Ted", replied the 'Colonel', after deliberating for a second or two. "It's thine."

The surprised mill owner handed over his money, and Wrigley, presenting him with the watch, added: "Tha's bin done lad."

....

On Saturday morning March 12th 1887 a motley assortment of people gathered at the Central Station Oldham. Though they seemed to be engaged in excited conversation, the voice of one man could be heard above all others. For there in the centre of the group stood the imposing figure of William Wrigley, who, on this rather special occasion was dressed more soberly than usual in a neatly cut black suit instead of the more familiar light-coloured one. He still wore the inevitable buttonhole and as always dominated the proceedings. Several passers-by called out to him, and quite a few were actually seen to salute the 'Colonel'. Those gathered around were most impressed as Wrigley outlined the role he proposed to play at Liverpool two days hence. Among them were several share brokers and suchlike who had not turned up specially, but who normally used the train to travel to Manchester each day in the course of business. Yet these men seemed just as captivated by the 'Colonel's' commanding presence as the rest of the gathering.

On the arrival of the 11-17 the 'Colonel' waved to his many admirers before boarding, and there was an instant rush of people all scrambling and pushing in an attempt to occupy the same compartment as the celebrated local character.

There was much joking and merriment as the train chugged slowly off in the direction of Manchester, the company hanging on to the 'Colonel's' every word. Of course the poisoning case was gone into at some length, Wrigley naturally having a great deal to say on the subject. But he was not a man to remain serious for very long and soon had his audience in stitches as he dug into his inexhaustable repertoire of humourous stories and anecdotes.

Before the journey came to an end ____ all too quickly for the 'Colonels' companions ____ Wrigley confirmed that the purpose of his trip was to make contact with Berry, the Executioner, whom he claimed had agreed to meet him at a certain public house in Salford. And although no definite arrangements had yet been made for him to act as assistant to the hangman, as far as the 'Colonel' was concerned Berry's final agreement to this was a mere formality. Moreover he said, he would welcome the company of any who cared to go along with him, and sure enough some did, trailing behind as the 'Colonel' swept majestically through Victoria Station Manchester like some visiting foreign dignitary surrounded by his minions. After being reinforced by several newcomers the entire retinue boarded carriages to be driven to the Bath Hotel Salford, where they found Berry at the bar as promised, in the centre of a group of interested customers. Of course he was the main attraction, but the 'Colonel' had no intention of being pushed into the background, and made his usual grand entrance. Striding haughtily into the room and producing one of his blandest smiles, he bowed gracefully, whereupon Berry immediately left the company to shake hands with the distinguished visitor from Oldham. On being asked what he would have to drink the 'Colonel' replied coyly: "Of course you know that I'm a religious man and a teetotaller...." " This remark of course was greeted with roars of laughter and a drink promptly set up for him.

From his appearance it would have been quite impossible to guess Berry's occupation. Thirty-five years of age, he was a little above medium height and thickset, weighing around 13 stone. He wore a stove pipe hat, dark grey tweed suit, crossover scarf and ankle length topcoat. His closely clipped red beard and side whiskers seemed to accentuate the broadness of his face, down the right side of which was a deep scar running from the cheekbone to above the eye.

With his broad Yorkshire accent and dry wit the hangman turned out to be an extremely interesting conversationalist, and could tell a good tale, even giving the 'Colonel' a run for his money. Naturally enough the pair of them were the centre of attention throughout the two hours spent in the tavern and although Berry did not seem too anxious to discuss his business it was not long before someone asked him the inevitable question. "Did he have any qualms about hanging a person?"

He answered that he did not, and added that in his opinion it was not wrong to execute a murderer. Of course he got no pleasure from it, but did it as a matter of duty, and if he did not do the job then somebody else would. He did admit though that the hanging of Mrs. Britland had had an effect on him, but said that the work did not usually worry him, apart from the fact that he was somewhat tense during the three or four days preceeding an execution. This, however, had nothing to do with any feelings for the condemned, but was simply an anxiety to carry out the work satisfactorily, as the hangman's job called for a great deal of skill, and any bungling could result in unnecessary suffering for the victim and leave him open to criticism by the authorities, the press and the public. For this reason, he said, he always felt a great sense of relief when a hanging had been successfully carried out. He got £10 for each job, with half fee in the event of a late reprieve coming through, and had travelled to Ireland in the course of his work no less than fourteen times.

During the conversation quite a number of people dropped into the pub for the sole purpose of seeing the hangman. One of them, a postman, stepped forward and asked if he might have the honour of shaking Berry's hand. The executioner had no objection to this and the 'Colonel' remarked; "I hope you'll never have to meet him before breakfast some morning lad."

As Berry was now ready to leave for Liverpool he and the 'Colonel' left the Bath Hotel, climbed into a cab along with three others, and set off to Exchange Station Manchester, calling at another public house on the way, where Berry had left a case containing his equipment. The case, though small, was quite heavy, and the hangman told his fellow passengers that inside was a new type of pinioning apparatus which he had had specially made and which he described as 'a beauty', its purpose being to prevent the victim moving his or her arms, although the hands were allowed a limited amount of freedom. He had also brought with him several ropes, all made of silk, as this, he said was the strongest material it was possible to find for the job.

The party duly arrived in Liverpool and from there took a cab to the prison three miles away. Several warders just coming off duty stopped to chat to the hangman who then went inside the gaol to inspect the scaffold, leaving his companions, including the 'Colonel', outside the gates.

After talking to the Governor, Berry was shown the gallows, which he tested by placing his bag on the trapdoor and pulling the lever. He was then taken inside to see the prisoner, observing her through an aperture in the cell door without her being aware of the fact. She was lying in bed, two warders being present, one of whom was reading to her.

Some forty minutes passed before Berry emerged from the prison, minus his bag, to announce that everything had gone off quite satisfactorily. The party now took a train back to Liverpool and during the course of the journey got into conversation with an old man, who, like most Liverpudlians, seemed very interested in the forthcoming execution. He claimed to have a fair knowledge of how such events were conducted; "Of course," said the old fellow, quite unaware that he was addressing the hangman himself, "in actual fact the Sheriff is really the executioner you know."

"Oh, yes?" said Berry, keeping a straight face.

"Yes, and the hangman is just his deputy."

"And a very capable deputy he is, I believe", said Berry.

"He most certainly is", said the 'Colonel', not wishing to be left out of it. "I know, I've spoken to him."

"Is that a fact?" asked the old man.

"I was there at the time", added Berry solemnly.

That evening the 'Colonel' and his friend ate and drank together and later on even shared the same bed, such a practice being quite common in those days. The 'Colonel' was no doubt behind the sleeping arrangements, for he later told many amusing stories of "the night I slept with the hangman". According to him Berry spent a very restless night indeed, tossing and turning continually and muttering in his sleep. In fact, claimed the 'Colonel' later, the room was literally a chamber of horrors. At times, in the middle of a bad dream, the hangman would suddenly sit bolt upright and call out: "There they are, eighty-one of them!" Wrigley assumed he meant eighty-one murderers whom he had executed, and whom he now saw coming towards him in his dream. From what the 'Colonel' could gather Mrs. Britland was in the front rank as they pointed an accusing finger at Berry and bore down on him.

The following night the 'Colonel' had the bed to himself, Berry now having taken up his quarters at the prison. There is no record of any conversation between them concerning the possibility of Wrigley being present at the execution, but it most certainly was discussed. From all the evidence it is quite clear that during their stay in Liverpool the two men became quite friendly. However, it was not in Berry's power to appoint the 'Colonel' as his temporary assistant, even if he had wished to, which is extremely unlikely anyway. In any event the hangman made the return journey to Walton alone. The 'Colonel' however, was not the sort of man to put off easily. His companions, by now firmly convinced that his boast had been a lot of hot air, had drifted away, but Wrigley himself was determined to make one last all-out bid to get into the prison.

CHAPTER 18
A LETTER FROM THE DOCTOR

No word had yet been received on the question of a reprieve for Mrs. Berry, although receipt of the petition had been acknowledged. Everyone knew though that the possibility was extremely remote, and perhaps because of this many people could not help but feel sorry for the prisoner.

The trial itself was at this point very much in the background, even if doubts still remained in some minds regarding the fairness of it. The main interest in the case as far as the public was concerned now centred on the execution, and if the newspapers were to be believed Mrs. Berry's health had now deteriorated to such a degree that there was even speculation as to whether or not she would have to be actually carried to the scaffold. These reports were certainly somewhat exaggerated, but there is no doubt that her health had suffered greatly over the past two weeks or so. She was now in fact no more than a pathetic shell of a woman, and this in itself was enough to draw expressions of sympathy from many members of the public in the form of letters to the newspapers.

One person though was in no mood to feel compassion, for amongst these letters of sympathy was a rather lengthy one from Dr. Patterson in which he sneeringly attacked almost everyone connected with the case whom he felt had opposed him. Any person reading the letter who had no knowledge of the result of the trial might well have gained the impression that the defendant had been acquitted and that the Oldham doctor was making desperate efforts to get the case re-opened, so vindictively was it worded.

The doctor posed the question: 'Was the medical evidence in the case conclusive?' He then went on to provide his own answer by stating that it had in the first place convinced the coroners jury. He went on:

We have no evidence that the medical testimony did not

convince the four amateurs who sat on the bench at Oldham Magistrates Court, led by the nose by Mr. Hesketh Booth, their clerk.

He then pointed out that the jury at Liverpool had been convinced, as had the medical men of Oldham, four of whom he claimed had been approached to testify for the defence but had declined to do so. He also claimed that three doctors from Manchester had agreed to speak for the defence, and had in fact been present at Liverpool, but had changed their minds and declined to enter the witness box.

He believed it had also convinced Mr. Cottingham, who, after the exhibition made by his principal witness William Thompson, had thrown in the sponge on the medical side of the case. Thompson, he said, had finished up admitting the case for the Crown.

Dr. Patterson now went painstakingly through the evidence all over again, though something was added: for the doctor now claimed to have pinpointed the very bottle out of which the girl had been poisoned, stating that the liquid had all gone down the sink except for a small portion which had fallen onto the carpet, and which the prisoner, "with good judgement," ordered to be washed twice.

On the Sunday morning, he said, he had been sure the girl would get well, but Mrs. Berry had got to her again that day, ordering Sarah Jane Knight out of the room so that she might be alone with her victim and using the opportunity to administer another dose of poison.

In mentioning the marks of corrosion on the throat he went on to state, rather melodramatically:

> The gullet had arrested for a moment the passage down of the flaming red hot draught, but the fiend pressed it down the child's throat.'

'Talk of a petition to reprieve her?' he went on.

'A woman who in twelve short months for greed of money slew her mother and daughter.......well, who in Oldham would sign it? Except perhaps the solicitor and Mr. Hesketh Booth, the advisor to the magistrates who would not committ her for trial and who are now in the hole which their lack of intelligence has dug for them.

Why did Dr. Patterson insist on convicting Mrs. Berry all over again? If a judge and jury had been satisfied, what was to be gained by digging the whole thing up once more? Did he still perhaps feel the need to justify his own actions? If so it was hardly necessary. For the majority of people, if perhaps somewhat perturbed at the way he had approached the case from a medical point of view, were in no doubt that but for his vigilance the affair might never have come to light, and the woman who had been found guilty of two brutal murders would still be going about quite freely and unsuspected.

Unfortunately the doctor could not have done his reputation any good by his letter to the press. The magistrates at Oldham had perhaps not been wrong in exonerating the defendant on the evidence as presented to them, but later events had led people to the conclusion that they had blundered badly in failing to commit her for trial. All this was plainly obvious and it did not become a man of the doctor's standing to twist the knife in so vicious and vindictive a manner. Also, there was certainly nothing to be achieved from a furthur verbal attack on the condemned woman, for she was now only hours away from paying the extreme penalty.

. . . .

Following Joseph Whittaker's efforts on behalf of Mrs. Berry, Mr. Cottingham also decided to make one final attempt to save her life, and travelled to London four days before the date set for the execution to deliver a personal plea to the Home Secretary. At the interview the Manchester barrister pointed out that the evidence on which his client had been convicted had been quite insufficient. The Home Secretary, Mr. Matthews, said he had already given the petition many hours anxious consideration and had been obliged to come to the conclusion that there were no grounds for a reprieve and that the execution must take place. Mr Cottingham was still not satisfied and urged several Lancashire M.P.'s to use all their power to prevent the sentence being carried out. A number of them did in fact go over the entire case again with Mr. Stuart Wortley, Under Secretary for the Home Department, following which representations were again made to Mr. Matthews, who replied that he was still unconvinced that there was any reason to change his mind.

It was reported at this point that a Manchester doctor had interviewed Mrs. Berry in the condemned cell and had then requested a meeting with the Home Secretary, claiming that the prisoner had confided in him certain information which he felt ought to be passed on. His request was said to be 'receiving attention' and that if the Home Secretary should consequently see fit to alter his decision confirmation of that fact would be immediately telegraphed to the prison. Whether the alleged 'new evidence' had any bearing at all on the case was never made known. It did not, however, make the slightest difference to the Home Secretary's decision and no telegram was ever received.

Mrs. Berry was now resigned to her fate and long past caring about any legal wrangling. There only remained the terrible ordeal of the hanging itself, which she was trying desperately to shut out of her mind, almost the whole of her last hours being spent in prayer with the prison chaplain, Mr. Morris. Though her parents had been Roman Catholic she herself followed the Church of England religion and seemed to find great comfort in the many prayer and hymn books which surrounded her during her time at Walton.

She received no visitors after the Thursday preceeding the execution, which was set for Monday the 14th. Mrs. Sanderson was to have travelled to see her on the Saturday, but it was decided that in view of the physical and mental state of the prisoner it would not be advisable. A telegram was therefore sent off to Miles Platting informing the sister-in-law of this decision and she was no doubt relieved to receive it. Mrs. Berry spent the greater part of Saturday in bed, either being read to by one of the warders or praying with the chaplain. On Sunday he gave her communion and stayed with her very late that night. She was at this time said to be in a very feeble condition and one report stated that a special chair with wheels had been built for the purpose of conveying her to the scaffold in the event of her being incapable of making the journey under her own steam.

CHAPTER 19
THE LAST WALK

Not unnaturally the prisoner slept very badly on her last night and was found to be in a heavy fitful doze when a female warder entered early in the morning to prepare her for the last walk she would ever take. She was to wear the clothes in which she had appeared in court.

Mrs. Berry was not the only one getting dressed up for the occasion, for in his hotel in Liverpool Colonel William Wrigley had risen very early and was preparing to leave for Walton. With James Berry now well beyond his reach he had attached himself to a reporter from the Oldham Standard, whom he fondly believed would be his passport into the gaol. The two of them travelled to Walton in a cab and on arrival the reporter presented his order of admission to the warder on duty through a small grating in the gate. The grating was slammed shut and the warder could be heard walking away. After several minutes his footsteps were heard again on the cobblestones and the gate was opened. The reporter was then told to step inside. Naturally the Colonel tried to follow, but was prevented from doing so, the warder politely informing him that he could not allow anyone to pass without an order. Of course the Colonel was extremely indignant at this and swore he would have the matter of his exclusion brought up in the House of Commons. The warder seemed unimpressed and shut the gate in his face, leaving the Colonel out in the cold, still arguing and issuing the direst threats.

Inside the prison Mrs. Berry was deep in prayer, closely attended by the chaplain. He had arrived at seven o'clock and remained with her until five minutes to eight, when the Governor, John Mills Anderson, entered the cell accompanied by the Executioner.

The chaplain stepped to one side and without any preliminaries Berry immediately pinnioned the prisoner, first buckling a broad leather belt around her waist. Her arms were then secured to the belt by means of straps just above the elbows. Finally the wrists were lashed together by a furthur strap which was then fastened into the body belt in front.* She seemed rather shocked at the sudden intrusion and became very distressed, almost delirious. The hangman did not speak to her, but went quickly and efficiently about his work, so that it was completed within a minute or so. Berry was by now a thoroughly skilled professional and was well aware that the quicker the job was done the less harrowing it would be for the victim. Normally he made a point of speaking quietly and in a kindly way to the condemned, often in the hope of getting them to admit to their crime, so that he would know for certain he was not about to hang an innocent person, though of course anything revealed to him would be in the strictest confidence. On this occasion though, because of the state of the prisoner, he must have realised this would be useless.

Before being led from the cell Mrs. Berry pitifully protested her innocence to the chaplain, who tried his best to sooth her, but without success. The Chief Warder now led the way as the little group formed up. After him came the chaplain, reading the burial service. He in turn was followed by the prisoner, who was supported on either side by a female warder, while bringing up the rear came the Executioner, the Goverenr, the Under Sheriff and his assistant, several more warders and doctors Beamish and Hammond, both attached to the prison.

The grim little procession moved slowly through the prison and into the crisp morning air. A fine snow had been falling for some hours and a thin carpet of white now covered the ground. The prisoner was seen to shiver as she stepped out into the yard. She now appeared weak and fragile and the two warders gripped her tightly by the arms, fearing she might collapse. But though her eyes were closed and she appeared barely conscious,

*My Experiences As An Executioner ____ David & Charles.

her legs did not give way, though there was very little strength left in them. As they moved slowly on towards the place of execution the chaplain continued to intone the prayer while Mrs. Berry answered him, her lips being seen to move though no sound could be heard coming from them.

A short distance away from the gallows a small knot of newspapermen stamped their feet and rubbed their hands to ward off the cold. The scaffold was a marked improvement on the one over at Kirkdale. There the condemned were forced to climb onto a high platform by means of a ladder or steps, an ordeal of the most trying nature. Here at Walton the arrangement was totally different. Two upright posts 10ft. tall supported a sturdy beam from which now hung one of Berry's best ropes. It was made of the finest silk he had told a warder and had only been used once before. The beam itself had been severely tested and was said to be capable of sustaining a pressure equal to five tons. As Mrs. Berry weighed less than eight stone it would appear to have been more than adequate. The two uprights were bolted to the beam and to the platform. The trapdoor on which the prisoner would stand was about 4ft. square. Beneath it was the well, ten feet in depth. Much thought had gone into the construction of it. As well as bricking up the sides the workmen had fitted a series of hooks which would grip the trapdoors as they dropped and prevent them banging against the sides of the well. This would help to ensure that the job was done as smoothly and silently as possible.

The distance from the condemned cell to the scaffold was considerable, and though the prisoner was very unsteady as the party slowly crossed the prison yard, she was still moving under her own power. On turning a corner, however, the coach house came into view and Mrs. Berry was suddenly faced with the terrible spectacle of the gallows. In spite of knowing what she was going to, the sight of it came as something of a shock and at once her head went back as if in a faint and her knees sagged. If it had not been for the support of the warders she would have fallen down. Seeing that she was now all but unconscious they hurried forward, half-carrying her the remaining few yards to the scaffold, where she was handed over to two male warders, who placed her on the drop and held her firmly while the executioner set about his work.

After pulling the white cap down over her head Berry swiftly lashed her legs together with the usual leather straps just below the knees. While the chaplain continued to read from the prayer book Berry slipped the rope over her head, adjusting the brass ring at the base of the noose carefully behind the victim's left ear.

All was ready and the hangman stepped back and took up his position by the lever. The condemned woman now uttered her last words, which were heard only by the chaplain, who then left her alone and stepped back. On the drop the fragile body of the condemned woman swayed like a leaf in the wind. Berry looked up at the prison clock. It was exactly eight a.m. The snow had ceased to fall and all was quiet. A sign was given and Berry pulled the fatal lever. There was a fearful bang as the trapdoor fell and Elizabeth Berry plummetted down into oblivion. She would be left hanging there for one hour before being cut down.

Several of the group moved forward and peered down into the dark hole. The limp body swung there forlornly like some grotesque pendulum. When it finally became still a ladder was lowered into the pit, down which the two doctors now descended for the purpose of pronouncing the woman dead. James Berry gave a deep sigh of relief. He had done his work well and was glad that it was all over.

. . . .

Outside the prison between seven and eight hundred people had gathered, among them some of the roughest types from the slums of the city as well as quite a number of well dressed people. There was plenty of talk and argument, the fate of Mrs. Berry being of course the subject under discussion, but as the hour drew near a hush fell over the crowd. They could now see that two warders had climbed the steps of the tower situated close to the main gate and upon which the flagpole was erected. There the warders stood and waited. Suddenly a muffled bang was heard by those just outside the gate, and they knew then that the trapdoor had fallen. As the black flag was hoisted women wept and made the sign of the cross, while men quietly removed their hats and stood with bowed heads.

After a minute or two the majority of the mob turned away and headed for home, but a number of people still lingered and had to be moved off by the police. It is a good bet that the 'Colonel' was one of them, for after being refused admittance he had remained outside the prison and attempted to regain a little of his lost prestige by informing all and sundry that he had only been left out of the proceedings because letters had been written to the authorities by certain influential gentlemen, who were in fact friends of his, suggesting that he be excluded so as to prevent him suffering any loss of character by becoming involved in such an unsavoury business as an execution.

....

After the necessary period of time had elapsed the body was cut down and removed from the well, being taken inside the prison to await the verdict of the Coroner's jury.

An inquest was opened that same afternoon by Mr. C. Aspinall, City Coroner, the jury first of all being required to go and view the body. They were accompanied by the Governor, the Coroner and several reporters, and were led from the jury room through several passages and down a flight of steps, emerging into the exercise yard, where a number of convicts were standing about. These men, as was the custom, were ordered by a warder to turn their faces to the wall until the visitors had passed.

The party eventually arrived at the building where the body had been laid out and a warder unlocked the door. As the jurymen filed into the mortuary, some of them rather apprehensively, they removed their hats. The room was completely bare except for a rough stone slab in the centre, on which the body lay, covered in a white sheet. This had been drawn well up over the neck so that the marks of the rope could not be seen. Slowly and timidly the jury members passed around the slab, venturing only as close as was necessary. They saw that the body had recently been washed, as the hair was still damp. It had been pushed back, but not combed, and lay in a tangled disorderly mess, which did not enhance the appearance of the corpse. The face, which had at times been so arrogant and defiant in life, now looked placid and serene in death, as if Mrs. Berry had died naturally rather than violently.

The party remained in the mortuary no more than a few minutes. They then trooped back across the exercise yard and the inquest was opened.

The Governor was the first witness and stated that the execution had been carried out efficiently and that death had been instantaneous. He was, however, contradicted slightly by the next witness, Dr. George Beamish, who stated that death had not in fact been immediate, the hearts action having continued for some six minutes after the body had entered the pit. "Death was in fact due to strangulation", he said.

After the usual formalities of identification had been dealt with the inquiry was terminated and the file on Elizabeth Berry officially closed.

Before leaving the prison the reporters present spoke to the Reverend Morris and were told by the chaplain that he had spent some time with the prisoner each morning and evening throughout her confinement at Walton.

"Did she ever speak of her guilt or innocence?" he was asked.

"Yes". he replied. "I was with her for a long period last night and she insisted to me that she was quite innocent."

"Did you believe her?"

"Well, it really seems unlikely that she would tell an untruth in the face of eternity. She said the only thing she gave to the child on that Sunday was the creosote mixture. I reminded her that in her statement to the police she said that she had not given the mixture. She answered __ Yes, but he asked me to sign it and I put my name to it without reading it. __ This can easily be done you know". went on the chaplain. "For instance, after it was all over this morning I was asked to sign a paper and I did so without reading it."

He was asked what books Mrs. Berry had read in the prison and said that they were mostly religious works, including Jeremy Taylors 'Holy living and Dying', and of course the Bible.

"On Sunday we held a special service when I gave her the sacrament and on going in this morning I found her more composed than I had expected. Again we prayed together and just before the Executioner came in to pinion her she put her head on my breast and asked me to bless her.

"Knowing how devoted she has been, how earnestly she has prayed and how she has spent the whole of her time here, I cannot understand how she could possibly tell me a lie just a few minutes before her death, for it was just before we left the cell that she protested her innocence."

"So what do you think Reverend". he was asked. "Is she guilty or not?"

"It is impossible for me to say. Her statement was emphatic that she was innocent and it seemed to me that her conduct was in keeping with her declaration. I just cannot believe that a woman who spends her latter days and passes away as she did this morning could die with a lie on her lips."

"What is the general opinion in the prison on this point?"

"There seems to be no doubt. The general opinion here is that there is something very mysterious about it all, and for my own part I would like to add that some of the vindictive letters that have appeared in the newspapers do not shed much credit on the writers."

Finally he was asked; "What were her last words Reverend. Can you tell us?"

"Yes", was the reply. "Just before she died she repeated several times, "God forgive Dr. Patterson."

CHAPTER 20
MORE ABOUT THE 'COLONEL'

Mrs. Berry was dead, and within a few short months her face would begin to fade from the public mind. But for the moment interest in her and the Oldham Poisoning case continued unabated.

The very evening of the execution the drama 'A Mothers Sin' opened at the Oldham Theatre Royal. Whether this was by coincidence or design is a matter for conjecture, but it certainly seemed a most appropriate and well timed choice.

Joseph Whittaker, meanwhile, who claimed that the whole affair had left him out of pocket, was busy organising an auction, at which Mrs. Berry's possessions would be put up for sale to the general public, and as the name of his former client was still on everyones lips he felt confident that this would go a long way towards re-embursing him for what had proved to be a very costly and time consuming case.

A Mr. Francis Thorburn of Salford wrote to the Oldham Chronicle describing himself as a 'lecturer and phrenologist', and claiming that he was in a position to define Mrs. Berry's 'phrenological cast' after studying a photograph of her.

"Her head is a large size". he stated. "It is about 21¾ inches, or a quarter of an inch more than an average female one. Her brain would therefore be a substantial weight, denoting the power to command and conceal to a considerable extent her true character. Her temperament is a combination of lymphatic / nervous, giving a tendency to be sensual, erratic and very emotional. She would be selfish, inclined to double dealing, fond of outward show and would not hesitate at doing a mean action provided she thought she might escape detection.

'She would have a great love of money and position. Spending on finery and anything else her fancy desired would be another strong trait in her character. The fullness of the under part of the eyes would give her a ready command of verbosity, which has served her lately to pretend that she is a thorough Christian.

'Another point to note is the extremely high forehead, although this is partly hidden by her fringe. She would be very superficial and would be quite capable of praying one moment and committing any sin the next. Finally, Mrs. Berry's ears are extremely low set, as is the case with all murderers of her class ____ a very bad sign."

Mr. Thorburn ended his very enlightening letter by pointing out that; "Phrenology shows up character traits in a person which the public ought to be warned against, and sounds the alarm."

A Professor Parrish, of 23 Mount Pleasant Liverpool, wrote in the Oldham Standard, also giving a phrenological delineation on Mrs. Berry and stating quite emphatically that the shape of her skull was virtually identical to that of various other murderers.

Though this sort of theorising would be laughed at today it was no doubt taken seriously by a good many people at the time.

'Colonel' William Wrigley was another who was obviously not prepared to let the dead woman rest in peace, for after returning to Liverpool from Walton Gaol he proceeded to inform the newspapers that he was offering his friend James Berry the sum of £5 for the dress in which she had been hanged, it being the accepted custom that the dead persons clothing became the property of the Executioner. When this item of news was relayed to the hangman he replied that he was not interested, saying he could get more than £10 for it. Had the 'Colonel' succeeded in obtaining the garment there is little doubt that it would have been prominently displayed in quite a number of public bars over the succeeding months, perhaps even on the Tommyfield, so it is just as well that his bid proved too low.

A day or two after this Wrigley was interviewed by the Oldham Standard and strongly denied that he had ever had the slightest intention of taking part in the execution. When reminded that he had made the trip to Liverpool he replied that he had had business there that weekend in any case. He was asked how long he had known James Berry and replied that they had been friends for the past year and often talked business together, the hangman apparently engaging in the buying and selling of watches as a sideline. During the interview it became clear just how the 'Colonel' had managed to bolster his image by getting the Executioner to meet him in Salford.

Although having been introduced to Berry at a gathering of Freemasons in Blackpool the previous year there is no evidence that the two struck up any sort of friendship. However, on Mrs. Berry being convicted, he had lost no time in communicating with the hangman. On his own admission he had written Berry a letter immediately after the trial, enquiring if the Executioner was by any chance a relative of the convicted woman, and had followed it up later with another, asking Berry to meet him on his way through to Liverpool as he wished to discuss some business with him, presumably involving watches. For this reason only Berry had agreed to the meeting and any talk of the 'Colonel' assisting in the execution would undoubtedly have been taken as a joke by the hangman.

So Wrigley had obviously set up the whole thing for the publicity to be gained from it and all but admitted the fact when he terminated the interview by remarking, with characteristic modesty; "Well anyway, I think I might have helped to sell a few thousand newspapers for you last Monday."

In his capacity as a member of the Board of Guardians he was in the news once more a few days later, this time as champion of the underdog, when, at the weekly meeting, he brought up the question of remuneration ____ or rather the lack of it, paid to the barber and the baker at the Workhouse.

In the case of the former Wrigley pointed out that he was paid only a shilling a week "and saw some terrible sights." In addition he had previously been given a mug of tea and a slice of bread and butter, but this had recently been stopped by the Master. The 'Colonel' said that he could not remember the Board having passed such an order to the Master. He was told that none of the Board recalled having allowed the barber his refreshments in the first place.

Passing on to the case of the baker the 'Colonel' stated that the old man worked fifteen hours a day and received not a penny in wages.

"Is he a pauper?" one of the Guardians asked.

"I suppose so", replied the 'Colonel'.

"Then he is not entitled to anything", snapped the Guardian, and there the matter rested.

The following week the irrepressible Wrigley was again in the public eye when he was sued by a local hay and feed merchant for the sum of £19.18s. The 'Colonel' put in a counter claim for £5.12s. which he stated the merchant owed him as commission on another transaction. The court found in favour of the plaintiff and the 'Colonel' was ordered to pay the feed bill plus costs.

The 'Colonel', however, was something more than just a glory-seeker and throughout his career did much commendable work both in his capacity as a guardian and also as a town councillor, almost always as champion of the underdog. As well as fighting for the rights of the downtrodden pauper it is claimed that he was instrumental in ensuring that for the first time all materials purchased and work allocated by the council were tendered for and not given out to friends of public officials.

There were of course some very lively exchanges in the council chamber once the 'Colonel' was elected, though his political career was not without its up and downs. He did not attain the eminence to which he aspired, which is perhaps not surprising. For to him the job was, in a way, just another passing fancy, although he did work extremely hard during his time in office. However, he made his fair share of blunders, not the least of which concerned the controversial affair of the Oldham Public Library.

He became a councillor after defeating the well-known William Bodden in what was considered a shock result and immediately set about opposing the council's plan to establish a free library, museum and art gallery, which he believed would be an unwarranted waste of public money on a building which would never be used by ordinary working people. Though quite wrong of course he was no doubt very sincere. After all, the proposed new building might be a very commendable idea, but with poverty in the town extremely acute and social services far from adequate, it is easy to see why Wrigley felt that the money could be better spent in other ways.

But the gallant member for St. Marys, or 'the people's William' as some now referred to him, was unsuccessful in his bid to stop the project going ahead, the memorial stone being laid in 1882 and the library opening officially on August 1st 1886. In 1887 a lending library was established, high over the entrance to which the stone figure of a woman was erected. Later on it was discovered that an unofficial inscription had been cut just below the figure, which read; 'Lady Wrigley'. Whether this was supposed to refer to the 'Colonel's' wife, in view of the fact that he had been such a strong opponent of the library scheme, can only be guessed at, but the general opinion would seen to be that some humourous workman was probably responsible.

There is no record of the distinguished councillor and his friend the hangman ever getting together again following their encounter in Liverpool. No doubt the 'Colonel' considered the Berry case yesterday's news following his return to Oldham. He certainly did not attend the sale of Mrs. Berry's effects, which is perhaps just as well, for he would no doubt have taken charge of the proceedings and made it even more of a carnival affair than it in fact turned out to be.

But you can't keep a good man down as they say, and the 'Colonel', ever on the lookout for something new to interest him, decided about this time to enter the licencing trade, taking over a well known local public house. Though his exhuberent personality ensured the success of the venture from the word go it was not very long before the 'Colonel's' need for variety and a wider audience drew him once more to the market grounds of the north, this time as a vendor of patent medicines. Of course he had to have something quite unique to offer, and as usual the 'Colonel' did not let his public down. He named his exciting new discovery the 'Golden Pill', a remedy guaranteed to cure all ills from backache to gout. 'A boon and a blessing to mankind' he called it, and naturally a fair number of the miraculous pills were sold, thanks to the 'Colonel's' remarkable way with a word and infectious enthusiam. But the novelty of the new game soon began to wear thin and Wrigley eventually gave it up, returning once more to the old watch and jewellery business. Unfortunately though, the 'Colonel' discovered that it was not so easy to pick up where he had left off. Possibly the public had found his excursion into the patent medicine field and quick about-face rather hard to swallow. In any event Wrigley was experiencing a very difficult time indeed. Trade had never been so hard to come by and even the presence of the great man on his famous platform was failing to pull in the crowds in quite such large numbers as formerly. Now in his fifties, the 'Colonel' was beginning to slow down a little and was not in the best of health. He decided therefore that a change of climate might benefit him, and in 1891, after his term of office came to an end, he left town and was not seen again in the area for some considerable time, it being rumoured that he had retired to the seaside, where he was still engaged in selling his watches and jewellery as a sideline.

At some time in 1894, however, Wrigley suddenly appeared again in Oldham and old friends were shocked at the great change in him. Instead of the ebullient fast-talking and smartly attired 'Colonel' of old they were now confronted by the sad spectacle of a beaten poverty-stricken shell of a man; for the former Mayor of Tommyfield had fallen on evil days indeed. With his wife Hetty he moved into a tiny terraced house at 36 Radcliffe Street near the town centre, and, partly due to occasional help from his friends, managed to eke out a living as best he could. He still frequented the public houses and sold watches, though his business was now conducted on a much smaller scale. The 'Colonel' was a very proud man and still managed to keep up some semblance of respectability. Though by now virtually penniless he refused to accept the relief he had worked so hard in the past to obtain for others. However, ill-health, bouts of depression and old age can defeat even the best of us, and after the turn of the century, the 'Colonel', whose few remaining friends now seemed to have drifted away, was reluctantly compelled to accept the hospitality of the Workhouse in whose boardroom he had once proudly sat as an elected 'Guardian of the Poor'. He did not stay permanently, but entered periodically and remained for a few weeks when things were at their most desperate. What a come-down for a man who had once been among the towns most respected and best-loved citizens. It was surprising how few people now recalled the pleasure he had brought or the good he had done just a few short years before. Even the recipients of the bread he had generously bought with his own money at the outbreak of the cotton famine were now conspicuously absent and there perhaps lay one of the reasons for his downfall. For there is no doubt that the 'Colonel' had made a good deal of money in his time and the fact that he was always fond of a 'tipple' could by no means fully account for the disappearance of it. His great generosity was most certainly to blame, for he could never say no when a hand was held out or a good cause was in need of support. Had he not been so open-handed to others he might well have ended his days in affluence.

By 1906 the once proud 'Colonel' was at his lowest ebb. He was seventy years of age, seldom left the house and constantly complained of stomach pains. His wife Hetty nursed him through many a difficult period, but on January 23rd he became so ill that she sent for the doctor, who promptly arranged for his transfer to the Workhouse, where he was found a bed in the institution's infirmary. For the next few weeks he remained a patient, and proved quite a handful at times. He was obviously not very happy to be there and suffered again from periods of acute depression. It was sad and ironic that the 'Colonel' should end up here in the Oldham Workhouse Infirmary and one wonders if the spector of Mrs. Berry ever entered his thoughts or his dreams as he lay there during those last grim days of his life.

On Tuesday March 20th Hetty Wrigley visited her husband and handed over to him sixpennyworth of brandy which he had asked her to bring in. She had no idea that alcohol was not permitted in the wards and went away completely unaware of having broken the rules. On returning the following day she was shocked to learn that Wrigley had been moved to the imbecile ward after attempting to cut his throat with a borrowed pocket knife. However, he had bungled the job and was now under restraint. Hetty was taken to him and remained by his bedside for the rest of the day. The wound was slight and inconsequential, but the patient was in a restless and excited state and Hetty found it difficult to calm him. By early evening he had become delirious and eventually lost consciousness. The doctor was called and after a brief examination announced that the 'Colonel' was dead. Hetty slipped quietly out of the Workhouse and made her way sadly up the steep slope of Coldhurst Street to the town centre. The silent snow-covered stalls of Tommyfield must have brought back memories of happier times as she passed by the old market and descended the hill to Radcliffe Street.

William Wrigley, auctioneer, was elected councillor for St. Mary's Ward on November 1st 1882, re-elected in 1885 and 1888, and finally retired from office in November 1891.

The 'Colonel' was a true genius, who enriched the local scene with his colourful personality for more than half a century. There were some people who wondered why, with his love of entertaining and skill in handling an audience, he had never made the theatre his career. There is a many-sided answer to this of course. In the first place even the theatre could not have provided the 'Colonel' with enough variety to keep him interested. To have been stamped as a thespian and only that, would have been nowhere near enough for a man of such wide horizons. After all, soldier, policeman, auctioneer, guardian and councillor were just a few of the lives he lived. In any case the stage would have proved far too confining, and what script was ever written that the 'Colonel' could have stuck to? There is some doubt of course that he had the ability to stick to anything for very long. Yet despite his many faults he was well liked wherever he went, for beneath the tough hard-driving exterior was a warm vibrant personality and an impish sense of humour which was clearly apparent to all who ever met or listened to him. There have been many wonderful northern characters, but was there ever one to rival the man who was once described by a newspaper as possessing the subtle reasoning of a Tallyrand, the eloquence of a Beaconsfield, the histrionic abilities of an Irving, and the intellect of a John Stuart Mill? Well, all one can say is, the 'Colonel' could not have put it better himself.

CHAPTER 21

THE AUCTION

On Thursday evening March 24th, just ten days after Mrs. Berry's death, an auction was held at No. 15 Union Street Oldham, attended by a very large number of people. The crowd was so big in fact that for some time before the commencement of the proceedings the pavement outside was completely blocked. As might be gathered it was to be no ordinary auction. For the articles to be disposed of were the worldly possessions of the late Mrs. Berry, including her clothes and also those of the dead child.

The shop itself was excessively crowded long before the arrival of Mr. Liversage, the auctioneer, and it was quite evident that prospective buyers would be greatly outnumbered by the curiosity seekers.

Liversage duly made his appearance and seemed rather taken aback at the size of the turnout. After forcing his way through the milling mob he produced a list of the deceased womans effects and proceeded to cast his eye over it. The crowd, however, was in no mood to be kept waiting and he was immediately pressed to "Get on with it". Mr. Liversage though, was not one to be hurried, and replied that he had no intention of starting until the appointed time of 6.30. On hearing this some tried to get out of the shop but now found it quite impossible to elbow their way through the seething mass of bodies. One man commented - "It's just like a Wakes".

Opening the sale at last, Mr. Liversage announced that there was no reserve on any of the articles, and added; "Everything I have to offer belonged to Elizabeth Berry, and you do not need to be afraid that any of these clothes belonged to anyone else. Furthermore I do not expect you to pay ridiculous prices for these articles. Mind you, if Madame Tussauds had known of this auction____"

"Or the 'Colonel', someone cut in. (Laughter)

"They would probably have been here tonight", continued the auctioneer.

What he did not realise at that moment was that representatives from more than one museum were in fact outside the building, unable to gain admittance because of the densely packed crowd. For despite repeated requests not a single person was prepared to give up his position.

The first item offered was a ladies satchel or handbag and bidding commenced at one penny. Labouriously it went up to half-a-crown, at which figure it stuck.

"I believe it cost Mrs. Berry half-a-guinea", the auctioneer informed his audience, in an effort to wring a few more pennies out of the sale. The bidding was then renewed, the satchel finally going for three shillings. The next item was a crepe bonnet, for which the gathering seemed somewhat reluctant to bid.

"Come along now", urged Liversage. "There is no need to be afraid of it. The articles I have to offer have done no harm, whatever the woman was guilty of."

A bid of one shilling was called, and Liversage remarked; "If any milliner buys this and displays it in her window I'll guarantee she'll do a roaring business over the next few months."

This seemed to have the desired effect and the hat was finally sold for half-a-crown.

At this stage, with the people inside packed like sardines and the ones in the street pushing and straining to get a better view, shouting and arguing began to drown out the voice of the auctioneer, and Liversage, fearing damage to his premises, asked a colleague to try and keep the crowd from leaning against the window. Though this of course proved to be something of an impossibility, some semblence of order was restored following an appeal to the crowd, and the auction got under way again.

Holding aloft another, smaller, bonnet, Mr. Liversage

announced quite proudly; "This is the hat that Edith Annie Berry came to the Workhouse in." He could not, however, force the bidding over 1s. 7d, even after adding; "There is a pedigree connected with this hat."

The sale of a furthur hat and a pair of white women's gloves followed. Meanwhile the temperature inside the shop had risen to the level of a turkish bath and those trapped in the middle of the swaying straining mass were finding things extremely uncomfortable if not downright dangerous and several people made renewed and noisy efforts to fight their way out, but to no avail. Those inside were forced to remain there, while the ones struggling to get in were equally frustrated. A butcher from an adjoining shop who had come in 'just for a few minutes' made desperate efforts to leave via the front door, but without success. At last, his patience worn out, he somehow managed to climb over the counter, past the auctioneer, and get out the back way.

The general commotion did not help Mr. Liversage, who continually pleaded with his audience 'not to make such a row'. He was advised by one spectator to "Fetch the hosepipe. That'll drive 'em back."

After he had threatened to abandon the sale the crowd calmed down somewhat and he was able to continue, holding up a child's pinafore dress. One woman was heard to remark: "Ah... poor little thing."

The garment was disposed of for 9d, Edith Annie's dolman went for 2s. and a dress for 8s.3d, while "the frock she went to her grandmother's funeral in" was sold for 4s.6d.

Again the crowd became unruly and there were shouts of; "It's suffocating in here.

"Let's go over to the Salvation Army barracks", and, "Adjourn to yon spare ground o'er there."

"If you'll be quiet for a while", said the auctioneer, "I'll soon get through the items. It's impossible for me to make myself heard with all this row going on."

With that he picked up another pinafore dress. "Did it belong to the old 'un or the young 'un?" someone asked.

"To the old one" was the reply. "But it will let in or out. You will notice that all these garments are of good quality cloth. Mrs. Berry must have thought a lot of her child ____ as well as herself of course. If there are any people here from the Workhouse they will have seen the little girl running about in some of these things."

There was a further flurry of shouting and pushing, causing the auctioneer to yell: "Mind that window!"

At this point one man did somehow contrive to force his way inside the shop. He was Mrs. Berry's solicitor, Joseph Whittaker, to whom of course would go the proceeds of the auction. "Stop this sale while I've had a word with you!" he called out on reaching the doorway.

"All right sir". said Liversage. "Come forward please."

A whispered conversation now took place between the two of them, the audience meanwhile becoming more and more restless. The auctioneer eventually informed them that the sale was to be temporarily called off, an announcement which was greeted with some derision.

"Now we don't wish to make money out of it you understand."

"You're after making all you can", a voice in the crowd piped up.

"No no. The sale is simply to relieve the administrator."

Mr. Whittaker now intervened, and told them; "I think it would be far better to adjourn for tonight. There are hundreds outside who can't even hear what's going on, let alone make a bid!"

As there were at least half-a-dozen tin boxes filled with goods still to be disposed of it was decided to call off the whole affair and the spectators were told that an announcement would be made in the following evening's newspaper giving the venue and time at which the sale would be resumed.

"You can see the ball dress then". said Liversage. "Eighteen pounds worth."

A number of policemen were now on the scene and the assembly noisily dispersed, many of them remaining in the street outside, where they gathered in groups to discuss both the auction and the murder case itself.

On the following evening the adjourned sale was resumed at the Temperance Hall Horsedge Street Oldham, a building with an infinitely bigger capacity than the Union Street shop premises, which had of course proved totally inadequate due to the surprisingly large crowd.

Mr. Liversage began by saying; "It has come to my ears that a rumour is being banded about the town to the effect that not all the articles in this sale were the property of Elizabeth Berry. Well I can tell you folks that this is a downright lie. And if any person in this room or anywhere else for that matter can prove me a liar I'll gladly forfeit £50 to the Oldham Infirmary. Now what d'you say to that?"

"Get on with it", droned someone at the back.

"Very well, I will", snapped Liversage, having made his point. With that he proceeded with the sale, offering first an inkstand and two bottles of ink which he claimed were worth 'three half-crowns.' He got 1s. 10d for them. A box containing a substance 'for curing sore eyes', a workbasket and a pair of cashmere gloves were all rapidly disposed of, as were a pair of curling tongs "which would make any woman pretty", a piece of mistletoe "worn by Mrs. Berry at the ball" and a pair of women's cuff links which the auctioneer said he would not guarantee to be gold. "But knowing all about Mrs. Berry's tastes I should be very surprised if they were not."

A piece of material, part of a frock belonging to Edith Annie, was sold for fourpence. Unfastening a bundle, Liversage informed his audience; "These are what were sent back from Walton Gaol. They're just as they came. They haven't been touched by anyone."

From the bundle he produced a pair of pocket handkerchiefs. They looked somewhat grubby and he explained this away by remarking; "Of course you have to remember that she had no opportunity of washing them." The handkerchiefs realised the sum of 2s. 2d.

With each article he placed on offer the persuasive Mr. Liversage added some remark regarding the former owner and this of course had the effect of boosting the takings. The hat "worn by Mrs. Berry at her trial" was bought by the representative of a Liverpool Waxworks exhibition, while a couple of dresses were obtained by a showman. Of the dresses offered, a black one, said to have been "worn by the murderess when she attended her mother's funeral at Moston", brought in the comparatively large sum of 9s. 3d., the highest for any single item up to that point. However, there was still the 'piece de resistance' to be bid for, and after a quantity of high boots and a bible had been cleared the auctioneer at last came to the box containing it. Slowly and very deliberately he raised the lid and amid a chorus of exclamations drew forth the long awaited garment. The ball dress was of rich ruby red silk, draped with black lace and ribbons. The dead woman's dancing shoes, pink silk stockings, pink silk gloves and black fan, were included in the lot and were all eagerly examined by those close enough to touch them. At this point the auctioneer became rather alarmed, fearing that the dress might be pulled to pieces before he could sell it, and after dragging it to safety and giving forth with his usual spiel, he called confidently for the first bid and was not disappointed, for the sum of £5 was immediately offered. £7 was reached before the lot was knocked down to another firm of Waxworks exhibitors, also from Liverpool. This concluded the sale and the auctioneer wound up the evening by thanking everyone for their attendance and expressing the hope that he should never again be required to officiate on such a sad occasion, which seemed very strange, for he appeared to have thoroughly enjoyed himself.

The proceedings, which had begun at 6.30 p.m. did not end until after eleven o'clock, when the vultures finally dispersed and made their way home, still avidly discussing the notorious Mrs. Berry and her glittering ball dress. An ironic note perhaps was the fact that only a year before Elizabeth Berry herself had held a similar if somewhat less lucrative sale at the little house in Castleton, when, assisted by her aunt, Mrs. Pemberton, she had disposed of her mother's few modest possessions.

Just a few short weeks after the auction at Oldham the ball dress was on display to the public in Liverpool as part of a particularly unsavoury exhibition, the centrepiece of which was a miniature re-enactment of the execution. Not a single detail was missing which would import the full ghastliness of the performance. Even the prison officials were depicted, with the chaplain reading the prayer and of course the hangman about to dispatch his wretched victim.

At around this time, Dr. Thomas Harris, whose evidence had carried so much weight at the trial, was holding his own exhibition in Manchester, where the gullet of Edith Annie was on show at a meeting of the Medical Society.

A waxen figure of Mrs. Berry was destined to live on for many years at Reynolds famous Waxworks in Lime Street Liverpool, whose Chamber of Horrors was housed in a large cellar. Reynolds catalogue reveals that the Oldham nurse shared her quarters with some of the most notorious murderers in history, including the legendary Charlie Peace and Landru, the French Bluebeard.

In 1923, Turners, auctioneers, of 17/19 Renshaw Street Liverpool, a firm going back three generations to the reign of George III, sold off the entire contents of Reynolds waxworks. One lot, described as being suitable for a small and profitable exhibition in itself, was a set piece depicting a trio of infamous ladies seated around a table, among them Elizabeth Berry. Her two companions, Mrs. Flanagan and Mrs. Higgins, both executed in 1884, were from the very lowest strata of society. The arrogant Mrs. Berry would not have been flattered.

. . . .

Elizabeth Berry's name was mentioned again in the newspapers around that time in connection with another death in Oldham, this time a suicide, involving a young man named Robert Crap, aged 19, who had hanged himself in the house of his brother-in-law at No. 6 Millbrook Hollinwood. The deceased had been employed as a lap-carrier at the Glebe Mills, and no explanation for his drastic action could be found.

The house in which he died was that previously occupied by Mary Ann Finley and her daughter Lizzie when they had lived and worked in that part of the town.

CHAPTER 22
INCONCLUSIVE EVIDENCE

The theories of the phrenologists, the antics of the 'Colonel' and even the disgraceful and degrading scramble witnessed at the auction made very good copy and were no doubt widely discussed, but more serious minded people were very much concerned about the legal side of the case, and one question loomed large above all others. Had justice really been done?

Dr. Patterson's letter certainly did not help in providing an answer; far from it. As well as arousing the anger of many who found it extremely vindictive, not to mention offensive, it only served to sow the seeds of doubt in the minds of some who had previously been firmly convinced of Mrs. Berry's guilt, for the letter was blatantly biased in its view of the case and resulted in several replies being published in the newspapers, one of which gave the opinion;

> The doctor in his letter selects that portion of the evidence which suits his purpose and leaves the rest untouched.

One paragraph in Dr. Patterson's scathing missive was very disturbing to say the least. This was the piece about the 'red-hot draught', which ended with;

"......the fiend pressed it down her child's throat".

Now where was the evidence to support such a statement? Edith Annie certainly did not complain of any such treatment and she had every opportunity to do so, being left alone with various people at different times during her illness. Mrs. Sanderson for example, having been so close to the child for a number of years, would have been the ideal person in whom to confide.

Could it be that in referring to her as 'the fiend' Dr. Patterson had himself been influenced by the sensational stories regarding Mrs. Berry's past which filled the newspapers following her conviction? He was called on to attend her during her fit of hysteria at the Workhouse, yet he could not have been unduly alarmed by it at the time or he would surely have brought it to the attention of the Guardians and pressed for her dismissal.

As regards her alleged attempt to place her baby on the fire, could this too have been blown up out of all proportion? It was stated by a relative later to have been the result of 'milk feeding', and in following this up I learned that a certain percentage of mothers are affected mentally following a confinement, when a period of depression is not at all uncommon. It is a condition known as puerperal insanity and in the majority of cases is no more than a temporary condition. When in the grip of such a depression the mother will often turn away from the child and ignore it completely, or in rare cases perhaps even attempt to harm it. Could Mrs. Berry have been merely a victim of puerperal insanity following the birth of her son Harold?

Another relative, living in Manchester and not wishing to become involved in the case, did say that the stories of Mrs. Berry's past had been 'wildly exaggerated' and there is quite obviously some truth in this assertion.

The affair with the Miles Platting curate was corroborated by too many people to be disregarded and there is no doubt at all that Mrs. Berry told numerous lies and stories bordering on fantasy. But these facts alone do not make her a murderer.

The evidence at Liverpool certainly appeared less than conclusive. No poison was ever found in the body and no trace on the vomit–stained towel or any of the other articles referred to in court, despite extensive expert analysis. Yet there is still the black corroded patch on the gullet to be accounted for. So assuming that a poison was administered, had the prosecution shown beyond doubt that Mrs. Berry was responsible? According to Ann Dillon the mother and child had been seen alone in the surgery prior to Edith Annies first sickness, but old Alice Alcroft was adamant in stating that Dillon could not possibly have gone into the surgery at the time mentioned, and this claim was borne out by the evidence of Beatrice Hall. Perhaps they were both mistaken — perhaps Dillon was. In any event it all boiled down to the word of one witness against the other. Or to be more accurate, two against one.

But if the mother had not administered the poison then who had? Mrs. Berry had certainly had the opportunity, but then so had various other people, Dr. Patterson himself having admitted that numerous bottles were left lying about in the surgery, not only in the poisons cupboard but also on the counter. Is it beyond the bounds of possibility that one of the inmates might have harboured a grudge? Some real or imagined grievance against Mrs. Berry which was taken out on the child? After all, the head nurse in a Workhouse in those days would be essentially a hard person and Mrs. Berry was known to possess a vicious and at times uncontrollable temper.

There may or may not be any merit in such a speculative theory. As a motive it is perhaps not a particularly powerful one. But is it any weaker than that suggested by the prosecution? To kill one's own child — or anyone elses for that matter — for the sake of £10 seems utterly inconceivable, even for those times. And Mrs. Berry was not exactly penniless, nor was she in debt. On the contrary. She had £64 in the bank at the time, plus such valuable possessions as a watch worth £14. So it could hardly be claimed that she was desperately in need of funds. If she did commit the crime then insurance money could not have been the motive. The other policy mentioned, for £100, certainly has to be dismissed, for surely no reasonably intelligent person could possibly remain under the impression that the insurance had been effected when no policy was issued after a lapse of nine months and no premiums ever paid.

Mrs. Berry was a reasonably intelligent person and this leads us to another highly significant point. Mr. Cottingham had fought every inch of the way for his client, but had possibly overlooked what might well have been a vital argument in her favour. Would Mrs. Berry, a trained nurse of some years experience have chosen a corrosive poison if she had planned to commit murder? A case of attempted homicide in 1862 gives some indication of the fierceness of such poisons.

Mrs. Sarah Cornell, an ailing elderly woman, was given a glass of what she believed to be medicine by her servant. The old lady took a small sip of the liquid, which burnt her mouth so badly that she immediately spat it out and screamed in agony. A quantity of the ejected matter, which turned out to be sulphuric acid, fell onto the bedcover and burnt several tiny holes in it.

Even without knowledge of the above case, Mrs. Berry, as a nurse, would almost certainly have been aware that sulphuric acid, or any other acid, would burn the victim and therefore arouse suspicion. Poisons in the surgery, on Dr. Patterson's own admission, included strychnine, opium and prussic acid. There was also of course sulphuric acid, and there would almost certainly be a quantity of arsenic. Of these the two to avoid would surely be the acids. Either arsenic or strychnine would have done the job much more cleanly and been less obvious. Arsenic in particular, if administered in small doses, can be exceedingly difficult to detect.

As regards the medical evidence at the trial it most certainly left much to be desired. Under cross-examination neither of the Oldham doctors could convincingly show that they had suspected sulphuric acid poisoning before it had been suggested to them by Dr. Harris, yet both had given it as their considered medical opinion that such a poison was the cause of death. Dr. Harris himself, a stubborn hard-headed man, had proved immovable, despite Mr. Cottinghams persistance. Yet even his evidence left many questions unanswered. Last and most certainly least came Charles Estcourt, whose exhaustive analysis, occupying many days, had revealed precisely nothing. Even so he had still been brought to Liverpool to state that sulphuric acid could have killed the girl without leaving any trace. He could offer no proof whatsoever though — only an opinion.

Circumstantially perhaps the finger of guilt did point to Mrs. Berry. Or did it? For surely the Castleton affair was the deciding factor in the minds of the Liverpool jurymen. As the Oldham Standard put it:–

> Mrs. Berry has not had the fair play given to her at Liverpool which she ought to have received. The raising of the Castleton inquiry kindled an unwarrantable sensation against a presumably innocent woman, who may be the wretched victim of prejudice and suspicion. But what can be done in such cases? There is no Criminal Appeals Court in this country, and more's the pity. Questions of life and death should not be scampered through on circumstantial evidence alone when science is so much at fault. The woman would not confess her guilt, and in fact protested her innocence to the very end. No greater reproach could be heaped on the status of scientific research in this country than to hang a woman for administering a poison, no trace of which can be found. It is only suspected, not proven. Mr. Justice Hawkins disposed of Mr. Cottingham's eloquent appeal by telling the jury to 'look at the facts.' What facts? Suspicions are not facts, and the whole case against Mrs. Berry remains shrouded in suspicion.

Now to the Castleton enquiry. Even there no positive proof of poison was ever discovered. Dr. Paul stated that he suspected atropa, but had not found any. Only a substance which he took to be atropa after testing out its effect on animals. Yet he would not swear that it was in fact atropa.

The Rochdale chemist, John Taylor, with his strange 'mania', could perhaps not be considered the most reliable of witnesses, but even if his story is fully accepted, what proof is there that the mysterious 'Ellen Saunders' and Elizabeth Berry were one and the same person? Dark complexion, between 28 and 30. This description could have fitted hundreds of women. The signature in the chemist's book was, in the opinion of William Henry Lawson, written by Mrs. Berry. But the Workhouse Master was no handwriting expert, and even they can be mistaken — as in the case of the Howard Hughes hoax, when experts supported Clifford Irving's claim that certain letters he had passed on to his publishers had been written by the elusive tycoon, only to learn later that they themselves had been taken in, for Irving eventually admitted to writing the letters himself. Not that anyone would have had a reason to copy Mrs. Berry's style of writing, but if a firm of modern handwriting experts can be wrong the evidence of the Master on this point should at least be viewed with a certain amount of caution.

Bearing in mind the Rochdale chemist's somewhat puzzling and erratic behaviour, it might be have been better if his testimony had been corroborated. Unfortunately his apprentice had died in the interim, or further evidence of identification might have been forthcoming.

The only other testimony was that supplied by the neighbours, and here again, as with some of the tales of Mrs. Berry's past, we wander off into the realms of dreams and fantasy.

None of this is to say that Elizabeth Berry was innocent, but merely to examine the strength of the case against her. At Castleton the jury was asked to consider its inquest verdict in the prior knowledge that the dead woman's daughter had already been convicted of murder. With the Liverpool trial influencing the Castleton inquest and vice versa, Mrs. Berry was caught up in a whirlpool from which there was no escape.

Perhaps she was guilty of the murder of the child. But was the evidence produced to prove it? In my opinion it was not. And if any reasonable doubt exists, particularly in a case built entirely on circumstantial evidence, then surely the benefit of that doubt should not be given to the prosecution, but to the accused.

CHAPTER 23

THE PRINCIPALS

So ended the highly controversial Oldham Poisoning Case. James Cottingham, who had fought so fiercely for his client's life could not have had very happy memories of the town. In 1883 he had defended a man named Harry Swindells who was charged with having shot and killed James Wild, aged sixty, a relative of Swindells' estranged wife, at a house in Henthorn Street, Shaw Road, Oldham. He was found guilty and hanged.

Five years after the poisoning case Cottingham was on the Oldham scene again, when in 1892 he represented Joseph Mellor, the Hollins Road murderer, in a particularly gruesome case.

After Mellor's wife, Mary Jane, had been missed by her neighbours, one of them ventured into the back yard of her terraced house and pushed open the door. There was no sign of either of the Mellors, but several flags had been removed from the centre of the kitchen floor and a hole dug in the earth beneath. the hole was empty, but under the cellar steps the neighbour made a grim discovery. The mutilated body of Mary Jane Mellor lay huddled there.

The police were quickly on hand and found that the body, which was already partly decomposed, showed seven stab wounds. Some teeth had been knocked out and the head was almost severed. The missing husband was soon tracked down and charged with the killing. The case caused quite a stir and within a couple of weeks the landlord had repossessed the house and was charging sightseers twopence a time to view the scene of the crime.

Mr. Cottingham was briefed by the defence, but had little chance of success from the outset, and sure enough he again proved to be a loser as far as Oldham was concerned. Mellor was hanged, but a replica of him lived on ____ at Madame Tussauds in London, the famous waxworks sending a representative to

Oldham to buy up the furniture and take soil from the hole in the kitchen, which Mellor had undoubtedly intended to be his wife's final resting place.

Mr. James Cottingham died at his home in Chorlton-Cum-Hardy, Manchester, in 1906, aged 89. He served on the Northern Circuit for the best part of forty years, being involved in most of the major criminal trials during that time. He was married twice, but had no children, and, remarkably, was active in the legal profession up to the age of eighty-seven, holding the position of Revising Barrister for Preston, Blackpool and the Rossendale Valley until 1904.

Coincidentally, Dr. Thomas Harris, the man who had proved such a formidable prosecution witness at the trial of Elizabeth Berry, died suddenly the same year at his home 'Oakley', in Brewood, Staffordshire.

A keen sportsman, excellent at shooting and cricket, he had often practiced at the Old Trafford nets during his time in Manchester, Dr. Harris, who was believed to have overworked himself, died following a days shooting on one of the hottest September days ever recorded. He was survived by a wife, three daughters and a son, who later became a physician on the staff of University College Hospital.

As for James Berry, a rather self-righteous type of man, quite proud of his profession, he continued to do his job at least as competently as his predecessor. Mrs. Berry was not the last woman he would hang, though he still showed a strong distaste for such executions.

Before he retired from the business he was to play a major role in a further unfortunate mishap while hanging John Conway, the murderer of a child, at Kirkdale Prison Liverpool in 1891.

After visiting the prisoner and being given his weight, Berry worked out a drop of 4ft. 6ins. and was rather taken aback when

Dr. Barr, medical man at the gaol, queried this and insisted that Berry give a drop of 6ft. 9ins. The hangman argued but was eventually forced to compromise. The alternative would have been to back out of the job. This he was obviously not prepared to do. He therefore reluctantly agreed on a drop of just under 6ft, with disastrous results. As Conway's weight was 11 stones 2 lbs. Berry's original calculation would probably have been about right. As things turned out the longer drop resulted in a spectacle almost as horrific as the one at Norwich Castle six years before. Though Conway was not completely decapitated his head had in fact been almost torn from his body and there was blood all over the floor of the pit.

Following his retirement in 1892, Berry undertook a lecture tour, during which he described his experiences as a hangman. Later, no doubt because of these experiences, he became a strong advocate for the abolition of capital punishment. James Berry died at his home in Bradford in 1913, aged 61.

Justice Henry Hawkins, sometimes referred to as 'Hanging Hawkins', later became Lord Brampton, and died in 1907 at the age of ninety.

Certainly a most pathetic and silent figure in the Elizabeth Berry case had been Mary Ann Finley. By all accounts a decent hard working woman, she had gone to her death without any knowledge of the terrible events surrounding it.

She had been afforded what amounted to no more than a pauper's grave. When the coffin was raised at the exhumation and the lid removed, it was seen that she had not even warranted a shroud, her body being wrapped in a newspaper, an old copy of the Rochdale Star. For Mary Ann Finley it was indeed the final indignity.

While researching this book I visited Chadderton Cemetery and talked to Malcolm Bardsley, the Superintendent, whom I found to be very helpful and well informed.

This cemetery, opened on August 1st 1857, is a comparatively small one, but is very neat and has the appearance of being well cared for. From Mr. Bardsley I learned that a Mr. George Buckley had been his counterpart at the time of Edith Annie's burial. In an old register kept by him we found an entry January 10th. 1887 and details of the interment. The cost of the grave amounted to £1.10s., added to which of course would be gravediggers fees, cost of the coffin and carriage etc. The grave number is also listed, 14-39.

With this information to help us track it down we set off along the path in brilliant sunshine, up the hill past the little chapel, then along another path, on the left of which stands a magnificent marble tomb belonging to the Platt family of textile fame. Directly opposite this another, narrower path, dips down towards the centre of the cemetery. As we went along this I knew by the numbers that we were getting close. I was eager to see the grave and photograph the headstone, but it proved rather difficult to find. At last, however, the Superintendent did manage to locate the spot, but there was no sign of any headstone. Only a small piece of bare ground covered by a thatch of stubbly grass indicates the spot where Annie is buried, and a small section of this has been cut out where the path has been widened to make way for a wooden seat.

After assertaining beyond doubt that this was the grave in question, the Superintendent returned to his duties and I was left alone to take in the scene. As his footsteps receded into the distance all was quiet except for the rustling of branches in the wind. It was mid-morning on a bright but bitterly cold day and no one seemed to be about as I stood there and tried to imagine how the little band of mourners must have looked on just such a morning as this in 1887, as they clustered together for warmth and listened to the minister intoning the words of the burial service.

After a few minutes I left the path and wandered just a few paces past the sad little grave to look at a nearby headstone which had caught my eye. By a strange coincidence the body buried beneath it was that of a little girl who had died not many years before Edith Annie, and who had also been eleven years of age. It was a neat headstone. Nothing grand like the Platts' tomb, yet there was a certain quiet dignity about it. And though well aware that moments such as these are very conducive to foolish sentimentality, I could not help thinking how nice it would have been if Edith Annie had had one like it.

SELECTED BIBLIOGRAPHY

OLDHAM CHRONICLE
OLDHAM STANDARD
MANCHESTER EVENING CHRONICLE
MANCHESTER EVENING NEWS
MANCHESTER GUARDIAN
LIVERPOOL MERCURY
MY EXPERIENCES AS AN EXECUTIONER by James Berry- David & Charles
ROCHDALE STAR

INDEX

Aberdeen, University of, 69
Acid, 157
Act of Union, 36
Albion St. Castleton, 88
Albion St. Miles Platting, 56
Alcroft, Alice, 47-49, 59-61, 77, 126, 128, 131, 138, 168, 173, 180, 217, 278
Alexians, 96
Alkali, 157
Alkrington, Manchester, 16
Allen, William Philip, 96
'Alone in London' (play), 41
America, 198, 230, 240
American War Office, 200
Ancoats, Manchester, 199
Anderson, John Mills, (Governor, Walton Gaol), 129, 211, 253, 256-257
Anderson, Sarah, 133
Andover Workhouse, Hampshire, 14, 17
Angel Inn, Oldham, 15
Anglo-Irish, 36
Armley Gaol, Leeds, 232
Arsenic, 280
Ashton-under-Lyne, 34
Aspinall, C. (Liverpool City Coroner), 256
Atropa, 192-194, 281
Australia, 57, 130, 195

Babbacombe, Devon, 233

Bacup, Lancs, 21
Back Albion St, Castleton, 86, 88, 89
Banks Alexander, 117, 118
Bardsley, Malcolm, 287
Barr, Dr. 286
Barker St. Oldham, 47
Barlow, George, 15
Bath Hotel, Salford, 242, 244
Beaconsfield, Earl of (Benjamin Disraeli), 268
Beamish, Dr. George, 253, 257
Belgium, 240
Belle Vue Gaol, Manchester, 201
Bennett, Miss, 208
Berry, Edith Annie, 7-8, 26-32, 40, 42-43, 45, 54-57, 59, 61, 86, 117, 120-125, 128, 135, 195, 204, 207, 271, 274-275, 278, 287-288
Berry, Elizabeth, 7-8, 25-35, 37, 39, 44, 47-63, (Magistrates Court) 67-68, 72, 74, 76-78, 80, 83-85, 87-95, 103-104, 106-107, 109, 111-113, (116-122, 125-126, 128, 130, 134-136, 138-139, 145, 151, 153-156, 164, 170, 173-174, 176, 180, 182, 184-188 – Trial, Liverpool Assizes) 189, 191-193, 195-230, 236, 247-262, 267, 269-270, 272-282, 285
Berry, Harold, 8, 203, 207, 278

Berry, James (Public Executioner), 188, 225, 232-236, 242-246, 252-255, 261-262, 285-286
Berry, Thomas, 118-119, 203-205, 218
Bible, 258
Bicarbonate of soda, 138, 172, 175
Bilton Place, Bradford, Yorks, 235
Binns, Bartholemew, 232
Birmingham, 192
Birmingham Union Workhouse, 87, 192
Bismuth 158, 176
Blackburn, Lancs, 209
Blackburne, John George, 15
Black Horse, Public House, Oldham, 16
Blackpool, 207, 221, 262, 285
'Blind Justice' (play), 115
Blue Bell Inn, Royton, 209
Blue Pitts Inn, 88, 100, 102, 108, 191
Bodden, William, 264
Bottomley, P.C. 106
Booth, Hesketh (Magistrates Clerk), 53, 127, 129, 248-249
Boundary Park, Oldham, 25
Bradford, Yorks, 232, 286
Bradford Borough Police, 230
Brampton, Lord (Mr. Justice Hawkins), 286
Brewood, Staffordshire, 285
Brighton, 228
British Isles, 235

Britland, Elizabeth, 34
Britland, Mary Ann, 34, 236, 243, 246
Britland, Thomas, 34
Britland Poisoning Trial, 34
Bulls Head, Oldham, 106
Buckley, George, 287
Buckleys Mill, Royton, 202
Burslem, 195, 213
Burton-on-Trent, 104, 208, 217
Burton-on-Trent Workhouse, 208
Bury Rd, Rochdale, 86
Butterworth, Fred, 110
Butterworth & Murgatroyd, 200
Byrne, Mr. 168, 170, 173
Byrom, Mr.(Relieving Officer), 22

Calcraft, William, 231
Calton Gaol, Edinburgh, 232
Calvary, 97
Campo Santo, 96
Casual Wards, 24-25
Castleton, 79, 86-88, 94, 100-101, 103-104, 106, 111, 113, 155, 164, 173, 191-196, 208-209, 214, 275, 281-282
Central Station, Oldham, 241
Chadderton, 16, 20
Chadderton, Joseph, 195
Chadderton Cemetery, 20, 40, 233, 287
Chamber of Horrors, 246, 275
Chapel Lane, Royton, 202
Chief Warder, Walton Gaol, 253
Chorlton, Alice, 93, 110

Church of England, 199, 250
Chesterfield Union Workhouse, 192, 208
Chorlton-cum-Hardy, Manchester, 285
Clegg, Mr. Kay, 15
Clogs, 17
Coldhurst Street, Oldham, 267
Collinge, Magistrate, 75
Conway, John, 285-286
Coombs, George, 196
Cornell, Sarah, 280
Cottingham, James, Barrister, 36-37, 39, 44-50, (52-54, 58-59, 61-63, 65-69, 71-78 – Magistrates Court), 96, 107, (114-136, 142-186 – Trial Liverpool Assizes), 248, 250, 284-285
Cottingham, James, Courtney, 36
Cottingham, James, Henry, 36
County Police Authority, 102
Courtenay, Lindo, 41
Crap, Robert, 276
Creosote, 64, 72, 80-84, 168, 171-173
Crimea, 198
Criminal Appeals Court, 281
Crompton, Lancs, 16
Cross St. Castleton, 94
Crouch, James, 52
Crown, The, 248
Curate, St. Lukes, 206, 219, 278

'Dead House', 20

Derby, 218
Devonshire St, Manchester, 135
Dillan, Ann, 56-57, 76, 124-127, 180, 217, 278-279
Dixon, Mary, 34
Dixon, Thomas, 34
Dorrick, Harriet, 92, 110
Drummond, Dr, 22
Drury Lane, Hollinwood, Oldham, 200, 221
Drury Lane, Original Company, 42
Dublin, Freeman of, 36
Dublin, Freemasons Roll, 36
Dublin Stout, 240
Duke of Lancasters Own Yeomanry Cavalry, 237
Duodenum, 162, 167
Durnford, Rev. Richard, 15

East View, Burslem, 195
Eaves, Alice, 90, 109
Edinburgh, 233
Edinburgh, Royal Institute of, 170
Emmott, Joseph, 221, 222, 223
England, 231
Estcourt, Charles, 34, 43, 46, 49, 52, 58, 63, 168, 178, 280
Estcourt, Philip Anderson, 36, 45, 52, 58
Evett, Lydia, 133
Exchange Station, Manchester, 244
Exeter, Devon, 233

'Famine, The', (Play), 42

Fawcett, Mrs. 15
Fenians, 96
Finley, Mary, Ann, 79, 86-95, 97-104, 108-110, 112, 135, 191, 193, 195-196, 198-204, 208-209, 276, 286
Finley, William, 199-202, 209-210
Fire Station, Castleton, 88
Five Arches, Spotland Bridge, Rochdale, 110
Flake Lane, Royton, 21
Flanagan, Mrs. 276
Fletcher, 227-229
'For One Under Sentence Of Death', (Poem), 235
Freehold, Castleton, 111, 196
Freemasons, 262

Gastro Enteritis, 176
Genoa, Italy, 96
George lll, 276
Glebe Mills, Hollinwood, 200, 276
Glodwick Road, Oldham, 16
Golden Pill, 265
Goodale, Robert, 234-235
Goodall, Chemist, Oldham, 64
Goulden St. Manchester, 198
Grand Hotel, Liverpool, 129
Grand Jury, 104
Grange Ave. Oldham, 25
Gregory's Powder, 119, 121
Guardians of the Poor, 13-15, 23-24, 36, 43, 47, 51, 192, 201, 207, 208, 215, 226, 262-263, 266, 278

Hall, Beatrice, 27-28, 30-31, 46, 57, 59, 61, 71, 121-124, 169, 180, 184, 279
Hammond Dr. 253
Harbes Labaitia, 159
Harpurhey Cemetery, Manchester, 205
Harris, Dr.Thomas, 34-36, 38, 43-46, 56, 58, 69, 74, 79, 100-103, 151, 156, 159-160, 164-168, 174, 177, 181, 184, 192, 194, 275, 285
Harrison's Vermin Powder, 34
Hawaii, 240
Hawkins, Mr.Justice Henry, 104-105, 115, 120, 126-127, 129, 131-134, 139-140, 145-146, 150-152, 156-157, 164, 169-170, 172, 177-179, 182-186 (Summing up), 187, 190, 281, 286
Heckmondwyke, Yorkshire, 232
Henderson, James, 36
Henley-on-Thames Workhouse, 208
Henthorn St, Shaw Rd. Oldham, 284
Highley, Mr, Chemist, Rochdale, 94-95
High St. Castleton, 196
High St. Oldham, 82
Higginbottom, Joseph, 40
Higgins, Mrs. 276
Hilton, Betty, 18
Hodgkinson, Charles, Chief

- 293 -

Constable, 34-35, 39, 44, 48, 50, 62-64, 79, 127, 134, 154
Holden Fold, Royton, 21
Hollins Rd. Oldham, 200, 284
Hollinwood, Oldham, 200-201, 221-223, 276
'Holy Living and Dying' (Jeremy Taylor), 258
Home Office, 226, 230
Home Secretary, 102
Horrobin, W.Alderman, 36
Horsedge St. Oldham, 41, 273
House of Commons, 252

India, 240
Inmates, Workhouse, 13, 15
Innes, William, 232-233
Inspector of Prisons, 228
Ireland, 228, 244
Irish House of Commons, 36
Irving, Clifford, 282
Irving, Sir Henry, 268

Jackson, Henry, 112, 135, 169
Jackson, Dr. Samuel, 18
Jackson St. Miles Platting, Manchester 205
Jacksons Pitt, Oldham, 41
Jones, Betty, 19-20

Kelsall, Alderman, 36
Kershaw, Dr.John, 79, 82-84, 103, 116, 154, 203
Keneally, Dr. 115
King St. Oldham, 29, 33, 147

Kirkdale Prison, Liverpool, 188, 254
Kleppell, Brother, 97-99, 100
Knight, Sarah Jane, 31, 49, 61, 217

Lamb, Detective, 79
Lancashire, 238, 250
Landru (French Bluebeard), 275
Langrish, Sir Hercules, 36
Larkin Micheal, 96
Lawson, William Henry, Workhouse Master, 26, 35-36, 111, 118, 196, 215, 282
Leach, Jun, Dr.Abraham, 154
Lee, John, 233-234
Lees, Magistrate, 75
Lees Rd. Oldham, 16
Lever, Mrs. 90
Lime St. Liverpool, 275
Limeside, Oldham, 25
Lincolns Inn, 37
Liquor Atropia Sulph, 110
Liverpool, 85, 104, 115, 129, 136, 154-155, 190-192, 211, 222, 225-226, 230, 236, 240-241, 244, 248, 252, 262, 274-276, 278, 281
Liverpool Assizes, 85, 104
Liverpool Mercury, 190
Liverpool, University of, 192
Liverpudlians, 245
Liversage, Auctioneer, Oldham, 269-274
London, 10, 250, 284
Louisiana, 200

Lowe, Thomas, Undertaker, 20
Lyons, Mary Ann, 89, 100, 102, 108
Lyons, Thomas, 89

MadameTussauds, 269, 284
Manchester, 82, 85, 87-88, 96, 135, 144, 179, 189, 195-196, 198-199, 203, 205-209, 218, 242, 285
Manchester Assizes, 53, 59, 85
Manchester Guardian, 189-190
Manchester Rd. Castleton, 88
Manchester St. Oldham, 64
March, Dr.Edward, 163
Marwood, William, 231-232
Master, Workhouse, 12-16, 19-23, 35-36, 111, 196, 208, 263, 282
Matron, Workhouse, 13, 16
Matron, Walton Gaol, 228
Matthews, Home Secretary, 250
Matty, 202
'Mayor of Tommyfield', 239, 266
McConnell, W.R., Barrister, 115-116, 118, 124, 132-134, 136, 151, 155-156, 162, 164, 168-169, 171, 173, 181-184
Megee, Annie, 41
Mellor, Betty, 21-22
Mellor, F.H., 115, 118, 131, 135, 137, 139-140, 164
Mellor, Joseph, 284-285
Mellor, J.W.,(Clerk to Guardians), 36, 52, 54, 59, 61-66, 71, 76, 115, 215
Mellor, Mary Jane, 284
Middleton, Manchester, 16
Middleton Road, Oldham, 26
Miles Platting, Manchester, 7, 26, 31, 35, 55, 86, 199, 204, 206-208, 213, 219, 251, 278
Mill, John Stuart, 268
Millbrook, Oldham, 200, 276
Mill St. Oldham, 52
Milne, Mr. Workhouse Master, 19-22
Minahan, 227-229
Misentary, 159, 166-167
Molesworth, Frederick Nassau, (District Coroner),36, 39, 48, 78-79, 86, 100, 102, 112
'Mothers Sin, A' (Play), 260
Morris, Rev.(Chaplain, Walton Gaol), 250, 252-253, 255, 257, 259
Morton, Henrietta, 94, 110
Morphia, 66-67, 69-70, 73, 147, 158
Mount Pleasant, Oldham, 16
Mount St. Liverpool, 261
Moston, Manchester, 96-98, 100, 103
Moston Cemetery, Manchester, 87, 95-96, 100,194
Mucus membrane, 161

Neville, Henry, 42
New Cross, Manchester, 198
New St. Rochdale, 209

Northern Circuit, 285
Northmoor, Oldham, 17
North Pole, 240
Norwich Castle, 234, 286

O'Brien, Michael, 96
Oldham, 8-9, 15-17, 21-25, 26-30, 34-40, 80, 82, 87, 96, 98-100, 104-107, 113, 115, 117, 122, 127, 129, 133-134, 136, 140, 154, 175, 177, 196, 199-201, 208, 215, 217, 219, 224-225, 237-238, 241, 243, 247-249, 260, 264, 267, 269, 273, 275-276, 284
Oldham Borough Police, 134
Oldham Chronicle, 7, 24, 79, 82-83, 95, 97-98, 113, 129, 189-190, 260
Oldham Magistrates, 226
Oldham Magistrates Court, 248
Oldham Market, 27, 122
Oldham Police Court, 40, 50, 213
Oldham Police Station, 34, 39
Oldham Poorhouse, 16
Oldham Public Library, 264
Oldham Royal Infirmary, 69, 273
Oldham Standard, 113, 117, 130, 190, 252, 261, 281
Oldham Town Hall, 47, 50, 52, 219
Oldham Twist Company, 200
Oldham Union Workhouse, 7, 9, 15-33, 36-40, 43-44, 47, 50-51, 56, 68, 71, 80-83, 105, 111, 117-118, 124, 130, 131, 133, 136, 147, 214-217, 219, 226-228, 262, 266-267, 271, 278
Opium, 217, 280
'Owd Betty's', 202
Owens College, 45
Oxalic acid, 157-159

Parish Poorhouse, 16-17
Parrish, Prof, 261
Park and Sandy Lane Spinning Co. 202
Parliament, 240
Partland, Ann, 68, 133
Paul, Dr. Frank Thomas, 192, 194, 281
Patterson, Dr. Thomas, 7, 26-33, 36, 38, 44-45, 55, 62, (64-77 – Magistrates Court), 79-84, (116, 128, 137-154, 156, 161, 170, 175-177, 179, 183 – Trial Liverpool Assizes), 190, 197, 216, 218, 247-249, 259, 277
Peace, Charles, 232, 275
Pemberton, Mrs. 91, 109-110, 195, 213, 226, 275
Pharmaceutical Society, 82
Phlegm, 172
Phrenology, 260-261
Phythians Mill, Castleton, 86, 88
Pickford, James, 135
Platts (textiles), 287-288
Poor Law Amendment Act, 9, 11, 15
Poor Law Commissioners, 10

Poor Law Inspector, 19
Preston, Lancs. 285
Prestwich Asylum, Manchester, 207
Prudential Agent, 91, 109
Prudential Assurance Co. 56, 105
Prussic acid, 280
Public Assistance Committee, 24
Puerperal insanity, 278
Purser, Charles, Detective-Inspector, 34, 37, 47, 50, 79, 125, 134, 168
Pyott, Mrs. 208

Queens University, Ireland, 64
Queensway, Rochdale, 88
Queen Victoria, 239

Radcliffe St. Oldham, 266, 268
Rational Sick and Burial Society, 135, 196
Rawlins, Detective, 79
Read, Betty, 40
Read, John Samuel, 40
Relieving Officer, 22-23
Renshaw St. Liverpool, 276
'Resignation' (Longfellow), 228
Revising Barrister, 285
Reynolds Waxworks, Lime St. Liverpool, 276
Robertson, Dr. John George, 29, 33, 38, 45-46, 55, 65, 67, 69-71, 138-141, 144, 147, 153, 155-162, 173-176
Robinson, George, 50, 77, 211-212, 225-226
Rochdale, 79, 86, 88-89, 92, 95, 110, 113, 115, 128, 135, 207-209, 281-282
Rochdale Police, 79
Rochdale Rd. Castleton, 88
Rochdale Rd. Oldham, 25
Rochdale Star, 286
Rochdale Workhouse, 207
Roman Catholic, 250
Rossendale Valley, 285
Royal Infirmary, Manchester, 8, 34, 45, 206
Royal College of Surgeons, 192
Royton, 16, 20-21, 23, 82, 84, 116, 154, 199-203, 208-209, 219
Royton Medical Officer, 84
Rishton, Lancs, 209
Rylands, Manchester, 218

Salford, 242, 260
Salvation Army, 271
Sanderson, Ann, 8, 27, 29-32, 37, 56, 79, 86, 117-121, 154, 169, 174, 185, 189, 213, 215, 251, 277
Sanderson, John, 8, 30-31, 37
Sandy Lane, Royton, 202
Saunders, Ellen, 111, 196, 282
Saville St. Miles Platting, 204, 213
Saville, Thomas, and Sons, Royton, 199
Scotland, 232
Scotland Yard, 155

Secretary of State, 21
Sebastapol, 198
Sedgley Park, Prestwich, Manchester, 82
Seidlitz Powder, 125
Sharples, Dr. William Henry, 95, 100, 110, 193-194
Shaw, nr Oldham, 18
Shaw, Dr. 206
Shaw, George, 192
Shaw, Mr. 200
Shaw Rd. Oldham, 36
Sheriff, 235, 245
Simpson, Thomas, 18-19
Singapore, 240
Somerville, County Cavan, 36
Springbank, Cobden Rd. Chesterfield, 192
Springhill Mill, Royton, 199
Star Inn, Oldham, 40
Strangeways Gaol, Manchester, 236
Stretford Rd, Manchester, 8, 208
St. Joseph's Roman Catholic Cemetery, Moston, Manchester, 96
St. Luke's Church, Manchester, 205-206
St. Margaret's Church, Hollinwood, Oldham, 200
St. Mary's Rd. Moston, Manchester, 96
St. Mary's Ward, Oldham, 223, 264, 268
St. Paul's Royton, 20

St. Peter's St. Chambers, Oldham, 103
Strychnine, 280
Sulphuric acid, 149, 158, 161, 165, 167-169, 176-178, 280
Sulphate of Atropa, 111
Swindells, Harry, 36, 284
Swires, John, 17

Talbot Rd. Old Trafford, Manchester, 168
Tallyrand, 268
Taylor, John, Chemist, 110, 115, 163, 196, 281
Taylor, William, 196
Temperance Hall, Oldham, 273
Theatre Royal, Oldham, 41, 115, 260
Thompson, Ellen, 31, 57, 128, 130-131, 217-218
Thompson, William, 170-171, 173, 178, 248
Thorburn, Francis, 260-261
Thornham, 16
Thorpe, William Henry, photographer, 133
Tichbourne, perjury case, 115
Tinchure of Iron and Cinchona, 137
Tindall, Supt. 79, 86-93
Tommyfield Market, Oldham, 224, 238-239, 261, 266-267
Tonge, Manchester, 16
'Tramp Weaver', 199
Trinity College, Dublin, 36

Tuberolosis, 160, 166, 174, 178, 184
Turner, Alfred William, 106-107
Turners, Auctioneers, Liverpool, 276
Tyson, Matthew, 99

Under Secretary for the Home Department, 250
Under Sheriff, 224, 253
Union Mill, Royton, 201
Union St. Oldham, 269, 273

Vicar St. Miles Platting, Manchester, 27
Vickers, Robert, 232-233
Victoria, Act 33 & 34 (21st section), 225
Victoria Station, Manchester, 205, 242
Viscera, 171

Waddington, Magistrate, 75
Wallwork, Frederick, 112
Walsh, Caleb, 20-23
Walton Gaol, Liverpool, 85, 188, 191, 211, 221, 224, 227, 246, 251-252, 261, 274
Waxworks Exhibition, Liverpool, 274
Welfare Services Committee, 25
Wellington Infirmary, Shropshire, 207
Welsh, Joseph, 198, 200

Welsh, Lizzie, 86-87, 221
Welsh, Mary Ann, 86, 198-200
Wesleyan and General Assurance Society, 112, 195
Westlands, Grange Ave, Oldham, 25
West End St. Oldham, 41
Wheeler, William, 24
Whipp and Bourne Ltd. Castleton, 88
Whittaker, Joseph, Solicitor, 36-37, 50, 52-54, 58-59, 77, 103, 106-108, 211, 225-227, 249, 272
Whitworth Rd. Rochdale, 135
Wild, John, Magistrate, 52, 68, 75, 77
Wild, Richard, 20
Wilmot St. Manchester, 208
Wolfenden, Sarah, 89, 91, 100, 102, 109
Workhouse Croft, 16
Workhouse Infirmary, 267
Workhouse Undertaker, 20
Wood, C. Granville, 82
Wortley, Stuart, Under Secretary for Home Dept. 250
Wrigley, William, 223-224, 237-246, 252, 261-269, 277
Wrigley, Hetty, 266-267
Wrigley, 'Lady', 264
Yorkshire, 232
Yorkshire St. Oldham, 133, 237
Yorkshire St. Rochdale, 110